BLANDTRAP
CHRONICLES
BOOK 1

LETTERS TO THE EDITOR OF THE TISKILWA
BUREAU VALLEY CHIEF

HARRY GRAFTON

BLANDTRAP CHRONICLES

BOOK 1

CITIOFBOOKS, INC.
3736 Eubank NE Suite A1
Albuquerque, NM 87111-3579
www.citiofbooks.com
Hotline: 1 (877) 389-2759
Fax: 1 (505) 930-7244

Ordering Information:
Quantity sales. Special discounts are available on quantity purchases by corporations, associations, and others. For details, contact the publisher at the address above.

Printed in the United States of America.

ISBN-13:   Softcover   979-8-89391-125-1
                        eBook   979-8-89391-126-8
Library of Congress Control Number: 2024909848

TABLE OF CONTENTS

January

Snicked from the desk of Calvin Farnsworth:

If you couldn't figure out how the dog, with his mouth tied shut and calmly cuddling withthe cat, could manage to drink an entire gallon of milk, wouldn't that be

... a muzzle nuzzle guzzle puzzle?

Harry Ellis

238 Persimmon Street

Blandtrap

To the Editor of the Tiskilwa Bureau Valley Chief

RE: Subscription Woes

Dear Sir:

Over the recent holidays I had the experience of reading your newspaper. A curious mind, the frequency of fish in our diet, and three house cats require us to subscribe to a local periodical and use them in ways not recommended by the publisher.

A wise and curious editor would concern himself with what happens to issues after they leave the press. I hope to add to your knowledge. In my home your paper lives two lives. After it is delivered to our door, the sometimes-interesting and occasionally well-written columns provide information that is often accurate. We appreciate the effort.

The next day, your newspaper, like a phoenix rising from the ashes, is reincarnated to live a new life destined to line a birdcage, cat box, or wrap the heads of fish. A new home is found for your articles among the ingredients of my trash. This kind of synergy is rare in today's world.

My recent perusal of your product was disappointing. I found no mention of news from my village, Blandtrap. That omission is what has prompted this vigorous protest of your paper's coverage, or lack of coverage of smaller communities surrounding your city. Focus is a wonderful talent but it is peripheral vision that expands our vistas. It allows us see where we fit within the larger order of things.

While Blandtrap remains the smallest and most quiet village in the vicinity of your fair city, its citizenry and its goings-on are certainly worthy of inclusion in your paper. At least mere mention, from time to time, is warranted by our village's devotion to your periodical. Each village comprises a small percentage of your total readership. Collectively, though, we must represent a significant portion of your circulation. At the very least we must be worthy financially if not by our humanitarian endeavors of mention amid articles about your many advertisers. I shall endeavor to remind you of the more noteworthy events of our local celebrations as soon as I quell the incessant knocking at my door.

I apologize for a lack of continuity in my letter. The door needed to be answered if I was to find the peace I needed to pen this communication. As I rose from my chair, and took my first stride, progress was impeded by one of our cats, causing me to stumble into the wall. I righted myself and prepared to return the favor to the feline via a mighty kick. My foot would have delivered the package, too, but the leg of the desk signed for the parcel.

Hopping on my "good foot," I answered the knock to discover your young carrier at my door. The lad is nice enough and I suppose he is even charming, in a boyish sort of way. As they so often do, the troublesome details of finance quickly arose and began to muddy our budding conversation.

It seems there was a matter of thirty-five cents regarding my account. Edith, my wife, normally handles matters of this sort so I found myself on unfamiliar ground. Still, it seemed foolish to ask the boy to return over such a trivial matter so I dove right in to resolve the deficiency.

Now, I try to be precise in matters of money because it is a serious topic. I asked for an explanation of the charges. It should have been a simple accounting of the events to date and the sums involved. Apparently, matters of subscription are more complicated than I was prepared to handle, but I decided to dispatch the matter by paying up, whether I believed I owed it or not. Assuming arrears, I reached for cash.

The thought occurred to me, "Does one tip for such services? If so, what is an appropriate gratuity?" Having always felt that the cliché mongers had it wrong - that valor is often the better part of discretion - I thrust a few small bills in the boys hand, patted his head, and quickly closed the door to return to this duty.

Back to the matter at hand, it seems inexcusable that your paper would ignore our village. Is there an ulterior motive? What advantage would your ignorance of our affairs produce for you or your readers? Perhaps it is envy over our annual Labor Day Hog Roast and Quilt Show, or perhaps you covet our Fourth of July flag display made out of red and white peony stripes with white carnation stars on a blue eggplant field. Seeing the lateness of the hour, I'll have to pack this letter and finish your rebuke after my standing breakfast engagement at Plow Boy Diner.

Rushing out my door, I stumbled over your paper carrier. Excusing myself and explaining that I had little time to explore our new found rapport, I tried to give him the slip. He was like a broken record, that kid, again and again mumbling something about the 'wrong amount.' Time was working against me there, and in an effort to expedite the transaction, I pressed a few more bills in the child's hand. While muttering appropriate pleasantries over the boy's protestations and nodding in agreement to matters unknown, I scurried on my way. The kid tried to follow me but was distracted when some cash slipped from his hand, allowing the escape I so desperately needed.

With a brisk walk to the corner, a quick left turn, and down Main Street I fled. I caught what I believed was a flash of plaid through a clump of trees down by Big Bureau Creek. Nearly following the urge to explore the sighting, it was more important to be prompt.

Continuing on my way to the diner, I happened to spot Clovis Beagle heading straight for me. Clovis is a large young man with larger problems, at least they seem large to him. A friend he was, but I simply didn't have time for him.

Evasive maneuvers were unsuccessful. He must have mirrored my movements as I crossed the street to avoid him. I lost track of the character, complicating defensive action. Peeking out from behind the large maple in front of the library to get a bead on his position, I was startled when he spoke from behind me.

"She did it to me again!" Clovis babbled, loud and upset.

"Who did what, Clovis?" I said retrieving my composure from its hiding place. If I had been on time I would be at my seat in the diner, surrounded by friends who could distract him. As it was I was late and I could hear my watch ticking on my wrist.

"Maybelle Oufsbacher! She's killed me off again!" Clovis was clearly agitated so I attempted to soothe him. I had two masters. The desire to console Clovis was one; my precious routine was the second. Breaking free from both was unlikely. It was a two-birds-with-one-stone moment. I asked him to accompany me to breakfast.

His answer humbled me. "What makes you think I haven't eaten already?"

Clovis was on his game and I was not. Continuing with my earlier plan, I assured him that he looked remarkably well and, if he hadn't offered it up front, I would have testified under oath that he was quite alive. Indeed, he looked just like himself, and, although I was not experienced in these matters, he appeared to be the best-traveled and agreeable cadaver I had conversed with recently. I told him I was impressed with the work of the undertaker and would hire him for my own purposes when the time came. In the interim, the mortician should be recognized for his work and receive an award or some other recognition for his extraordinary talent.

It has always amazed me how condolence, even if it is offered with all sincerity and innocence, or shrouded in sarcasm, can have the exact opposite of the intended effect. Grief is a cruel master.

"I'm not dead, you old coot!" he rudely shouted, "Maybelle's waggin' her tongue all over the village tellin' folks I died last night. Everybody I see is walkin' around with a hankie, dabbin' their eyes real sad like, 'till they see me. Then, they pale up like they're seein' a ghost. Ya gotta help me Harry. Ya gotta tell folks I'm still alive before I scare 'em to death! Some of the older folks are fragile. They can't take a scare like that."

I suggested he might want to delay correcting the matter, at least until the casseroles began piling up on his doorstep. And wouldn't some flowers around his place brighten these gloomy winter days? Clovis wouldn't hear of it. He insisted on rectifying matters immediately, so I agreed to spread the word and hustled off toward Plow Boy Diner. I'm not sure he was done with me, but I had all I wanted for the moment.

Passing the bank, my eyes were drawn to Seth Hugginbough, owner of the Hardware Store and Lumberyard. He was in an animated discussion with Tom Holdfast, Blandtrap's banker. Merchant and banker in obvious dispute in the lobby of the bank was a tempting diversion. On another day, I would slip into the lobby and slowly transact an unnecessary deposit while extracting the details of the argument. Matters pressing as they were and eavesdropping eating time as it does, I would have to rely on others for the nitty-gritty.

Reaching my goal at last, I found Stu Brewer sitting at our usual table. Stu has been a good friend throughout the years. You don't always like everything about your friends. They are your friends because they care about you. That is the key element of a friend. Their annoying characteristics don't matter so much when compared to their concern for you.

I always knew what I was in for. You see, Stu had a horrible birth defect. It wasn't apparent when you first met him, but once you got to know him you could see it plainly. He was born without a wallet. Modern medicine, even as advanced as it is today, was unable to correct this deformity. Many transplants had been attempted, but the rigors of Stu's constitution rejected them all. When it was time to pay, Stu would be unable to produce a form of payment. He had buckets of excuses, but no cash came forward.

I didn't know what we would eat today. I didn't know what we would discuss. I didn't even know where I was going when I left the diner. One thing was sure: when I left the diner the check would be mine. No amount of inference, no amount of suggestion, or even the most thinly veiled insults could move him. The end result would be the same. The check would be in my hand and I would pay it..

"Hey 'Spendthrift'," Stu mocked. "You finally got here, huh?"

"Please excuse the lateness of my arrival, Stu. I was unavoidably detained." I began with a synopsis of my morning.

"Don't sweat it, Harry. I didn't start without you. What happened?"

Having the time, I explained in great detail how Clovis had treed me over by the library. Recapping the earlier episode with your paper carrier brought nods of agreement from Stu. He had encountered similar difficulty with the boy.

Getting back to the Clovis soap opera, Stu challenged me, "Didn't you see him coming, Harry? He's as big as a house!"

"I couldn't shake him. He was awfully agitated; it must have heightened his senses. Somehow the behemoth was able to fly under my radar." I explained.

"Agitated, huh? Maybelle didn't kill him off again, did she?" Stu chuckled.

"She sure did," I offered. "I wonder how she killed him this time. Do you remember the last time? She had him drowning in his oatmeal. Clovis said he wouldn't have minded so much if she'd killed him by burning in a building while saving a baby or maybe drowning while swimming the English Channel, but to drown in your oatmeal just didn't seem respectable."

"No, it didn't," Stu wanted to be on the record with his position. I had said at the time I didn't think he got a fair shake.

I went on. "That drowning in his oatmeal sounded suspicious to me right from the start. In fact, I was on my way to investigate it when I ran into Clovis. He was screaming at Maybelle over at the IGA." It's surprising how many of Maybelle's corpses are still walking around and breathing. She needs to develop a new standard for determining life or death. Flipping a coin would be more reliable than her present system.

"I agree." Stu said as he nodded.

"I think Clovis looked healthier the first time he died than he did this time. Maybe he needs some vitamins. Anyway, the matter is becoming repetitive. I confess: the next time Maybelle knocks off Clovis, I'll be tempted to do him in myself and so fulfill the prophecy and end the mystery. Stu worried that Maybelle had cried wolf too often. If Clovis should actually meet his demise, it may be days before anyone bothers to validate the rumor. The odor may arrive well before the wreaths. Pall bearers would have no time to train for the anticipated physical strain of toting Clovis' huge remains to their final resting place. There is no doubt about it, Clovis' demise should be well planned and carefully scheduled in order to inconvenience the fewest mourners.

Gene Prince was sitting in the diner with his wife, Maude. He is a gem of a man and a saint in every sense of the word. I said hello to the couple and he blessed me in a way I can't describe. He is an anchor to the moral and spiritual ship that is Blandtrap.

After paying the check, as I was leaving the diner, the rascal you hired to deliver papers and haunt my life cornered me again. His dogged determination is admirable, particularly in a young person, but his persistence in this matter was becoming wearisome. I gave him a moment, but your lad doesn't get directly to the point. My mind was consumed with more important business of my day. He was yammering something about "paid into the middle of next year." Unfamiliar and disinterested as I was with matters of subscription amortization and time being my enemy, I tucked some more bills into his shirt pocket, larger bills this time, hoping they could do the job their little brothers had failed to do: put this matter to rest once and for all. Ever striving to be polite, I rarely walk away from someone while they are still talking, but this was the exception. With time flying, I hurried on leaving the lad to convince himself of his argument.

Following a spirited discussion with the Postmaster regarding the increasing cost of postage and the regularity of delivery, I procured the necessary stamp in an interesting design, and stand here at the patron's work counter completing your letter.

Consider yourself fortunate. You have avoided the wrath of this author because I am trying to catch the noon post, but I assure you, reprieve is only temporary. I promise you, I'll write again soon and give you the proper down-dressing you so richly deserve for overlooking our flourishing community. I bid you good day.

Respectfully Submitted,

Harry Ellis

P.S.

I see your carrier through the window and he's headed this way. He seems to have the bit in his teeth today. I am unable to predict or control his behavior, in spite of my best efforts. He's gone to the well too often, and he's met his match in me, I tell you! I'd like to go out there and settle this matter once and for all, but I find myself a bit light on funds. Empty pockets are an embarrassment to the well prepared gentleman. So, in order to spare the lad any humiliation in front of the village folk, I'll slip out the back door and stop by the bank to replenish my supply of cash before I face your beast again.

Good day.

Harry Ellis

Harry Ellis

238 Persimmon Street

Blandtrap

To the Editor of the Tiskilwa Bureau Valley Chief

RE: Enterprise – Bob and Ruth Woods

Dear Sir or Madam;

I was unavoidably interrupted from expressing my discontent in my last letter. It was rude of me and I herewith apologize and mend my error by continuing the job here. Your kind letter was, I assume, a thinly veiled attempt to placate my wrath over your paper's continued neglect of the affairs of Blandtrap.

You suggest, from time to time, our citizens are without business or discernable enterprise. Nothing could be further from the truth. Our thriving Village Square, the entire block, is filled with small businesses operated by capable management. Yes, the entrepreneurial spirit is alive in Blandtrap and is exercised by business neophytes and the more experienced as well.

Bob Woods regularly chased one of his grand schemes for getting rich. He was unaware he was already rich. Many of his ideas were reasonable and made him a profit, but the big idea, the one that would make him wealthy beyond his wildest dreams, never materialized. He kept trying and most of his get-rich-quick schemes neither made him rich nor could be executed in a short amount of time. Usually, Bob's ideas required a monumental amount of work and the payoff was so far down the road that it would be easier to predict the weather than accurately forecast earnings.

As a dairy farmer, Bob was successful. He maintained and milked the usual dairy herds. He also processed his milk into cheese and marketed his dairy products. All this was lucrative, but Bob was not satisfied with success alone, he craved fame. When he pursued more grounded goals, his relentless efforts paid off and he eventually became well known, but true fame escaped his grasp.

Bob was not like Bill Whittacre who was a truly humble man, never seeking praise for his work nor accepting it when it was offered. He was content to work hard and remain unnoticed. You could look in Bill's eyes and see the loneliness. Young as he was, he was unwilling or unable to do anything to relieve the pain of his solitude.

Nothing Bob did was ever easy for him or on him. He started out with less than zero, no money and fewer prospects. He had a good upbringing, though, which taught him to be honest and industrious. He learned those lessons and others and it added to his inborn stubborn determination. He set about to succeed in a field where nearly all the best practitioners inherited their farms. Bob earned every acre of his, along with the respect of the town.

Investment isn't easy, involving some degree of speculation at best and is often simply a wild guess. California investments were cruel to Bob and Ruth. They had observed that those who made the most money tended to do so through a monopoly. Competition spurs innovation and creativity, but monopoly delivers the profit. The very wealthy were the first to fill a niche or the first to provide a service to an untapped market. Seizing the opportunity when it arose, they opened the first dollar store on Rodeo Drive. It opened to critical ridicule and closed quickly without making a sale and with the blessing of fellow merchants.

Bob and Ruth had a tendency to flaunt their fortune; Bob more than Ruth. He just liked to show off. When he proved his earning capability to the bankers, they lent him more money. When he showcased his product quality, consumers and distributors bought more of his product. It only stood to reason that if he showed off his wealth, his friends and fellow villagers would love him all the more.

People don't react that way. The flaw in Bob's logic wasn't clear in his mind. Showy displays of wealth tend to put people on the other side and tend to make them cheer against the rich. Villagers of Blandtrap didn't exactly wish Bob and Ruth harm as much as they wanted to see them taken down a peg or two.

Deep in his heart Bob was never satisfied with his achievement or his status in the community. He worked night and day to earn the respect he already had from the community, but didn't realize he possessed.

Ruth had come from money and she endured the hard times admirably, but felt she deserved better. Times of hardship were brief. When finances began to supply more than the necessities, Ruth preferred to buy the best but not to let others know what she had was the best. She had learned from her mother it was better to conceal their wealth and offend others less. It was a sign of their maturity, yet they broke from the practice of humility every once in a while.

I remember a few years back, maybe ten years or so, when Bob had another of his grand ideas. He and his wife, Ruth, had driven to Florida for vacation. Along the way they would stop, periodically, for gas and meals. At truck stops and fuel marts Bob noticed displays of air fresheners for cars. The usual aromas were available everywhere: pine, cinnamon, new car, and lemon were popular at the time. This very narrow selection of scents seemed to present a business opportunity to Bob. When an opportunity knocks on Bob's door, he runs to see who's there.

He thought, the more options on the shelf, the more air fresheners would be purchased. Many, probably, had not ventured into the air freshener market simply because new and exciting scents were unavailable. "Variety is the spice of life, "he thought. "If I could find an aroma that would capture even a small percentage of the car air freshener market, I could make a fortune.

Research, in a formal sense, was expensive, time consuming, and did not always deliver the desired quality of product. Bob knew there must be a shortcut. It had been his experience that after all the research was completed, the recommended course of action was usually one of the logical options before research began. Rarely did it point in a new direction. Reason and common sense, he determined, would replace research.

He thought painstakingly about potential unique scents, although none he could conjure would have wide appeal. But in July, during a family reunion picnic he noticed how many of his relatives had grown up on dairy farms, and then moved into cities.

An aroma that could evoke the fond memories of growing up on a dairy farm seemed like a lead pipe cinch to succeed. All the children, hundreds of thousands of them, who grew up on dairy farms could enjoy the aroma of a dairy farm in the comfort of their car. The stress of commuting, traffic jams, parking woes and repair bills would all be relieved when the driver leaned back, closed his eyes, and breathed in the scents and memories of childhood. The safety and calm of those days would soothe the wounds of a hectic life.

Bob set to work on the formula for the perfume. First, he had to select the odor he was shooting for - not all aromas on a dairy farm are desirable. He secluded himself in the basement of his house, neglecting some of his favorite duties and cherished hobbies. He came up only for nourishment and bourbon. It was all very secret. No one, not even Ruth was allowed near his workbench.

Ruth got a chance to review Bob's work while laundering his lab clothes. She later confessed her doubts concerning the direction of his experiments. There was a time she worried he would never create a scent with more appeal than the disinfectant required to remove his less successful attempts from his clothing.

At last he had it! This was a sure thing - guaranteed success. He quietly allowed Ruth to sample the scent after swearing her to secrecy. As the fume wafted to her nostrils, Bob saw the broad smile of approval a man doesn't often see from a wife of many years. They were on the same page in this respect. Success, real success was just around the corner.

Once he had developed the scent for the air freshener, a snazzy marketing plan was next. Bob had favorably marketed his dairy products, so it seemed he was more than qualified to hawk the air freshener based upon a dairy farm. Bob's biggest mistake was in keeping his marketing plan a secret, at least keeping it a secret from those a little more worldly than his rural experience had made him. Our perceptions of ourselves are often blinded by our own innocence and ignorance. I certainly could have helped if I had only known.

Bob made arrangements with a manufacturer to produce the cow and barn shaped air fresheners. He designed a utilitarian clip to distinguish his product from the more common fuzzy dice suspended from the rear view mirror. Packaging for the product was colorful, bright, and caught the eye at the moment it was seen. His slogan, though, needed some work.

He opted for a billboard campaign. He started with six billboards around Blandtrap. Out by Lusty Hill was the site of the first unveiling. The billboard company pasted the sign while Bob and Ruth sat in the diner waiting for customers to come in to comment.

Bob was never very good with words. He could communicate well enough, but you couldn't call him a wordsmith. The precise words that made him completely understood often eluded him. Yet, he could normally make due with its first cousin. This occasion was more challenging than his previous experience had prepared him to handle. The billboard was a beautiful work of art. There was a picture of Bob and Ruth in either upper corner. The backdrop was a photo of their dairy, a stately home, a beautiful barn, and a pastoral field with a grazing herd. Truly, this was an artistic masterpiece, but the signage read boldly:

Bob and Ruth Woods
Say,
"SMELL OUR DAIRY AIR"

The morning of the unveiling, Bob and Ruth drove to the diner and sat at the large booth, even though they were only two. The large table fashioned a kind of 'throne room,' of sorts, where Bob imagined he would receive those coming to offer praise and adoration for his triumph. The couple was expecting many to stop by. They were not disappointed.

The Woods were finishing their first cup of coffee when Maybelle Oufsbacher of the Ladies Aid Society came in. Maybelle seemed disturbed and didn't go over to greet Ruth right away, like there was a job to do and she was hoping some one else would do it. Like most of the older ladies in Blandtrap, Maybelle was known to be direct when she spoke. It was unlike her to be shy.

Looking around the room, Maybelle witnessed the stifled snickers and concealed grins from patrons as they accumulated like a crowd around an accident scene. Responsibilities such as this fell on Maybelle's shoulders because she so often took liberties with the truth in trivial matters like she did when she killed Clovis every few months.

Must she always be the one to bear bad news? Maybelle knew her self pity would be nothing compared to the mortification Ruth would feel especially if the charade continued any longer. Making eye contact with Ruth, Maybelle saw the job was hers alone, so she crossed the diner without the usual formalities and quickly whispered in Ruth's ear.

One's countenance, particularly in victory, seems as solid as a rock, but when tipped off the shelf by the finger of humiliation; it shatters like blown glass on the floor of reality. Ruth became a stone - a rapidly reddening stone. Bob was perplexed. Ruth, after collecting her composure, leaned over and whispered to Bob and experienced the slow fade of his facial expression as it changed from pride to horror.

There was no place to run. They had positioned themselves at the head of the table, back to the wall, normally a place of honor; and now they had to stay. Bob took his medicine pretty well. Bob and Ruth sat in their booth while the village, one at a time and with little compassion, filed by and registered creative comments of their own invention. You can guess the sport they had with the two. After a while Bob & Ruth rose to their feet, dignity tattered like a mainsail in a hurricane, and politely departed. Bob stopped at Hugginbough Hardware and Lumber on his way out of town. Seth had three gallons of paint and rollers on the counter waiting for him.

From the door of the hardware store to the door of their car Bob listened to the moan of a bagpipe playing in the distance, down by Big Bureau Creek. Fog near the river concealed the musician from sight. Ruth rolled her window down a crack to listen while she waited for Bob. He resisted the urge to drive around and solve the mystery of the bagpipe player.

Bob wanted to run him down with his car. He wasn't upset with the bagpipe player but he wanted to strike out in any way to assuage his hurt. There is no salve to treat the self-inflicted wound that is our own stupidity. Only the most wise and humble understand their own ignorance.

Ruth had to cancel plans they had for a victory celebration. Jose Wong's Ye Olde Fashioned Chuck Wagon Smorgasbord Buffet had a room reserved for them. Ironically, they had decided to serve ham to their guests, along with sweet and sour chicken, camp stew, jambalaya, and couscous, a typical Jose Wong presentation. She asked Jose to deliver the food they had purchased to the nursing home in time for dinner. Ruth believed someone should benefit from their indiscretion. Jose agreed and it was done as she wished.

Her mind hadn't been working as quickly as usual while she was trapped at the table with Bob. Free from that confinement, she had time to think as she drove from Jose Wong's. Ruth made a mental list of things to undo. They had balloons imprinted with their motto. She would have to destroy all of those. That's just the sort of thing that would resurface at inopportune moments if they fell into the wrong hands. Also, she could save the expense of the helium if she caught them before balloons were inflated. Five hundred 'smell our dairy air' balloons covering the ceiling of the large meeting room was a vision she had looked forward to for weeks. The thought now haunted her.

You in the city, no doubt, had some communication with them during this event and perhaps this will jog your memory. A last minute plea to have their flyer removed, pulled from your paper probably crossed your desk. It was too late. The papers were already on doorsteps and in newsstands by the time the Woods discovered their error. I would think, given the confiscatory rates you charge for advertising, a client would expect some counseling in the quality and perception of the finished product. I'm sure you saw the entire train wreck coming and stood off to the side to watch the carnage. Newspaper people are like that, you know.

Bob is bull headed and he would have kept this thing a secret. If he had sought your opinion, I'm sure he would have enjoyed another outcome. He was so convinced he had it right and had struck it rich, you probably couldn't resist going ahead with the ad once Bob had spurned your advice. It gives you a sense of superiority, doesn't it? You should be ashamed of yourself.

The relatives Bob and Ruth had invited to come to Blandtrap and share their joy were more troublesome than villagers. With a normal celebration, one is careful to invite only guests your are convinced will get along with each other, shunning more difficult and openly critical relatives who dampen fun at every turn. The Woods had focused on inviting mostly unfriendly relations in order to rub their noses in newfound success. All who could drive were already on the way. These relatives would not be much hassle since they would be gone by dark. Relative so distant they had to fly would be staying at the Woods' house for a few days until scheduled flights would depart. It would be a living hell in their own home.

By dawn the next day, the billboards had been whitewashed, and Bob's dreams of fame were realized. Hardly a week goes by without Bob meeting an old friend only to have them break down in howling laughter before Bob can shake their hand. Fame and infamy live next door to one another. It is amazing how often a package addressed to one is delivered to the other.

I enjoy Bob's company and we meet regularly to share coffee and a chat. I am careful never to mention the incident but from time to time, Bob would bring up the billboards during our private conversations. "As God is my witness, Harry, I never saw it that way." he would protest. Then, he would continue to mutter, his voice trailing off to silence.

Fortune doesn't fail to visit us in Blandtrap; we just prefer to keep our successes and our failures to ourselves. We are an industrious people here. We take economic chances and explore new business opportunities. They don't always work out well. Our village is a hotbed of enterprise and you would do well to recognize it.

Sincerely,

Harry Ellis

Harry Ellis

238 Persimmon Street

Blandtrap

To the Editor of the Tiskilwa Bureau Valley Chief

RE: The Flu Epidemic

Dear Sir:

This week, I fear, you must excuse me from my usual duties. My strong feelings regarding the happenings in Blandtrap must be put aside for the greater good of the community. I will resume reporting to your deaf ears next week.

Blandtrap is in the throes of a flu epidemic. Only a few healthy souls like me are wandering about today. At the Plow Boy Diner I had to make my own coffee and tend the register for my own check and ring up the few other customers able to make the trip. The menu had been reduced to oatmeal and toast due to lack of demand. The oatmeal was tasty, but most folks, those pretty well recovered from this plague, chose the toast. I had both.

Carla Dombrowski is a young nurse who works for a doctor in your city. In a small town, when you possess special skills, or normal skills for that matter, you are expected to use them to benefit villagers in need.

It is not the needy who expect you to help them, although they are not surprised when you do, it is that you have an expectation of yourself to help, a desire to ease the load of familiar fellows. It is another basic difference of attitude we have outside the city. In our village when we see another we tend to think of how we might help them as opposed to the methods of you in the city. When you spy a helpless citizen, you think of how you can make a buck off of them.

Neighbors strolling around Village Square were like the cast of a zombie movie. They acted as if they were alive, but if you looked into their eyes you could see they were dead from the shoulders up. Among the living were those, like me, who remained unaffected by disease. Not a sniffle or sneeze to sully our demeanor. We were a scant few. The dead consisted of two sorts. The first sort was in denial, refusing to admit they were ill. They feigned conversation without uttering a discernible syllable, all the while swaying as if there were a stiff breeze. They weren't good company.

The other sort staggered around with their heads down sniffling. Congestion made sinus cavities change the tone of their voice. Folks spoke an octave and a half lower than normal.

Still others, knowing it was going to come to that, started checking themselves in early with the undertaker. He didn't appreciate the advanced notice and attributed the illness he contracted to contact with these future clients.

The undertaker didn't seem to like people in general. He was sympathetic, trying to anticipate their needs but he really didn't care for them. He said he saw too many people at their worst to embrace them as a group. Two emotions quickly bring to the surface our most selfish thoughts and actions. They are grief and greed. With inheritance often an unknown at the time of the funeral, the undertaker dealt with the family of the deceased during such times. He often said he preferred his clients to their families because they were much more kind and cooperative.

As I passed the pharmacy, a sharp rap on the window glass startled me. It was Rudy Neddleless wagging his finger in my direction. I went to the door while he trotted over to unlock and let me in. "I'm in a bind, Harry," He said almost panting from the exercise. "Everyone is sick. I've got nobody to deliver medicine for me. If you could deliver three of these for me I would be ever so grateful."

I learned a long time ago that if one has a task that absolutely cannot be put off, one must give it to the busiest person they know because they don't have the time to do it later and must do it now. I was flattered Rudy considered me as such. But I really did have other matters to tend. I relented, in the end, given the urgent nature of his request.

It was surprising he was shorthanded. With a large number of in-laws without discernable employment, the availability of cheap, albeit unreliable, labor was usually found on his couch or with its head stuck in his refrigerator door.

I told Rudy I would help in any way I could. Secretly, of course, I was hoping he would restrict deliveries to addresses inside village limits and near my home. I was disappointed in that aspect. "Sure," I said, "Where do I go?"

"Here is the medicine and the addresses are on each sack. First go to Maybelle Oufsbacher's house. She's got it pretty bad. Next go to Lillian Crabtree's. Don't knock, just go on in. Get her a pitcher of water with some ice, if she has any, and take her a glass. She can't get up. She's also sleeping a lot and still forgetful. Make her take the medication while you are there then leave it on the bed stand. Write on the pad she keeps on the nightstand when she should take the next dose. Last, go to LaVonda's home. She won't be there but leave it for her. She's under strict orders from the doctor to remain in bed so she'll be over at the Carlson's, who are also under the weather, helping the old folks any way she can. She won't admit she's one of them herself."

I was a bit dumbfounded at the detail and rapidity of the instructions, yet I was confident I could execute them with results similar to those desired. I grabbed the box containing the sacks of medicine, rebuckled by boots and coat, and took my leave. Maybelle's house was a good three or four blocks away. As I turned North onto Paw Paw Street, I fondly remembered Ed Oufsbacher and what a kind and thoughtful fellow he was. I always felt I was profited by knowing him well.

Paw Paw was a delightful street. It had little traffic because it was not a through street. The brisk air, powerful sunshine, and sidewalks cleared of last night's snow made the journey a pleasant one. One of the benefits of small town life is that residents scoop their walks in a timely manner. But nearing Maybelle's house I saw that snow still covered her sidewalk and the walks on either side or hers.

It came back to me and I relished the memory of 'Ed Alley.' There was talk, for a time, of changing the name of the street. Ed Oufsbacher bought the house between Ed Wing and Ed Pomerene. That was coincidence. The fact that they each married women with, shall we say, extremely strong personalities was almost eerie. One couldn't say they were hen-pecked. That would not be properly descriptive. I am unfamiliar with a proper term so, even though I am unsure whether the word exists, I will say they were hen-hammered.

I only saw it myself on a few occasions, but I was amazed each time. The three Eds would be working in their yards: Ed Wing might be cleaning the windows on his house, Ed Oufsbacher might be tending his manicured yard and garden, and Ed Pomerene might be washing his car.

A shrill shriek would ring out, "Ed!!" The high pitched tone would echo off surrounding houses making it impossible to identify the direction or the personage of the source. The three Eds would snap to attention in unison in a way that would make a synchronized swimming coach green with envy. They would hustle, not run because running would lack dignity and may engender unwanted scrutiny, into the house to attempt to quell the latest brewing tempest.

The Ed who had actually been called would manage the emergency and escape further ridicule. The remaining Eds would be met with accusations of laziness and shooed back into the yard, sometimes fleeing from the end of a broom. They would return to their chores with expressions of visible relief on their faces. Yard work and outside tasks were a haven to them.

All the Eds are dead now and, understandably, the widows have trouble finding help for chores they can no longer handle themselves. As well off as the three ladies are it is surprising workers do not call on them as they do on other elderly in the neighborhood. They cannot understand why workers are so shy. They pride themselves on the way they treat people in their employ. They share freely that they treat workers with all the respect they treated their own husbands. Somehow, I think that knowledge is widespread among the Blandtrap labor market.

Ed Wing was the last to pass and at his funeral the subject of renaming the street resurfaced among some at the gathering. Since they lived on a cul de sac, many wanted to change the name to 'Dead Ed End,' or at least erect a memorial sign. The idea never got traction so nothing came of the matter.

I made a mental note about the state of the sidewalks and went in. Maybelle was in bed and looked quite ill. She had little color and no spunk. For a lady who was known to walk downtown three or four times a day just to share a bit of idle gossip, she was very still. She spoke more after the dentist wired her mouth shut when she fell and fractured her jaw.

I fetched a cup of water and watched her swallow her pills, settling into a chair for a moment until she crawled under her blankets. We chatted briefly but as I was leaving she muttered pathetically, "If anything should happen to me …"

I cut her off in mid whine, "Nothing's going to happen to you, Maybelle, except getting well. You'll be up and about and killing off Clovis again in no time." It was a private joke between Maybelle and me. A broad, sheepish grin spread across her face which I took as a good sign.

It's rare when you get the upper hand in a conversation with Maybelle, or a work in a word edgewise. Having her at this disadvantage, I considered telling her stories about my time as an apprentice. I enjoy telling those stories but Edith informs me they are universally considered boring. It was the perfect opportunity for payback for all the times I had to listen to her drivel. Thinking better of it, I relented and left her to rest.

I was out the door and heading up the street, making good time despite a couple of slips on the icy walkway. Once I hit clear concrete, my pace improved. While passing the hardware store on the way to Lillian's house, I poked my head in the door to talk to Tommy Hunter, the kid who minds the counter when Seth Hugginbough is out delivering lumber and hardware. The kid doesn't work weekdays because of school, but the high school was closed for the rest of the week due to the epidemic. The Hunters, though, are a hale and hardy lot with a strong work ethic. I knew Tommy would be there if he escaped ravages of the disease.

"Hey, Tommy!" I shouted toward the back, "The three widows, you know, around Maybelle Oufsbacher's house, don't have their walks or driveways scooped. Could you get a couple of friends to pop over there and clear those walks for the ladies?" With the flu and all...they just can't do it themselves." Tommy nodded in concession as I closed the door, then I realized I had not made myself entirely clear and ducked back inside. "Maybelle's sick in bed and the other two are nearly deaf." At that Tommy flashed me a big smile and the OK sign. He knew what I meant.

Lillian lived only a few blocks away. I knocked and let myself in. I called to Lillian as I entered. I didn't want to catch her by surprise, not that it would startle her but she would be greatly annoyed.

Lillian Crabtree had never married. She had no use for the male of the species. Perhaps her three brothers, notorious slackards with shameful morals and well trained by their father, had soured her for all time on the idea of men with virtue. She had no experience with men of integrity. The few times she dated in school reinforced her opinion of men. Thinking her as loose morally as her brothers, dates were quickly disappointed and sent packing. Given the character of her family, it was an easy error for an idiot to make.

Many in Blandtrap thought her profession was out of character for her. She had very little concern for children. As our finest elementary school teacher, her interest in children was entirely professional. No child ever looked up at her longingly and mistakenly called her 'Gramma' or 'Aunt.' She would have spurned the title if they tried to label her in that way.

In school she handled matters her way. When the bell rang she came out from behind her desk like a prize fighter from his corner. She jabbed the ignorance out of the little folks with mind-numbing repetition and an insistence on logical thought. She required manners in everything done from the way homework was handed in to the way they addressed one another. "Not Bad" was high praise from Lillian and "Well done" was doled out only a handful of times during her career. Former students looked back on their time with her not with love but with deep respect. That was her goal; nothing else would have satisfied her.

I grabbed a glass and made a pitcher of ice water delivering them with the pills to her bedside. "Put them over there." She said without motioning. Lillian had a way of speaking in the general sense that made it clear what she specifically wanted done. It was the nightstand to her right she was referring to, not the one to her left.

Explaining that no one else was available and the doctor wanted her to have the medicine immediately, I brought it straight away. Then, I gathered up my conviction and said, "I'm supposed to see you take the medicine. I'm not allowed to leave until I see you take it. These are doctor's orders. I don't have a say in it."

I could see her bristle at the suggestion even though she was hidden under the covers. At any other opportunity, she would have grabbed me by the ear and escorted me out the door at the suggestion that she needed to be watched at all, particularly by a man. It was testimony to how sick she really was when she submitted to my authority. She took the medicine without incident. Jotting a note on the pad, I told her when it was time to take the next dose. I would have stayed to chat, but she dismissed me with "Thank you Mr. Ellis. That will be all." I left. She could be much more direct if she needed to be. It was best to go quickly.

On the way to LaVonda's house I caught a glimpse of the rear of the hardware store. Seth had returned from deliveries and given Tommy a break. The boy was coming out the back door. He wasn't headed for the soda shop or the diner as one would suppose. He had a snow shovel in his hand and was headed toward Paw Paw Street and the widow's sidewalks. Good kid, that Tommy.

LaVonda's door was on the latch in anticipation of my arrival and I secured it as I entered. Retrieving a glass of water from the kitchen and placing it and the medicine on the nightstand, I began my search for the absent LaVonda. During a quick phone call to Edith, I noticed through the window over the kitchen sink a small path from LaVonda's back door, across the alley, and to the door of the Carlson's attached garage.

Following the trail I found LaVonda in the Carlson's kitchen washing dishes. Teetering from fever she had propped herself up using a kitchen stool. It enabled her to wash dishes without the danger of passing out and crashing to the floor. When she first got a glimpse of me she had an expression that was part 'caught in the act' and part 'reinforcements, at last.'

"How are the Carlsons doing?" I began.

"Fine, they are resting now…..I suppose the doctor sent you." She said as she leaned into the counter for support.

"In a manner of speaking, yes." I answered. "You sit down for a moment while I check in on the Carlsons."

"They're fine." She was insulted at the thought of her care being inadequate in any way.

"Pardon me if I don't take the opinion of one cadaver regarding the condition of the morgue." I responded. This seemed to amuse her in some way and she slumped into a kitchen chair as I checked on the Carlsons. I returned to chat with LaVonda at the kitchen table. I was killing time until she regained strength for the trip home.

I served the fresh coffee and muffins she had made in anticipation of visitors. She knew it wouldn't be long until someone showed up to drag her home and it would be impolite to receive them without refreshment. A chat with her was more exciting than one would think it would be with a church organist. I'm easily surprised on such occasions.

LaVonda's place, the parishioners believed, was behind the organ or piano on Sunday morning and you would find her there each week without exception. She also gave piano lessons to ungrateful children who refused to practice. I have some small personal knowledge of this as my parents could attest. No one suspected she had another side.

Friday and Saturday nights, she could be found, should anyone care to look for her, in some roadhouse or speakeasy tickling the ivories in a different style of music. Only a few of the men in the congregation ever ran into her in this setting and, as propriety would have it, they were in circumstances that made sharing the encounter with others, shall we say, awkward at best. No one knew for sure because it was impertinent to question a lady regarding such matters, but I always thought she never married because the gentlemen she met in taverns were unsettled and of low moral character and the ones she met at church were either already married or too dull to be of interest to her.

Edith eventually arrived and assumed the duties of tending to the Carlsons and I bundled up LaVonda and led her home. Once I was sure she was comfortable, I collected Edith and we had a very pleasant walk together. Passing the pharmacy, we stopped in to report our mission accomplished. Our reward for a job well done was, what it so often is: another job to do well. Rudy had another delivery for us. He had prepared a large box for the nursing home and it needed to go right away. Residents were in need and employees were dropping like flies making replenishing supplies impossible if they were to properly care for their charges. Their stockpile had dwindled to nothing and the need was great.

I trotted home to get the car, returning to pick up Edith and the box to begin our journey of mercy. We drove to the nursing home making quick work of the delivery. Since the shadows were getting long by then, we decided to eat out. Our restaurant of choice that evening was Jose Wong's Ye Olde Fashioned Chuck Wagon Smorgasbord Buffet. It was easy to find even in the gathering fog. With all the neon lights it takes for the name on the sign, the road around the place was lit up like an airport runway. Dining at Jose Wong's is an adventure as well as a culinary pleasure. As the name implies the menu is large and varied. I had herring and a taco while Edith enjoyed roast beef and pot stickers.

It is my sincere hope that the epidemic will have run its course by next week so I can return to reporting the news of Blandtrap to your deaf ears. Until then, feel free to continue to manufacture your misinformation.

Respectfully Submitted,
Harry Ellis

Harry Ellis

238 Persimmon Street

Blandtrap

To the Editor of the Tiskilwa Bureau Valley Chief

RE: Cold Rain Falling

Dear Sir:

Today I will have to dispense with the usual lambasting. We, of Blandtrap, are preoccupied today and I am unable to respond as I have in the past. A phone call last night has changed our normal routine and Blandtrap will not be today what it has been in the past.

As I left my home this morning the air was clear and the sun was shining, yet a heavy fog had settled over this community and a cold rain falls on our hearts. My steps to Village Square were not brisk and I did not look forward to the usual meeting with friends. Still, we must meet. No one would be absent. Regulars and irregulars would sit together along with men who only join us during times of testing.

I passed the quilting club standing on the sidewalk. Choosing not to interrupt, I nodded my head in respect and recognition as I went on my way. Words were not necessary; they may have even been an intrusion. The ladies of the quilting club were gathered outside the notion shop. Forming a somber circle, holding hands seeking guidance from the only One who can provide relief and understanding in matters such as these. I paused a moment to join them in their grief and their petitions to God, then entered the coffee shop.

Inside it was a little livelier, but still uncharacteristically quiet. On a normal day the large round table in the back would contain only few

30

patrons, mainly older men, such as me, while younger men would sit in groups of two to four at smaller tables scattered through the diner. They, like most young people, seem to quickly tire of the useful instruction, sage wisdom, and frequent stories of us older folks. Age will change their opinion on the matter.

But when events such as these occur, the younger men seek out our company. They desire our comments now, when normally they would try to avoid our suggestions. I'm not sure whether they seek us out for guidance, or whether they simply want to gauge their own feelings against ours, much like you might use a yard stick to measure your pace. The large table was already full, and they had pulled up an extra chair by the time I reached them.

There was a time when I recognized the faces of all the younger men at the table and knew all their names. It doesn't happen that way anymore. I'm not exactly sure I got them matched up correctly but I had the right number of names for the right number of people. Bill Whittacre was there, too. I bet I could count on one hand the number of times I've seen Bill in the diner. When young men join us, we older men collectively form an opinion regarding the wisdom youngsters have accumulated. We are usually impressed with their progress until they open their mouth to make a comment. That usually moves them back a square or two in our evaluation of them.

Bill Whittacre only absorbed what was happening around him and didn't intrude with his own conversation. He remained silent and was believed to be wise by the older guys. He was generally known as a good man and proved it regularly.

"What do we do now?" Bobby Allen asked. "Mom and Dad are on vacation. They'd know what to do, but I'm stuck here alone. Maybe my girlfriend, Alice, would know."

No one responded to Bobby. He didn't expect an answer. When women talk to themselves out loud it is important to pay attention, but when men do it, you should wait until they address you directly. What men say often has nothing to do with about whom they say it. It has less to do with content and more to do with heart.

"What was it?" Stu inquired.

"A girl, I think." Someone said. "I don't know any more."

"She was seven pounds, six ounces and eighteen inches long." Stu had the details.

"Did they have a name picked out?" I wondered out loud.

"If it was a girl, they were going to name her Roberta Ann." Clovis' father remembered out loud.

"That was her great grandmother's name, wasn't it?" I observed.

"Yeah, it was a great honor...regardless." Clovis father added.

"What should we do? Can we really be of help?" Bobby was lost for a plan.

"Whether it will help or not, we'll do what we can and try our best to keep out of the way while we do it. We'll handle this the way we handle everything else: start with what is most effective, then, move on to less important details until there's nothing left to do." Ray Solomon spoke up.

Men struggle at times like these. Women sympathize and are moved to comfort the distressed. If the Williams family were being attacked by an army, we had enough men ready to fight a respectable battle. If their child were stuck in a well, we had enough able bodied men to dig them out. It is when there is nothing that can be done, we men realize how little help we are, how limited our abilities, and how dependent on God we remain.

Ray wouldn't be your first pick for sainthood. He's had a checkered past having lead a fast life with questionable women and lots of booze, but in the last fifteen years he's straightened out pretty good. In his ignorance he was always impulsive. He thinks before he acts now. Sometimes, he just thinks.

There are people who can lead on a day to day basis and do a good or even brilliant job. Other leaders rise in times of crisis or tragedy. These are people that you would never suspect, from their daily activities, were capable of greatness. It is very rare for a person to be both. It is so rare you couldn't put up a museum to recognize their collective endeavors; a phone booth would be too large for the task.

"Pray with me." Ray ordered heads to bow and even men who don't regularly pray followed his lead. Ray was the perfect choice to lead the prayer. Ray had gotten himself into enough tight jambs from which only the Lord could save him that he was an expert in this type of situation. "Father, we don't know what to do. Please be with the family of Roberta Ann giving solace to her mother and strength to her father. Give us the wisdom to know the right thing to do and the opportunity to do it. We pray in Christ's name. Amen."

"Amen," we all joined in.

"Gentlemen", Ray started, "We will leave God to do his part, let's do ours." Turning to the man next to him and proceeding around the table he said, "Eldon, you live next door to them, so the minute they leave for the funeral home to make arrangements, you call Bobby. Bobby, you have the mower loaded into your truck and get over there and mow their lawn as soon as Eldon calls. Harry, go down to the hardware store and get a new welcome mat for the front door. They'll have a lot of people tracking in and they'll need a good one. Stu, you go to the bank and start a fund for the family. Blow the dust off that wallet on the way over and give the account a good seeding because I understand they didn't have much insurance. The rest of us will keep our eyes open and do what we can."

Ray seemed to be in charge and I guess he was, but it was more like the voice over the loudspeaker seems to be in charge at the train depot. You respond to directions when you don't know where to go. We finished our coffee. I got stiffed by Stu again. These were extraordinary circumstances. I didn't mind paying for Stu that day. Normally tighter with a dollar than a preacher's wife, I knew Stu to be generous to a fault when there was genuine need. It was likely Stu's seed money in the account would outshine any other contribution. Everyone with a heart has their own manner of philanthropy. This was Stu's way.

I caught sight of Carla Dombrowski sitting alone in a booth at the back of the diner. I nearly overlooked her, self-absorbed in grief as I was. She had her head down on the table and was not in her usual buoyant spirits. Edith had told me she worked for the doctor Mrs. Williams had been seeing and had been the nurse during several visits to the doctor. I'd seen the look on a hundred faces over the years. She was questioning herself.

I walked over and gave her a pat on the shoulder and she looked up at me with tearful eyes. I could tell she felt responsible in some way. Did she miss something? Was she attentive to the point where she could have foreseen this problem? In fact, Carla lacked the skill to see this coming and the power to do anything about it even if she possessed the skill. This type of foresight resides in the realm of God alone. Knowing this is not a comfort; it brings more tears.

Edith had trained me well. I knew the best I could do was to keep my heart open and my mouth shut. I made a mental note to have Edith call Carla. They knew each other from church. After a quiet moment, I headed for Hugginbough's Hardware.

It's a strange turnabout that occurs at times as these. Women know what should be done, but nothing they do seems to be exactly the right thing to do. Men don't have any idea what should be done, but what ever they do seems just right.

Some ladies from the Quilting Society were still in their circle of prayer. I put my hand on Mrs. Wing's shoulder interrupting the prayer while I told them of Carla and her suffering inside the establishment. They didn't mind the intrusion. Carla was in good hands now and would be later with Edith. I went about my duties. Mrs. Wing was soon on her way inside to tend to her. I left.

Clovis was wandering the streets looking for someone to talk to and, given the situation, I didn't try to avoid him as I would if I had more pressing business to manage. I knew he would have trouble working through this. His father, no doubt, had already talked with him about the matter, but Clovis often needed things explained to him many times in several different ways before he got a good grasp on what was going on. He fell in stride beside me. "Sad, huh?" He observed.

"Real sad." I answered.

"Anything I can do for them?" Clovis wanted to help like we all did. Like most of us, he didn't have the slightest inkling about what would be of help.

I stopped and thought for a moment. "Sure Clovis, you know that bramble the Williams' have back by the alley?"

"Yeah." He was paying close attention and I could see he knew what I was talking about. Clovis' face was a window into his mind. You could literally see what he was thinking if you took the time to know him well.

"They'd appreciate it if you could clean that out for them. Make sure you rake it up real good and take the brush with you when you leave. Put it in your truck and dump it on your farm. They have a little bit of a fence along the garage. See if you can take the lean out of it. Don't put in any new posts, even though you may have them, just prop it up and make it look good for now. Once things settle down you can go back and fix it proper."

"I could do that!" Clovis said excitedly. I'm sure he was glad to learn he could help. He started to paddle off. He couldn't wait to start his noble task.

"Clovis!" I yelled to him. He stopped and turned toward me, "You know how you can't always find the right words to explain how you feel?"

Clovis nodded. I swear I could see a tear in the corner of his eye. Maybe it was in mine.

"They're going to feel the same way, only worse. So, if you see them, maybe you should just wave and keep quiet. They'll know how you feel. No need to bother a grieving person with a lot of chit chat." Clovis could remember that from when his grandfather died. Everyone wanted to tell him how sorry they were for him when he just wanted to weep privately.

"Yeah," He sighed as he left. He wished he had a better command of the English language so he could better communicate what he felt. I do, too.

Bill Whittacre was paying as I reached the cash register. "What are you up to, now, Bill?" I asked to see how he was doing.

"I'm not good at consoling people. I hardly know what to say when I meet someone on the street. I know people will be dropping off a lot of food by the house; they always do at these times. I'm going to buy some plastic wrap, storage containers, and sandwich bags at the IGA and leave them on the stoop. They'll need them, I think." Bill mumbled, sort of in a question.

"That'll be good, Bill." I said as I patted him on the back. I believed it to be a most thoughtful gesture. Not many single men would be moved in this way or be so considerate of the needs of the family. He marched off toward the IGA.

At the hardware store, I quickly picked out an appropriate mat and took it to the counter. Tommy Hunter was tending the store by himself, which is a tribute to an eighteen year old boy. Few teenagers would be trusted to tend a store alone. He was up to that task and more.

"Hi Harry, are you buying another doormat? Didn't you buy a couple of mats last week?" Tommy quizzed. I was surprised he remembered previous purchases. No wonder Hugginbough keeps this kid around and gives him so much responsibility. He does as good a job as Seth would if he were here.

"Yes I did, Tommy. This one is for the Williams"

"Oh," he said stepping away from the cash register and holding up both hands, "In that case, it's on the house."

"Are you sure you're allowed to do that, Tommy?" I knew Hugginbough to be a generous man with his money, but not necessarily with his inventory. It not being Tommy's mat to give, I thought I should ask because I was uncomfortable with his offer. Teenagers always seem to be giving things away these days. Tommy was the exception to the rule.

"Its OK," he assured while he put the mat in a bag. As I left I heard him ringing up the item on that ancient cash register Hugginbough insists upon using in spite of advice to modernize. As I was passing the window, I saw Tommy pull his hand from his pocket and put the money for the mat in the cash drawer. Good kid that Tommy. Few lads his age would consider dipping into their own pocket to help others in trouble and fewer would actually do it. Not many grownups would do it either, now that you mention it.

On the way home I stopped by the Williams house and replaced their worn welcome mat taking the old mat with me as I departed. I didn't bother to knock, just did my business and left them to their grief. Nothing really helps and nothing seems to harm.

Passing the bank I saw Stu talking to Tom Holdfast, Blandtrap's banker. It was an amusing sight. The only person with a tighter grip on a dollar than Stu was Tom. Two famous skinflints were having a discussion on benevolence. It is true that God moves in strange ways and this is one of the proofs. Later I learned Stu had been more than generous in starting the fund and Tom got on the phone to the board of directors to obligate the bank to match his donation. Amen.

The aroma was overwhelming when I arrived home. It was a smell you only find during a holiday or at a funeral. Great joy and great sorrow have more in common than I can explain. Edith had been in the kitchen all day.

Cooking is an art which men can master. Women, however, master cooking as an abstract form of art. A man can make a casserole as well as any woman. But, when a man makes a casserole, all you have is something to eat. When a woman makes a casserole, you know a heart was poured into the mixing bowl along with the ingredients. With the lady's product, you have a casserole to eat and consolation as you dine. It's an entirely different matter.

Edith's sympathy was getting the best of her. When I kissed her from the side, she smiled at me but had to wipe a tear first. I just held her. There was nothing I could say to comfort her. She suggested we invite the Williams to go with us on our next trip. It would take their mind off things. I agreed and we did indeed extend the offer, knowing relief would come not from recreation or distraction, but they would appreciate the offer nonetheless.

The funeral was a small affair with just the family and only the closest friends in attendance. As the hearse passed Village Square, all heads bowed. At the church, the Ladies Service Circle was praying and planning meals for the family. Men stopped what they were doing. Those with hats removed them. Reverence was the order of the moment.

We never knew this child. No one held her in their arms and no one heard her cry or laugh. Why then does the loss seem so great? Regardless of what we do to ease the pain or to remember the child, we are changed by her passing as if she accomplished great deeds during the life she didn't enjoy. Then again, perhaps she did.

Some ask why God lets something like this happen. I mentioned that to Ray Solomon earlier today. He reminded me that I shouldn't be worried about what God was doing. God knows what he is about, even if we can't understand it. I should, instead, be worried about what I was doing. And so I will retire, and reflect on what I am doing.

Until next week you will be left to your usual resource of reporting only about your own city and imagining or manufacturing news of the surrounding residents. I will endeavor to be in better spirits later, however, today we will grieve, knowing that Roberta Ann Williams is with God, her parents are in shock, and we are all somehow diminished.

Respectfully Submitted,

Harry Ellis

Harry Ellis

238 Persimmon Street

Blandtrap

To the Editor of the Tiskilwa Bureau Chief

RE: The Big Snow

Dear Sir:

Your weather predictions are outrageous. Sure, you can argue that I should rely on something other than a weekly publication for my immediate weather needs, but other weather prognosticators maintain a better record than yours and publish on an annual rather than weekly basis. Almanacs, for instance, seem to do a pretty good job and were written years ago. You should be at least as reliable as an almanac.

Two weeks ago I had to shovel six inches of 'partly cloudy' off my driveway. Certainly with determination and attention to detail, you can improve your performance. It must seem out of character for me to encourage you rather than pasting you with sarcasm as is my habit. But, I live in fear that your dismal forecasts will leave me unprepared for more serious conditions. I worry that your next 'warm and sunny' prediction will conceal a cyclone of biblical proportions. You have won me over as a cheerleader, with fear instead of confidence, but you have won me over nonetheless.

Just last week your accuracy caught Blandtrap by surprise. You predicted 'cold with some snow.' After three days of continuous snowfall we saw the wisdom of your words. Everyone entering Plowboy Diner said the same thing as they shook the white fluffy stuff from their garments and shoes, "That was some snow!" You can count that forecast in the 'dead on' column in spite of the fact it left us unaware of pending conditions.

In the future, it would be more helpful if you could quantify your forecast. Qualitative terms like 'some snow' have literary significance and, I am sure, took several cups of herbal tea to conjure up appropriate words that artfully describe the event without offering any practical information to alert readers to responsibly prepare for its consequences.

May I suggest for snowfall you use more visual terms such as the traditional inches of accumulation. I can understand your reticence in being held to an accurate measure like inches. If you used feet of snow and told us you were rounding to the nearest foot it would be more helpful than descriptive language. Even if you measured snowfall in hernias per township it would be more useful than your present system.

The temperature dropped Tuesday evening and we battened the hatches against the cold. On my walk to the diner on Wednesday morning the snow began with a light white powder. After two cups of coffee and some hash browns it had begun to accumulate. Stu and I looked at each other with expectation as we stood on the street in front of the diner. We glanced up to gauge the clouds and drew on our limited knowledge of meteorology, "Could be a big one." Stu said prophetically. "Better get ready,"

I offered back, "I'm with you," I said and we headed for our respective homes.

Edith was up and about by the time I arrived home. She was well into her morning ritual of cleaning things that weren't really dirty and planning meals we were unlikely to consume. Some garden seed catalogues were spread out before her. She was making a list, so I sat at the table, thumbing through a catalogue until she finished her scribbling.

"You'd better check on the widows." I said when she was done, "It looks like this might pile up after a while. Find out what they need and I'll see how we can get it to them."

Edith turned the page on her note pad and reached for the phone. "Could you get the directory out of the drawer for me, please?" She asked. I complied with her request but it was wasted labor. Edith knew the widows' phone numbers by heart. She began dialing without referring to it.

I slipped out to Hugginbough's Hardware and Lumber to get a few bags of salt and sand for sidewalks and vehicles stuck in the snow. Tommy Hunter was in school so I got to deal with Hugginbough himself. He told me about the Phillipi boy getting married on Saturday. He was marrying a girl from Butte Crossing, but they were going to have Preacher Brimstone preside over the ceremony. I backed the car up to the dock to load bags into the trunk. Snow was coming down even harder and flakes were getting larger. It had become wet and snow started to stick to whatever it struck.

Hugginbough slapped the trunk closed expecting me to leave. "Maybe I should get an oil lamp or two and some oil. If this keeps sticking, power lines could come down." I said heading back inside from the loading dock. Seth rummaged around the stock shelves a while and came to the front with two dusty cases of lamps.

I decided on a case of high fluted lamps thinking the ladies would prefer them and added three bottles of oil: red, green, and clear. Sometimes color is important and I didn't want to take any chances. Fashion can interfere with rescue if one is not cautious. Edith and the widows tend to be particular about things like that. Personally, I would just be pleased to have the light.

On the way home, the car handled differently with the extra weight in the trunk. The car slid off the road a bit as I turned the corner on Persimmon Street. I was horsing around a little, but the effect was greater than I had anticipated. Roads were getting icy and slick. They were just at that fun stage now, but they were going to get worse. If I'd had more time I would have driven to the church parking lot to cut a few doughnuts. Remembering the deacons were meeting that morning, I ruled out horseplay to avoid having another one of 'those talks' again on Sunday.

It took Edith all morning to contact the widows and compile and complete their lists and she was not yet finished. As I ate the sandwich she had prepared for my lunch, I had an opportunity to overhear the pitfalls of Edith's task.

"Hello, Maybelle." Edith started. "The weather is getting pretty bad and we're afraid it will get worse. If it snows all night, you won't be able to get to the store. Give me a list and I'll have Harry pick up a few things for you. What do you need?"

"No, Maybelle, I can't see Sue Raney's driveway from my house and I don't know what kind of car her new boyfriend drives anyway. Is there anything you need?"

"Yes, Maybelle, it is shameful what the politicians are doing in Washington....No, I hadn't heard that...No, I hadn't heard that...No, I hadn't heard that. Maybelle, is there anything you need: milk, eggs, bread?"

"I agree, Alice Swanson does bake the best bread in the church. No, I don't know the recipe she uses. Maybelle, do you need any bread? OK, it's on the list."

How about medicine, do you need a prescription filled? Sure, prescription costs are high…Yes, I've noticed…Yes, very high…Are you expecting to be overcharged in the next few days, Maybelle?" Edith was swimming against the tide, fighting desperately not to be swept out to the sea that is Maybelle's world of concerns.

Edith struggled through arthritis, global warming, dryer sheets, and space exploration before she got the prescription that Maybelle needed.

I had been watching the clock. Edith picked up the receiver to dial Maybelle's number at 12:10 and returned it to the cradle at 1:05. It was an amazing exhibition of tenacity and endurance on Edith's part. I'm proud of the girl.

Sighing deeply, she looked a bit cross-eyed as she rewrote her notes on the pad in front of her. "Mrs. Wing wasn't home and Mrs. Pomerene was on the other line when I called. I only have those two left." I did the math on the number she had already contacted and the length of each call to determine Edith would not finish until sometime between 3:00

and 4:00. We chatted as she ate her sandwich and we parted ways, each to our own tasks.

Trotting down to the diner to get more news about the storm, I was in luck. The county road plow crew was finishing lunch as I walked in. The usual conversation ensued and I tried to sway them to my way of thinking. It was the contention of the Road Commissioner that snow could not be properly plowed until it was four inches in depth. "Salt and sand work best," he would say, "at depths of less than four inches."

The problem with that policy, which we in Blandtrap so often point out, is that snow deposits relatively evenly around the area. Once snow accumulates to four inches in depth, driving has already become extremely hazardous; even liberal application of salt and sand does not improve drivability of roads. By the time plow blades are dropped to pavement, roads are nearly impassable. By the time the plow gets to side streets, snow may be six to ten inches deep. The road crew smiles at this point in the argument. They rather like this arrangement because roads are much easier to plow when no cars are on the road.

The only other news at the diner was the Phillipi wedding on Saturday. The Phillipi boy was marrying some girl from Butte Crossing. I told Enrico, father of the groom, that's what happens if you don't keep a tight reign on your children. The first time you're not looking, they'll wander off and marry a girl from a wretched place like Butte Crossing!

I had to hit the road to evaluate resources needed to provide for the widows. Pausing to size up the food situation, I stuck my head in the door of the grocery to see how they were prepared. Leon Fezzizzi, the manager, was on the phone at the service counter. "How are you stocked?" I asked as soon as he hung up. He knew why I asked. It was a familiar drill during inclement weather.

"Pretty good," He said, "The bakery is going to crank out bread and rolls all night so they'll be ready by morning and tomorrow's truck from the dairy is coming tonight. We'll be all set." That settled, on my way I went.

Returning home, Edith and I spent the evening quietly. She baked some pies and a cake while I read to her from your newspaper and some magazines. I did the honor of icing the cake while Edith cleaned up around the kitchen. We both turned in early.

On Thursday the snow came with a vengeance. Flakes were large and fluffy and stacking up quickly. I scooted out the door before Edith rose and headed out for Plowboy Diner, taking a seat at the large round table rather than the usual table. Unable to perform any useful work, men who could make the trip would be showing up at the diner as soon as they could get away.

Snow had been deep on the way over. It had accumulated to mid-shin depth. I knew I would have to get home soon to shovel the walks and driveway before it was too deep to handle by myself. I also realized I would have to shovel more than once that day if weather continued its course.

Clovis' father showed up first, complaining of road conditions. He said snow was at least eight inches deep and hadn't seen a plow yet. When Stu arrived, he said he had called the City Garage to see why his street hadn't been cleared. They are known to be early birds unless there was some kind of trouble. Word was that both truck and plow were inoperable. The engine of the truck had been disassembled to replace seals and it would take several hours to get it up and running. At the same time, the plow was down until a part for the hydraulics came in. The part might make it in that day or, more likely; it would be Friday morning until they were back in business.

The whole gang started to gather: Craig Beeman, Simeon Swagg, Clovis himself, and Seth Hugginbough all came by at about the same time. Stu showed up later. News had become tainted from repetition and its reliability had been lowered to the level of rumor. Each person had a unique misunderstanding of what they believed to be the facts. Every newcomer had to be straightened out in one way or another. I left in mid correction to head for home.

Busying myself with snow shoveling duties, I couldn't stop worrying about widow's deliveries. It took more than an hour to clear the snow and by the time I was done, it was almost deep enough where I had to scoop again. I wasn't up to the task at the moment and slipped inside the house.

The ritual of warming up with a cup of Edith's cocoa was what drove me out into the snow in the first place. Nothing warms cold bones like a cup of Edith's cocoa, one of the great comforts of life. As I was walking out the door to make the first delivery, Edith yelled to me, "Don't forget your ear muffs!"

I shouted back, "I'm going to Maybelle's house. I'm going to need ear plugs long before I need ear muffs." I could hear Edith laugh as I left and filled the next couple of hours with pickups and deliveries all over town and out to the retirement home at the edge of town. It was slow, but I made steady progress.

Maybelle had been my last delivery of the day. She needed groceries and medicine. Decorum demanded I stay until she put up the groceries and stowed the pills. Before I could cut myself loose I had a stiff neck from nodding my head 'yes,' unable to get a word in edgewise. I wouldn't have gotten away at all if Edith hadn't called to see if I had made it that far yet. While Maybelle answered the phone I made my escape out the back door and around the outside of the house to my car. I had to wade through hip-deep drifts to get away, but any price was worth the reward of freedom.

I had to shovel walks again as soon as I made it back home. Edith and I finished the evening with soup for supper and a rematch of a bitterly contested Scrabble defeat I suffered last week. I still seek revenge for the insult. One last shovel before bed let me sleep more soundly and wake up pretty stiff.

Friday morning the snow was still coming down. It had snowed enough I needed to shovel the walks before I could, in good conscience, leave for the diner. It would have been too deep for me if I waited until I returned. I was stiff and sore all over by the time I finished. It was foolhardy to clear the driveway since the streets had not been plowed but I did it anyway. The walk to Village Square took me through thigh-deep snow and past houses who hadn't kept up with the downfall.

A seat in the second row around the large table was the best I could do after arriving as late as I had. The main topic of conversation involved the ability of the Cubs shortstop to cleanly field hot grounders. I had missed much with my tardiness. Obviously I had missed the topics of weather, crops, politics, religion, and scandal. They were all the way down the list to baseball. Clovis' father launched into a familiar discourse about the great shortstops of all time. When he paused to recall a particularly obscure name from baseball antiquity, I took the opportunity to ask for an update on road conditions. Every one jumped in like a chorus to help me out rather than listen to the shortstop story again, since many had heard it three times that week.

Stu said the city garage had their part for the plow and the truck was almost back together. They expected to be plowing within the hour. No word had come from the county road crew. Conversation languished several minutes. No one got up to leave because there was nothing to do. Taking turns calling home to our wives and families to check on them, we were encouraged to stay. No wife, it seems, wants a husband with time on his hands hanging around the house. We tend to do things like shut off the water to fix a leak or remove doors to relieve a sticky jamb and lose interest before the job is complete and parts reassembled. The average man has no trouble at all starting, without finishing, five or six home improvement projects before turning in for the evening. I'm not as handy as most. My personal record is three.

From outside the diner, we heard a much anticipated scraping sound coming down the street. It was the plow! Men got up and moved to the window to watch. You would have thought it was a presidential motorcade the way we amassed to get a glimpse. It was a thing of beauty, the cleared road behind the truck.

Admiring what he saw, someone said "You could drive on that."

The plow passed by the restaurant to the cheers of the diners. As soon as the plow was out of sight a loud boom echoed off buildings surrounding Village Square and rattled the glass in the windows. We held our breath in horror, fearing the worst. From the direction of the plow, a cloud of dark, dense, black smoke passed by the window from the direction of the plow. We all hung our heads and shuffled back to our seats utterly defeated. The plow was no more.

A while later, Enrico Phillipi hustled through the door and stomped snow off his boots onto the welcome mat. In light of the looming wedding, Enrico was immediately granted a prominent seat at the large table. He had to get out of the house, it seemed, because his son and wife were in a tizzy about the snow. The rehearsal and dinner were that night in Butte Crossing with the wedding on Saturday at 11:00. "I know we won't make it tonight; and now, with the city plow down again, I'm sure we won't make it tomorrow either." He slumped in this chair thinking about reception hall deposits and bills for an uneaten dinner. Clovis trotted over and brought him a cup of coffee.

Enrico's problem seemed to perk up the crowd of idle men. "Didn't they close the high school today?" Stu remembered, "I mean sports and everything. The basketball and wrestling teams don't have anything to do right?"

Clovis' father said, "We had to bring the tractor today and I've got the end loader on it. I could take Clovis back and bring in the dump truck."

"My father-in-law has a dump truck too." Simeon Swagg added.

Stu was in good form and organization was a way of life for him. "Hugginbough, is Tommy Hunter at the store today?"

"I haven't been by the shop yet, but if there's no school and no sports, then he's there." Hugginbough said with confidence.

Stu directed, "Have him call the wrestling team and meet us at the Phillipi house. Tell him to bring all the snow shovels you've got in stock." Seth was out the door like lightening. He would deliver the message in person.

Men were standing up, putting on coats and buckling boots. They were alive again because life had purpose. Enrico was confused about what was going on. "Finish your coffee and head for home, Enrico." Stu promised, "We'll get you to Butte Crossing in time for rehearsal. You have our word on it."

I went home, but had to shovel my own walks again before I could leave for the Phillipi home. Edith insisted on coming with me in case there was anything she could do in support of the effort. It was three and a half blocks down sometimes unshoveled walks. When we got there, Bob and Ruth, who store their motor home in town, had it fired up and parked in front of the Phillipi house. Men and boys had cleared the road to the end of the block with scoops and shovels. Clovis turned the corner in the end loader, with his father following closely in the dump truck. Simeon Swagg was already waiting in his father-in-law's dump truck. Work began in earnest.

Stu came out of the Phillipi house to announce he had gotten through to the county road crew and pled our case. If we could get them out to the county highway, they would have a path cleared all the way into Butte Crossing. With a goal clearly in sight, the men were inspired to new heights of performance.

Several more men appeared and they were ready to work. From a few blocks away we heard the moan of the bagpipes before a tune began to play. We don't know anything about Celtic or Highland music but we agreed it was a song about marching into battle. Encouraged, we cleared snow all the faster. The bagpipes, at a distance, stayed with us until the job was done.

As workers became cold and tired they were rotated through the motor home. Workers would warm in the heat and get a cup of Edith's cocoa to rest and recover. Bob and Ruth had stopped by to get Maybelle on their way to the worksite. Maybelle was seated at the table to make sure men didn't dally after they rested.

The motor home rolled along with the progress of the workers. At 6:30 PM we connected with the county road and they had been as good as their word. They were waiting for us and began to clear the road into Butte Crossing. The motor home returned to the Phillipi house to inform them of our success.

Workers applauded to salute the Phillipis as they left on their trek to the wedding. I got a glimpse of Pastor Brimstone in the back of the van as it passed by. We dispersed to our homes feeling pretty good about the way the town came together. The bagpipe finished with a song of victory to serenade villagers returning to their homes.

Back in the kitchen, Edith informed me we were invited to the ceremony. I made a mental note to pick a toaster on the way back from the diner in the morning. Nothing says you're married like five or six toasters and a few bathroom scales.

The events of yesterday have sapped the venom from my pen. Relenting to fatigue, rest is the medicine to relieve the stress of endless shoveling. I encourage you to do better in your forecast of the weather, or, perhaps, consider replacing the column with an article on fashion or a bridge column. I hear crossword puzzles are quite the rage these days.

Respectfully submitted,

Harry Ellis

February

Purloined from the property of Calvin Farnsworth:

If you were to do a pretty good job of performing a popular roller rink dance to prerecorded music in a swamp in mid-Florida, wouldn't that be...

…an okey dokey Okeefenokee Karaoke hokey pokey?

Harry Ellis

238 Persimmon Street

Blandtrap

To the Editor of the Tiskilwa Bureau Valley Chief

RE: Groundhog Day

Dear Sir:

I read in your pages about the Groundhog Day celebration in your city. From the story I gleaned you have purchased your own rodent for the festivities and have been flaunting your pet for the townspeople's pleasure. The photos are particularly interesting. It makes me wonder how you select the pictures you use for publication. The image of the groundhog is much more flattering than yours as you hold the beast. I would have chosen a photograph that put me in a better light than the rat, but that, I guess, is why I am a subscriber and you are the professional!

We recognize Groundhog Day in Blandtrap, but it is not the gala event that your city observes. It does not consume our thoughts for days at a time nor do we spend weeks planning for the event. A simple recognition of the day is all we feel it deserves. Your perception of Groundhog Day as an august occasion escapes our reason, consequently our observation of the holiday lacks the tradition and ceremony you enjoy.

I began the day with my usual walk to Plowboy Diner for coffee and conversation. When I arrived, Clovis and his father were already seated at the table and Stu was at the coffee pot getting his first cup. By the time I got my cup and made it to my seat, being waylaid by a couple of ladies from the Quilting Society inquiring about Edith's health, Calvin Farnsworth and Simeon Swagg had beaten me to the table.

It was one of those nondescript years so far, except for the big snow which had worn a hole in conversation lately. Normal routine takes a toll on men's conversation. The weather was normal for the season, crops weren't in nor should they be, crop prices were just about where they should be, football season was long over, and basketball season hadn't gotten interesting yet leaving little spark to the spoken word.

When I brought up the fact it was Groundhog Day, the farmers began to bristle at the thought and berated the day. "You can't expect a farmer to celebrate Groundhog Day, can you? It doesn't make sense to celebrate a mortal enemy. The groundhog feasts on our labors in the field and it rewards us for feeding it by leaving holes that break the legs of our cattle. We spend hours of time and hundreds of dollars trying to eradicate the varmint and town folk want us to recognize the rodent as having some redeeming value!" Clovis' father railed. This was just the sort of entertainment I had been hoping for. It's why God made diners. It seemed to perk up the others, too.

He continued, "How can any sane person highly regard a creature dedicated to the destruction of both crop and livestock without a wink of concern for its host. Would lake fish celebrate the swooping eagle? Would an isolated deer celebrate the wolf pack?" His voice was in crescendo, clearly audible at surrounding tables. "Would a mouse stop in his flight of panic to laud the praises of the cat? I say no!"

Now he had the attention of the entire diner, except for Frank and Alvin, the owners, who had heard this kind of talk before. It had become an annual event. Not an important event like an anniversary or Independence Day, but a less prestigious moment like Aardvark Day or Guy Fawkes Day.

"The groundhog is an animal without any discernable value whatsoever. You can't pet it, you can't eat it, and you can't even train it to guard your house. It goes on eating, digging, and destroying property with full approval of most folks. I, for one, will stand against the beast!"

He rose to his feet for emphasis. I thought about offering him my chair to stand upon but he's getting up there in years and probably shouldn't be climbing anymore.

"As long as I tend my fields, this animal will meet the back of a shovel before it serves as grand marshal of a parade in this village." The oratory garnered applause from diner patrons. I was disappointed he didn't at least put a foot on his chair and a finger in the air. That's the kind of thing that really catches a crowd's attention and burns a moment into their memory. I think he dropped the ball there.

The patrons didn't necessarily agree with his position but they recognized a well constructed argument delivered with zeal. Clovis' father had become merely an idle threat to the groundhog population. He was wise but getting old now. Personally, I would pay a handsome fee to see old man Beagle chase a groundhog with a shovel. The groundhog would be as safe as money in a bank vault. A better match would be the old man against a snail. You could probably get even money on that one were you inclined to wager.

Frank, one of the owners, stopped by our table to see what all the hubbub was about. We convinced Frank to tell us the Groundhog Day story. We were like little children. "Tell us a story, Uncle Frank," was the consensus of the group.

"Look at yourselves - grown men looking for a fairy tale!" Frank feigned protest as he continued. It was clear he enjoyed these moments as much as we did. "The story goes that on every February second, the groundhog sticks his head out of his hole. If he sees his shadow, it scares him and he goes back in his hole and we have six more weeks of winter. If he doesn't see his shadow, spring begins immediately. Everyone knows that part of the story.

"What is more interesting to me is how the groundhog knows it is February second. I'm pretty sure they don't have calendars down those holes. Even if they had calendars, who would tear off the pages or mark off the days while they hibernate?

"It's a pretty story and we all like to hear it, but its goal is to mislead us, to distract from the horrible evil the groundhog represents.

Something else must be at work here. What about the shadow? Why does it scare the groundhog? The creature is not entirely nocturnal. At night, while feasting my vegetable garden into oblivion I have seen a groundhog sit directly under my pole light. The shadow doesn't scare him then. If I flick the switch on and off: shadow, no shadow, it doesn't appear to interfere with the intruder's dinner." One of the waitresses came over and dragged Frank back behind the counter, still muttering to himself. Alvin knew he would have to settle Frank down or he would be no help the rest of the day.

Frank had passionate opinions regarding the groundhog. In his eighties, now, he had learned that passion was the spice of life, but conviction was what got things done. Together and unchecked by reason, these two spawn a fanaticism dangerous to the owner. This lethal combination had been the cause of death for several of his acquaintances. So, Frank had learned to spout off freely, and forget about an incident rather than hold a grudge or obsess.

Over the years, Frank had delivered many speeches on the evils of groundhogs, well rodents in general anyway. He had an elaborate theory regarding them that was every bit as intricate and intriguing as alien conspiracy theorists present for their cause. He seldom had an opportunity to hear similar theories to his own discussed in a national forum.

"I always thought Groundhog Day should be in the fall. That's when we make sausage at our farm." Clovis offered out loud. Clovis wasn't always on the topic, but didn't usually have much trouble staying near it. He was off the mark here and it seemed out of character.

Stu saw the bait in the water and, against better judgment acquired over years of experience, bit, grabbed the hook, and ran with it. "What does sausage have to do with Groundhog Day?"

"For a while, I wouldn't eat sausage. Remember, dad?" Clovis looked to his father who nodded in agreement while puffing on his pipe even though it wasn't lit. "Dad taught me to do things right. He said if I couldn't do something the right way, have somebody else do it. I shouldn't have anything to do with it myself. That's when I had trouble with sausage." This was a conclusion to Clovis. We weren't sure what the question was, but Clovis thought he had answered it.

We all felt like we should help Clovis land the fish he had on the line. If only we could make him reel it in, we could get to the bottom of the matter. We didn't dare use analogies like this one. Clovis was on a tangent to the conversation now. If we put him on another so soon, it might be days before we got back to our original topic, providing we could remember it.

Voles, moles, and mice were the target of Frank's wrath whenever they came up in conversation. Rats and rabbits got the same treatment when it was their turn. Groundhogs were different in that they were the only rodent with a day dedicated to them. Of course, there is Easter sporting the Easter Bunny, but popularity of this character with young children put that particular rodent off limits to him. He could hold his opinion if he held his tongue. He had been silenced by young mothers protecting the ears of their offspring often enough to discontinue the practice.

He used to launch into the same kind of degradation he saved for rats. Little boys and girls would burst into tears and remain inconsolable after hearing the full brunt of his ire. He was, around the holidays, considered a pariah, unwelcome at family gatherings and in public places such as grocery stores until mention of the day had faded from memory. It intensified his hatred of other rodents.

"Why did sausage disturb you?" Remo Astapacas piped in. Remo usually sits by himself so we weren't expecting him to join in the conversation. The only clean table available when Remo arrived was the one next to the large table around which we were seated. His preference was to sit alone at breakfast. That day he was trapped, having to sit next to the old guys and being distracted by their conversation. Clovis had sucked him into his logic stream and he had to know more.

"Well," Clovis was suddenly aware he had the attention of all. It made him uncomfortable. There was no way out so he forged ahead. "You know, Groundhog Day..........ground....hog.....day. Isn't that what sausage is? Its ground hog! You grind it don't you? I thought if there was a ground hog day and you were going to make sausage, you should make it on ground hog day. It's only right." Looking down at his shoes, "It made sense at the time, anyway." Clovis ended by shaking his head. He didn't want to be the center of attention any more.

Clovis' father was smiling. Not knowing the exact words his son would speak didn't prevent him from knowing the route he would take to arrive at his conclusion. Fatherhood had been one sleigh ride of loose logic after another. If Clovis moved along to another topic it was never a smooth transition. To talk to a neighbor most would simply walk next door. For Clovis to walk next door his path would pass farm fields and wander through forests before he would get there.

I remembered one summer when I was a child; we had overheard high school athletes complaining about groundhog holes on the practice football field. When I was a child summer was a remarkable time spent playing with friends all day. After a few quick chores were done we had all day to ourselves and would go full tilt until after dark.

In the middle of summer, families would take vacations. If one family was gone it had only a minor impact on us, but when three or more families vacationed at the same time, life got lonely and boring. That summer was such a time.

We couldn't muster enough kids to field a baseball game, even with just three on a side. Trying to use younger kids in the neighborhood didn't work either. They'd get hit by the ball, forget how to run the bases, or wet themselves and we'd have to stop the game to tend to their needs. It angered us because summer was a time for fun and irresponsibility, not a venue for babysitting.

Grass on the practice and playing fields was allowed to grow longer during the summer. It made the surface more durable and able to span the inevitable short periods of drought the season brings. Shuffling through the grass with Mead, Corky, and Neal we noticed the heads of many groundhogs peeking above the green blades as they kept track of our movements.

I can't remember whose idea it was to rid the practice field of vermin but we all jumped on board in short order. Sitting down in the grass with our useless baseball gloves and bats, we pooled our collective intelligence regarding groundhogs and their capture. Being young, our warehouse of knowledge was still mostly empty so we got up and walked around the neighborhood seeking advice from older kids. Like mixing metaphors, we gathered information without regard for source or validity, confusing rumor and misinformation with wives tales and outright lies. Jumbling sound reason with seemingly good ideas we fashioned a plan of attack.

Phase One was to identify the location of the beast's holes. Sharp kids as we were we believed we could look across the field and remember where we saw groundhogs standing. Two major flaws haunted this plan were that groundhogs don't stand right outside their holes and, more importantly, without landmark or other identifying characteristic, it was impossible to locate a distant groundhog hole unless you were lucky enough to fall into it as you searched.

It took two days to complete our next plan. We got a piece of paper and drew a map of the practice field putting X's where we found holes. Getting down on our hands and knees we crawled across the field to make sure we discovered and charted every groundhog hole. It worked and we were ready to move on to something more exciting than crawling in the grass.

Phase Two was capture of the creatures. The plan was to dump water down their holes to drown them out. We were told groundhogs always have two entrances to their tunnels. We planned to pour water down one hole and put a fishing net over the other. When the groundhog came out of the second hole to get some air, we had him in the net. It seemed foolproof and we were the fellows for a job like that.

There was more work to that scheme than we realized. It required carrying buckets of water to the field because, even when we combined all our garden hoses, we fell about a quarter of a mile short stretching to the nearest groundhog hole.

Each managed to get permission to use two buckets from our homes. When asked why we wanted buckets, we thought it better to be evasive rather than straight forward, not wanting our plan squashed after we already had two days of hard labor invested in it. Falling back on our usual tactic of a long-winded, vague, wandering explanation resulted in the expected parental response, "Just take the buckets but make sure you bring them back…and don't dent them." Nothing works quite as well as a tried and true scheme.

Careful calculation of the volume of a groundhog hole might have discouraged us from attempting this feat. More work was involved than we would have committed to had we known. None of us were strong enough to carry two buckets of water at the same time so it took two trips each to fully supply our water stores. The second bucket was a struggle since carrying the first sapped most of out strength. Returning home was fraught with danger. Parents can't stand to see an idle child and will instinctively assign new chores when they find one. We had to be careful to look busy as we dropped by home for more water.

Mead, Corky, Neal, and I were each looking forward to keeping one of the groundhogs we caught as pets. It had become a status symbol of sorts in our little minds. Gathering around the tattered map of vermin abodes, barely any negotiation was involved with each of us claiming a groundhog hole we had our eye on. Each trudged off dragging our buckets of water and fishing nets, setting our own traps.

Success was a mystery that morning. Two buckets of water wasn't sufficient to flush a groundhog out of his hole. By the time we ran home and brought another bucket of water, what we had poured down the hole had soaked into the soil, no longer posing a problem to the resident. Our gritty individualism would have to give way to a more cooperative spirit.

Resting from the wasted effort of three trips of heavy lifting we pondered the possibilities. Corky and Mead worked out the problem while Neal and I lay back on the grass. I was distracted by the fluffy white clouds that brought periodic shade and comfort to our hot, weary bodies. I didn't hear how they arrived at the plan but we were all to return for two more buckets of water and meet back at the first groundhog hole.

Teamwork was what we needed. We had to use four buckets of water to chase the animal into the open to learn that we had placed the net over the wrong hole. Expanding our plan and allowing for more error than we anticipated, we tried again. Having four nets at our disposal we placed them over the four holes nearest the pour hole.

Our next attempt yielded a crop and we snagged a groundhog in a net. Foresight is a wonderful luxury but we were living a frugal life. Believing we would capture an animal should have alerted us to the need for a container to hold it. Sadly, we had no such vision. Neal scrounged around the band building and found a box with a lid. Dumping the beast in the box, we savored sweet success at last.

Nothing energizes a team like victory. Trips back home for empty boxes was a task much easier than fetching water. Trying our plan again gave us two groundhogs for the price of one. We all had our groundhog except for Mead.

Low on water, we vowed to continue until Mead had his groundhog too, even if it meant more grueling trips for water. Mead's house was closest so we all headed there with our buckets, an idea that would have served us well earlier in the day.

We met Mead's dad halfway. The family was off to an outing of some kind ending our day's expedition. Mead's dad caught wind of what we had been doing and wouldn't let Mead have a groundhog. Feeling strongly about the matter he used colorful language that I have omitted here but made his beliefs crystal clear in our minds. Since we didn't need to catch one for Mead, our quota was satisfied.

Loved ones at home don't see triumph in the same way troops in the field appreciate it. Grateful for their efforts, those at home can't know the pain and hardship endured in a foray. So it was with us as we returned home with our boxes of groundhogs.

Mother was on the phone when I came in and I waited patiently for her to end her conversation so I wouldn't rudely interrupt her. She had trained me well and I took to that kind of instruction naturally. I put the box on the dining room table and began leafing through a magazine, waiting as calmly as I could.

Sidetracked by a page of cartoons, I failed to notice when mother hung up the receiver. She walked to the table and flipped open the lid to the box. I don't know if that particular animal was clairvoyant or just ready to take advantage of any opportunity but as soon as it saw daylight, it jumped from its prison.

Mother was not foul mouthed by nature but she let loose with a four letter word she reserved for special occasions like this one. Her shriek frightened me into awareness. Not completely sure of what was going on, I tried to survey the situation: mother was screaming, the box lid was on the floor, and I caught a glimpse of a groundhog rump rounding the corner into my bedroom. It took hours to rectify the wrong I had committed and days to calm my mother. The groundhog survived. I wasn't sure I would.

Neal left his box in their garage. His father was surprised in much the same way mother had been. Hearing the commotion, Neal ran to the garage to see his father in hot pursuit of the escaped pet. Neal's dad tried to use a walking stick to inflict pain on the critter. Finding an open window, the groundhog made good on his escape.

Corky's parents dispatched the dilemma with haste. I couldn't know how it was handled because his parents said they wouldn't speak of it again and they didn't, except for five or six times a day for the next month or so. It is enough to note that a cardboard box is not as secure as a steel cage.

Comparing notes later we realized we each had listened to a similar lecture about how wild animals don't make good pets because they would never become tame, never could we play with them, or handle them safely. Besides, they weren't groundhogs. They were ground squirrels or chipmunks, entirely different from the game we thought we were hunting.

We learned a valuable lesson that summer. Of course, we went on to get into trouble following other stupid schemes. As a group we were given to capers. To our credit, none of us has ever confused a groundhog with a ground squirrel since that summer.

I'm confident you city dwellers will celebrate your holiday with the same revelry you reserve for other important occasions like Cinco de Mayo and Bastille Day. I'll never understand city folks, but to each his own.

Respectfully submitted,

Harry Ellis

Harry Ellis

238 Persimmon Street

Blandtrap

To the Editor of the Tiskilwa Bureau Valley Chief

RE: Valentines Day

Dear Sir:

We find ourselves at that most holy time of year for the greeting card industry. The growers of flowers and makers of chocolates have been slaving away for months in preparation for this very moment. Valentines Day has for weeks been inspiring the thoughts of young ladies imagining how that special someone or, better yet, that secret admirer will make himself known in a thrilling way or will honor them from afar. It's like a cat and mouse game for the younger ones. Love provides a rainbow of experience, causing ordinary people to display the strength of commitment to one another. I will try to relate a few stories to you of what love has accomplished in this small community.

Maggie Thompson is the first to spring to mind. Maggie's love for her husband was unyielding. She worked at the grocery store for years and was known by everyone. She was somewhat of a character, being clever and outgoing. When she was not at work, she could be seen walking back and forth across town to her husband's grave. He was buried in the cemetery at the end of town and her small home sat at the opposite end of town. She would pay her respects daily, or more often, walking the distance across town in any and all weather. Many would stop to offer her a ride. Occasionally she would accept, but usually she would decline the offer preferring to walk alone. Her son, Donnie, found it increasingly difficult to keep track of her as she grew older. No longer able to work, Maggie had more time on her hands to visit the cemetery. As time passed Maggie's mind began to slip steadily and she was known to say the most unspeakable things about Donnie to anyone who would listen. In fact, she was longing for Donnie's company. He lavished attention on her regularly, yet her failing faculties kept her from remembering it. That kind of devotion is worthy of recognition.

They buried Maggie recently. It was an affair that was well attended for a lady of such modest means. Those who could not attend, I am sure, paused to remember their favorite Maggie story. Everyone in town had one. When she took up residence in the cemetery, I am convinced she immediately took a position of prominence. After all, she had already spent more time in the cemetery than half the people buried there. Reunited with her God and her husband, she had no more reason to wander.

Another example of love's endurance is the story of Jim and Paula. Jim has been in love with Paula for as long as anyone can remember. Paula did not reciprocate with the same emotion as Jim. She enjoyed Jim's company but didn't consider it much beyond that. Jim busied himself with the affairs of the church and with God's work. He had a small bookstore in the church that sold books at a loss. It was a very modest loss so Jim was able to augment the income of the bookstore to sustain it for many years. He sold Bibles and books about the Bible, song books and books about songs, and other items, like recordings of music and bookmarks. It was a great service to the church and very time consuming, but with Paula out of country, Jim seemed to have quite a bit of time on his hands. In addition to the bookstore, Jim owned a large house. It was a very large home for a single gentleman. He took in graduating college students, befriending and mentoring them until they acclimated to adult, self-sustaining life. We called it a halfway house for the well-educated. He, at times had as many as six young men living in his home.

They moved up through the house as they adapted to the real world. Arriving in the basement were the newcomers. No one lived on the first floor. It was a common area where guests were received and entertained. An occasional houseguest or a brother in dire and desperate circumstances would occupy the couch, but it was only a temporary station. Jim provided spiritual and practical advice to his wards. Graduates would move in and instantly be plagued with the usual distractions: women and money. Thrills also tend to turn a young man's head. Thrills, like drugs and alcohol, have allure that is difficult to see and nearly impossible for some to escape. A young knight, once he leaves the castle for adventure will face many dragons before he is recognized by others or even himself as a knight. It is comforting to have the advice of one who has already battled some of those dragons. If he cannot explain how to kill the dragon, he may be able to relate what is ineffective or at the very least, how to escape the fight altogether. Jim was such a man.

The group functioned as a mirror for many who lived there. One could be struggling with a temptation that seemed serious and nearly impossible to overcome alone; but the same problem, when seen in the life of another, seems simple and the solution obvious and easy. In this way one man helped another as steel sharpens steel.

Paula was dedicated to the work of God. She was a nurse and a competent one at that. She was also a missionary tending to spiritual needs in the mountains of Honduras. Medical assistance in a remote community is rare and special to the residents. First aid for cuts and other accidents is foremost. It is probably the only contact with health care for many of the men. Children and women would come to Paula for help. Men would only come if their injury was life threatening. Men are men everywhere.

When Paula would return from mission trips, she would see Jim. They kept company in this way for many years. Jim made his feelings known but Paula didn't return the same sentiment for more than a decade. Jim waited, patiently at times, not so patiently at other times. Even then he waited more until Paula agreed to be his wife. It is an encouragement beyond description to see Jim and Paula sitting in the pew together with their two children. Nearly middle-aged before they started their family, they are content together. Sure, there are the usual problems that married couples share. All must endure those problems, but when faced together and with God, they draw a couple together rather than push them apart.

Edith and I met while working on a local amateur theater production. She had a leading role and I was working makeup and the spotlights. Somehow she summoned the strength to resist my charm, at least for a while. I would bring her coffee and take extra care and time with her makeup. She noticed the attention but attributed it to a zeal for the theater. We would be in the company of a group after rehearsals but she was under the impression that I was married. Indeed, it is my natural state. I was several years older than her, so she assumed I was married. It took time to convince her I was not. It took even longer to convince her I was worthy of marrying. And it seemed forever to convince her that I should be the one she should marry. In the end she relented, threw caution and reason to the wind, and agreed to marry me.

Edith has been talking, lately, about romance among the young people of Blandtrap. Tommy Hunter, the lad who works for Seth Hugginbough at the hardware store, was taking a girl from town to the spring dance. She didn't know the girl's name but she was a Paar, a family that moved to the edge of town about a year ago. Ladies of the church had been speculating about the date. Tommy was so dedicated to work he let nothing interfere with his hours except sports. This date would require Tommy to take a Saturday afternoon and evening off. He had never done that in two years of employment, even if he was ill. Half the ladies thought, regardless that this was a first date, that Tommy was very serious about the Paar girl and this might lead to marriage. The other half speculated that Tommy finally realized his social inadequacies and determined it was time to enter high school society in a proper way. The arguments were strong on both sides, each side capable of citing many examples of similar couples to defend their positions. Providing examples to argue their side seemed, in their minds, to elevate their arguments above the realm of gossip.

I overheard Tommy's mother talking to Mrs. Brimstone last week in the diner. It turned out his mom was making him go. He wanted to work Prom night. She arranged it with Hugginbough to not schedule him that Saturday and spread the word around town to leave her son alone that weekend. Tommy was really steamed at his mom and miffed at Hugginbough too. "Some reward for total dedication!" he thought.

It was only his mother's ultimatum that motivated him to ask out a girl. Her demands were, "You ask a girl to the dance by Friday or I will arrange a date for you by Monday." The threat of a humiliating Sunday in church as his mother went from girl to girl asking them if they wanted to date her son was more than he was willing to endure. Tommy had a date by Friday. It was even money on his red face; whether it was from his embarrassment at asking his first girl out, or anger at his mother.

I chose not to pass this information on to Edith and the ladies. I get a warm feeling when I know something Edith doesn't know. They are rare occasions. The debate was far more entertaining than the truth. You don't pour water on a fire while it's still keeping you warm.

Bob and Ruth Woods have a story of enduring love. Bob was a gangly lad and his family ardent church goers. They were also insufferably poor. Old man Woods had a good heart but money slipped through his fingers like water. He didn't waste money because he never had any money to waste. He did, however, regularly encounter those less fortunate than himself. With a heart of gold and an abiding love for mankind, he would give generously to ease the need of someone down on their luck or legitimately oppressed. Every now and then, some plagued soul would wander into town with no money or place to live. When the matter was brought before the church on Sunday, Mr. Woods would have already met the needs of food and shelter. It was a natural result from living his faith every day. He didn't just suit-up for the game on Sunday, he practiced every day.

Mr. Woods was never down on his luck, he didn't have any luck to be down on. His faith was unending. "You can bet on the cards, or dice, or the stock market if you like; I will put my faith in God and his ability to provide." Some thought it was scandalous the way he gave away his meager resources that he should have used to provide for his family rather than sharing them so freely with characters who were suspicious at best. He would just smile when someone would confront him about his over-generosity. Never responding, he would thank them for their concern. "You can't talk to someone if they don't understand your language," he would say.

The work ethic of Mr. Woods was enviable. He often held two jobs: One at the lumberyard long before Hugginbough bought it and combined it with the Hardware Store and another that was catch as catch can. His four children could and did stop by on their way to and from school. Anytime they wanted to talk to him, he was available. His second job, and there might be more than one second job, would be something like stocking groceries or light ground work around the square. Always somewhere he could be found if he was needed.

Pastor Brimstone used him as an example of charity and hospitality and it was a challenge to all of us who were better off, wealthy really, in comparison to Mr. Woods. It was humbling and led us all to keep on our toes regarding the needs of others. The preacher kept using Mr. Woods as the example until he took stock of his own situation. He realized, next to Mr. Woods, he seemed like a skinflint. Admiration turned to respect, where it should have been all along. We were changed by his example.

Bob Woods grew up in the shadow of this man. Bob and Ruth were generous but they had a much firmer grip on a dollar than Bob's father. Most people can't live the way Mr. Woods did. They simply lack faith and the commitment to that faith that allows such behavior. Bob was always worried about where the next meal was coming from. Leftovers are saved to minimize waste for most families. Often, leftovers in the fridge were the only food in the Wood's house. It didn't happen often, but every once in awhile they would miss a meal. "It doesn't seem to hurt them," Mr. Woods would comment looking at his family, "And the benefit to the poor outweighs our discomfort."

Ruth did not come from poverty. Her family had a large farm by the standards of that day and Ruth had two older brothers. Her father, Kaiser Olavson, provided generously for his family. They weren't "maids and coachman" rich but they were quite comfortable with a couple of hired farmhands. Livestock included a couple of dozen dairy cows, always a champion bull, and two chicken coops. Sweet corn, beans, and occasionally other vegetables were grown for the cannery in Princeville. They had a few cabins for migrant workers when they decided to plant vegetables. The large work force was necessary at harvest. In order to support the community and trim migrant worker expense, they hired local youth to put up hay in the summer.

The Olavsons hired Bob as a migrant worker. Someone had suggested Bob would make an excellent worker. Kaiser didn't turn up his nose at a hard working farm hand, provided they knew their place. It was a good deal for both. Bob needed the work and the Olavsons didn't have to feed and house Bob for the summer.

That was where Bob got his first glimpse of Ruth. He had been aware of her in school but never shared a class nor did they have any friends in common. Once Bob had a chance to watch her and hear her the way she spoke, he was lost to other girls. She noticed him for the first time as he outworked grown men around him and became intrigued with the boy.

Kaiser always kept a keen eye out for his only daughter, as did her two older brothers. Once the two heirs noticed Ruth's interest in Bob, they nearly worked Bob to death. If their sister's head turned in Bob's direction, they wanted to see what kind of stuff he was made of.

While putting up hay, the boys kept bales flying at Bob. He was quickly buried in bales and they kept it up for a few hours before Bob got the rhythm of the task. The challenge caught Bob by surprise. He was a quick study, able to catch up and keep up after half a hayrack was unloaded. From then on he handled anything the brothers threw at him.

To gain an advantage, they threw an untied bale to see how he would handle it. If you throw an untied bale just right it holds together in flight but when caught, it explodes into a cloud that envelops the recipient. The other brother let loose with another bale that clocked Bob pretty hard. He dropped like a sack of potatoes, his face cut up a bit.

They dragged Bob down from the hayloft to let him revive in a more comfortable environment. It was a cheap shot so cold the brothers nearly regretted doing it. Mrs. Olavson was in town on errands so Ruth came out to tend to Bob. She was impressed with Bob's gentle nature, a contrast to her brash brothers. Bob was mesmerized by her beauty and captured by her sincere character. Although it was the first time they had formally met and had a chance to talk, it was plain for all to see they were taken with each other. The brothers' plan had taken an ugly turn in their minds.

Their meeting became a solemn time, a time of vows. Ruth vowed to get to know Bob well. Bob vowed to pursue Ruth with honorable intentions. Kaiser vowed to keep them apart whenever possible and Mrs. Olavson vowed to reign in Kaiser's ire, as she did every day of her life. The brothers vowed to beat him regularly until he went away. Each of them kept their vows as if their very salvation depended on it.

Bob was at the classroom door when Ruth left a room and he walked her to her next class. He met her this way all day, every day, except for lunch and after school when one or both of the brothers would beat him bloody. Ruth told Kaiser about her brother's fisticuffs at school. Kaiser was a tough man but didn't tolerate bullying. When he confronted the boys regarding the fighting at school and learned who it was they were beating and why, he gave his sons a stern lecture about fighting but leveled no punishment, ending the speech with a wink..

Beatings continued for a while. The brothers laughed about how poor a fighter Bob was. He never got a punch through. At first, they bragged between themselves of their pugilistic prowess. "Can't be touched," they would tell each other. After a while it became apparent Bob was not fighting back. This took all the air out of their balloon. They finally asked him one day after a beating, "Why don't you fight back?"

"Aside from the fact that this is just savage, you mean?" Bob asked. They looked at each other and nodded back to Bob. "I could not force myself to strike a brother of the woman I love." Bob answered frankly. This made the brothers feel silly which is worse than having an unsavory character courting your sister. They each hit him one more time, out of frustration this time rather than anger, and that was the end of the matter. They never beat him again. From then on, whenever Kaiser began to rail against Bob, they would not add their voices to the derision. He had earned their respect, if not their admiration.

The Olavson's were a proud people and Kaiser was the most proud of all. When he looked into the Woods family, he found two things: an impeccable reputation and poverty. The first was good but the second was unacceptable.

Kaiser had worked hard and provided for his family, making a good life for them. Some could say he made an easy life for his family, free of most financial worries. He was not about to let his daughter get tangled up with a boy from a family like the Woods. He had bigger plans for her than a good-hearted boy.

Mr. Olavson tried to hunt Bob down for a couple of weeks, always narrowly missing him. Bob was either in school or working at one of the three jobs he juggled. He didn't have a spare moment in the day. With school, homework, numerous part-time jobs, and whatever wandering souls his father brought home; all Bob's time was accounted for. He often thought it was a good thing Kaiser didn't let him see Ruth. He was sure he was falling in love with her; however, another demand on his time might have done him in.

By the last term of his senior year Bob had things going his way. He was holding a "B" average in school. He was working 40 hours a week and earning more per hour than any other kid in town. Bob had arranged his schedule so he didn't miss church on Sunday. Possessing more than self respect, he had the respect of others and was considered a man by the other men in town. He was no longer referred to as Mr. Wood's kid, just as Bob. That's strong recognition in this village.

Kaiser did not relent in the face of Bob's reputation and accomplishments. He still forbade Ruth to see Bob. They both turned 18 that year just before Prom. Ruth approached her father one evening as he sat at his desk doing business. She said Bob was coming over to speak to him and would arrive in a few minutes. Kaiser began to protest but Ruth held up her hands and said, "Tell it to Bob. He's on his way" Mrs. Olavson stood behind her daughter in support and gave Kaiser that "you will see this thing through" stare.

When the knock at the door sounded, Kaiser took his seat in the Parlor. He would not answer the door. Perhaps the lad would be intimidated and go away. Mrs. Olavson walked past the grand patriarch. She welcomed Bob to their home. Kaiser rose to his feet to forbid his wife to let him in. She pretended not to hear him as she pulled the boy inside.

Bob came in and offered his hand to Kaiser, who grudgingly accepted it. Kaiser motioned to a chair, but Bob remained standing and addressed him eye to eye, as if they were equals. Kaiser would have no part of the idea that Bob was on par with him and sat down to distinguish himself as superior. Bob remained standing as a show of strength and respect.

"Sir, I have admired your daughter for several years now. We see each other in school whenever we can. I have respected your wishes that we not see each other socially although I disagree most vigorously with the decision. This is the end of our senior year in high school and I wanted to tell you face-to-face that I intend to take your daughter to Prom. With your permission, sir, I pray, but I intend to take her without your permission, if that is your choice. She is safe with me, sir. My intentions are honorable and I will keep her best interests before mine."

Kaiser finished fiddling with the pipe he had been lighting as Bob spoke. He intended to take a couple peaceful puffs before he threw Bob out into the yard. He opened his mouth to answer but heard words that were not his.

"We would be proud to have Ruth accompany you to Prom, Bob." Mrs. Olavson answered before Kaiser could rise or speak. Mrs. Olavson was generally submissive, yielding to the discretion of Kaiser. It was easy because he generally exercised good judgment and showed keen discernment in almost everything he attempted. On the rare occasion when Kaiser was wrong, he had trouble seeing his error. Unfortunately, he was as stubborn as he was wise. She knew when it was time to step in; confident Kaiser would cave to her judgment. Mrs. Olavson could be even more unreasonable than Kaiser, and more obstinate as well if the situation demanded it. When she interjected her opinion this strongly, Kaiser knew he had to relent. The stakes were too high here. He would give ground for the moment but keep track of the situation in secret and from a distance.

Bristling at his wife's interference in the matter, Kaiser yielded to her discretion.

"Thank you, sir. You won't regret your decision." Bob gave Ruth a peck on the forehead as he left. He would have rather eaten glass than have that talk with Kaiser, but it was over and it went well. He was all the better for the experience.

Ruth and her mother went off to the kitchen to talk; it would not serve them well to appear to gloat in front of Kaiser. With the ladies out of earshot, Mr. Olavson turned to his boys who had been watching open-mouthed through the verbal exchange. Never had they heard anyone speak so directly to their father in that way. Certainly they lacked the courage to do so. "You're both going to Prom. Get dates. You two are going to keep an eye on them. Never let them out of your sight!" were his orders to his heir and his henchman.

Bob and Ruth had a wonderful evening at Prom. Bob was a perfect gentleman. When he saw Ruth's brother hovering nearby, he was concerned not so much about the beating he expected but about ruining his only suit. Replacing it would require another job. He need not have worried. He had won the brothers over to his side.

Kaiser extracted details of the evening as soon as the boys arrived home. They said Bob had behaved admirably, which is more that than could be said about one of the brothers who was wearing a bright red hand-shaped slap mark on the side of his face.

Kaiser didn't change his mind about Bob. He reinstituted the ban on Ruth seeing him socially. They finished the school year honoring his decree. Bob again came again several times to talk with Mr. Olavson but he refused to see him. All other avenues exhausted, they eloped on a Friday, a couple of weeks after graduation.

When they returned on Sunday evening, Kaiser, in a rage, snatched Ruth before they could get home to Bob's new apartment. He kept them apart for about a month, with Bob showing up at the door to claim his bride every morning and evening. Kaiser had all his plans in place to have the marriage dissolved when his wife announced Ruth was expecting. Defeated by Bob's tenacity, his daughter's resilience, and now God's own hand, he relented and sent Ruth back to her husband.

Bob became very successful; aggressively taking every opportunity that came his way and eventually making his own opportunities. He obtained a lease on some farmland and became a respected farmer buying the land he leased and several surrounding tracts of land until his spread rivaled Kaiser's farm.

The city is not the only repository for stories of the heart. As you see, we have our own examples of unfailing love. Blandtrap may be off the beaten path, but the highway of love and devotion runs right through the center of Village Square. You and your town would do well to heed our example.

I wish you and your wife well this Valentines Day.

Respectfully Submitted.

Harry Ellis

Harry Ellis

238 Persimmon Street

Blandtrap

To the Editor of the Tiskilwa Bureau Valley Chief

RE: A Scathing Sermon

Dear Sir:

Another week has passed in Blandtrap and I have spent much of this week under the weather. While I am not the perfect patient, I am among the best. Placing a minimum of burden on my loving wife, I disturb her only for the most urgent needs. Edith had to leave frequently to tell neighbors how well I was doing and brag about how considerate I had been.

The secret to being a perfect patient lies in making your needs clearly known and removing all doubt as to what is required to ease your suffering. For instance, many would simply ask for a tissue. While any tissue could do the rudimentary job, if you really want the quilted tissues, or perhaps the kind of tissue which has lotion in it to soothe your weary nose, you should ask. One would think that this kind of specificity would be received with eager admiration by those nursing one back to health, however, the usual reaction has become predictable but not with the fanfare originally anticipated.

I'm afraid that my unfortunate illness has left me ignorant of most of Blandtrap's activities this week. Unaware of what has happened about the village, I must report only on the Sunday activities at church. Unable to get around and not willing to rely on rumor, I shall report from the pews of the church about matters familiar.

A Sunday suit is at least as comfortable as wool underwear in a heat wave and is just as suited to the task. Yet, each Sunday, we don our finest clothes, put smiles where long faces typically hang, parade in tastefully flashy cars, eagerly approach people against which we often hold secret grudges, and compete to sit in desirable places among the pews. What is our purpose in doing this? The reason often escapes me and I blush when I remember.

Edith and I arrived at the church building early. I would like to say that is our custom but it is only our intention. On Saturday evening it is a simple enough matter. The next morning we will get up early, shower and dress, and leave in plenty of time to walk to the building at a relaxed pace. More often than not, we oversleep, dawdle, or lose track of time until we must hurriedly drive and are late. Today we avoided the pitfalls and had time to fellowship before services began.

As Edith was chatting with one of the old ladies, I noticed a quarter laying on a table in the rear foyer we use to seat the overflow on Easter and Christmas Eve. None of us is without sin, but many who attend each week regret what they have done and are working on changing their heart and behavior. On Easter and Christmas Eve we pack the joint pretty tight with the unrepentant stacking "vice" next to "ignorance" next to "bad habit" until some have to stand for lack of room for a chair. It's a testimony to God's grace that he doesn't rain fire down on the event. Then again, every Sunday probably represents the same opportunity.

They would run if they knew what was waiting for them if they don't turn, but they don't seem to realize their fate. They are content to stand and they are entertained by the songs and self-comforted because they are no worse than others in attendance.

If they only knew or cared now desperately the rest of us needed them each day, I would like to think they would spend more time with us. They let family, business, or sport come between them and us, and probably between them and God. I would like to say the loss is theirs. In reality, the loss belongs to both.

The lone quarter on the table occupied my mind. I wondered what it could be doing there on the table. Was someone taking up a collection of some kind? What was the purpose of the collection? Perhaps the church had some unexpected expenses it was trying to defray or a parishioner had fallen on hard times. Did it matter? If there was a need and I was able, would I not lend a hand? I placed some more change on the table next to the quarter. I felt better.

Stu saw me put the change on the table and walked over to see what I was doing. I told him I didn't know what the collection was for but there was only twenty-five cents offered when I found the contribution so I added some more change to form a pile. Church is the only place where Stu can look at another person as if they were cheap and he generous. He extracted his money from his pocket and unfolded a couple of bills placing them next to my pile of change. I was going to question Stu about his giving but another church member grabbed his arm and seemed to be asking him something. I didn't want to interfere with what may have been a personal matter.

Stu's philanthropy made me feel as like I was being a little tight-fisted with my money so I snatched a few bills from my wallet and tossed them with his. Bob Townsend, sober by two or three hours, quizzed me on the money on the table. I gave him my understanding of the situation and he was moved. Maybe he was hung over, but he gave every indication he was moved.

He may have had problems, but success never glued Bob Townsend's billfold shut. He plucked out several bills and they had zeros on them. Walking away, Bob seemed satisfied with himself. He didn't often feel that way on Sunday morning. It was a new experience for him. Simeon Swagg caught Bob's ear before he had gotten too far from the table and heard about the donation.

Clovis' father cornered me over by the ushers. I explained what I believed to be the story while the ushers eavesdropped on our conversation to learn the details. Clovis joined us and got the gist of the conversation from the tail end of it. Not one to procrastinate, Clovis' father went right over to stand in the line that had formed to contribute to the fund. Two ushers followed close behind.

Brimstone caught wind of the apparent need and delayed services until he and others could participate. Everyone was feeling quite jolly and smug given the opportunity to help the less fortunate. People were chatting with one another and not just with those who sit next to them in the pew. No, they were talking with people who sit on the other side of the aisle! It was a beautiful tableau, a picture of what a congregation should be.

The Conklin boy walked in from the Sunday school area and asked rather loudly, "Has anyone seen my quarter? I think I must have dropped it somewhere around here. My pocket's got a hole in it."

Mrs. Wing spoke back to the child, "Why, yes, Robbie, I found a quarter on the floor and put it on the table over there." She was pointing to the mound of money cascading off the table.

I pulled the last remaining coin from my pants and handed it to the boy, sheepishly trying to divert the obvious gaff I had made, "Here. This might be it." I told him. The kid was pleased to have his money back but the congregation felt betrayed.

Off the boy went, happy as a clam as the congregation stood around in groups of two or three, chatting with scowls on their faces and pointing at me as they spoke. I don't believe they were wishing me well. I took Edith by the arm and headed for our pew before they could form a posse.

Brimstone started corralling the membership into the sanctuary so services could begin. He had not yet heard of the child and the lost coin. He had been so moved by the generosity of the parishioners he preached off the cuff for thirty minutes before he launched into his prepared sermon.

He would have an entire week to prepare a sermon on jumping to conclusions directed at me. I was wrong. I took the down-dressing like a man.

Later, the ushers totaled the contribution and it came to $462.83. Not bad for a misplaced quarter. Before we could recoup our investment, the church treasurer scooped up the money, claiming it for the church. "What a lovely special contribution." She said.

"These are the spoils of pride." I thought to myself.

We gather together, if I hear my Bible correctly, to worship our God who gave everything He had to those who didn't have any thing. He gave His life so that I would be free from, among many others, the sin of hypocrisy.

If I came here to confess my sins and to build up other hapless saps like myself, why am I so grandly dressed? Who am I trying to impress?

My God knows me as sinful, yet looks on me as forgiven. My wife knows I'm not perfect, although I'm sure she's in error over several points, but she loves me in spite of them. My neighbors, yes there are those who look up to me, know I can lose my temper on occasion, and still do not try to avoid me. Even strangers who give me the "hairy eyeball" once in a while, they treat me fairly. Who, then, do I think I am fooling? Only myself, I guess. Next week I will dress differently and, no doubt, suffer ridicule reserved for the unconventional.

Old LaVonda runs the music program for the church. She's taught just about everybody in town how to sing. For some it took, but for others it doesn't show so much. She directs the adult and teen choirs, and has small choruses for each grade of children. She's taught singing for even longer than she can remember. There's probably not a single knuckle in town that, at one time or another, hasn't suffered the rap of her ruler. Rap music meant something else to LaVonda than it does to others today.

The choir sings "Joyful, Joyful We Adore Thee" while the deacons scurry about and talk quietly to one another. You would think, since the routine is the same each week, that the position of the lectern would be somewhat standard and well understood. And, in time, the person responsible for positioning the lectern could place it while blindfolded in a driving snowstorm without missing the mark, but since a committee of deacons has charge of this simple task, it assumes the complexity of brain surgery on a rolling ship.

One will move the lectern to one side of the platform, another will move it back. Quiet yet quite animated discussion among the deacons continues for a while until, I suppose, they tire of the routine or perhaps exhaust all polite vocabulary and sit at last. If I were a visitor, I am sure I would think they had never done this before.

The preacher, the Reverend Brimstone, doesn't use a lectern. He prefers to get close to his listeners. He's a straight shooter who doesn't mince words, sometimes to his embarrassment but always to his integrity. If it comes into his mind, it goes out his mouth. Fortunately, his thoughts are usually pure enough for congregational ears.

The fundamental conflict among the deacons is as old as mankind itself. Some fear the entrapment of traditions and the rest fear change for change's sake. They fear something important may be discarded as an idle tradition. Like it is with most matters that don't impact a man's salvation, both sides are right and both sides are wrong. It's no wonder resolution escapes them.

Now that the deacons have the lectern properly sited, we have a prayer, some scripture, and the collection. Gil Stamen has passed the collection plate for two decades. No one remembers why anymore. But those who assist him know of his strategy. Stu and I have seen him do this same routine every week. Gil will place a twenty dollar bill in the collection plate before he passes it. "Baiting the trap" as Gil calls it. Upon retrieving the plates, Gil will remove his twenty and replace it with a five. Since the fall in the garden the shameless have preyed upon the guilty, and so it continues today.

After communion, and the sharing of concerns, we are on to the sermon. Preacher Brimstone has a direct nature about himself. He doesn't mince words nor ask a lot of unnecessary questions. He rarely tries to entrap anyone and that was what caught so many off guard today.

I enjoy sitting in the pew and surveying the group of wholly unworthy individuals God has chosen to do his bidding in this village. It's not so different than you might find anywhere else like the mall or propping up the bar at Skinny's Tap. The difference is that this group is trying to serve God. Sure, they may be unsuccessful at nearly every turn, but they keep trying. It matters little where you are on the journey as long as you keep pressing on to the goal.

Before Brimstone got rolling, he made the announcements. Turning to the back of the service bulletin, I read the announcements in about 45 seconds. Brimstone, though, embellishes freely when announcing events. He lauds the value of the group performing the function, extols the urgent need for the event, and, at last, compels the congregation to attend.

He opened by reminding the congregation that last week he had asked them to read a certain chapter of the Bible before this week's sermon. He then asked for a show of hands of all those who had read Mark 17 this week. An impressive portion of the flock raised their hands. When backed into a corner and without testimony to the contrary, most people will confess to being obedient.

Preacher Brimstone reminded the congregation that the Book of Mark only has 16 chapters then preached a blistering sermon on the evils of lying and deception. He was in full form today with broad pontification and wincing volume which he increased for emphasis. The congregation reacted typically. The necks of the congregation began to disappear into their shoulders in an attempt to become inconspicuous. Brimstone had learned that the fear of finger pointing held a congregation's attention. Napping or eye resting was simply out of the question. Even babies seemed too fearful to whimper.

No one dared glance at the clock on the wall but time found a way to pass anyway. The sermon was finally over. The collective deep breath that was drawn by the audience was deafening. After a prayer and a serenade from LaVonda's Legion, we were dismissed.

I don't envy the job of a preacher. He must render soul-searching, heart-wrenching, life- changing lectures, week after week, and must get it done before the roast burns.

Since Brimstone shakes hands with those who leave through the main doors, I knew the side exits would be busy this morning. Edith and I always leave through the main doors and fiery sermon or not, we would use them today as well.

Standing in the reception line I tried to think of some pleasant comment to permit an unencumbered escape. It's not easy, particularly in so short a time, to come up with a one sentence remark that not only demonstrates that I had a profound understanding of the sermon, but so insightful that it discourages further discussion.

I rarely ask preachers theological questions when I'm in a hurry or urgently need advice because, as a group, preachers are consistently unwilling or unable to proffer the "yes" or "no" answer I'm seeking. Also, their answers tend to be excessively wordy while also being as vague and complex as to require significant examination before they can be applied to a specific situation. I find that the butcher renders a more concise response to these kinds of questions.

"Edith and Harry," he said when we reached the front of the line. "How nice to see you again."

"Wonderful sermon!" I blurted.

"I'm glad you liked it. As a matter of fact, I thought of you while I wrote it." He responded.

We drove home in silence.

Respectfully submitted,

Harry Ellis

Harry Ellis

238 Persimmon Street

Blandtrap

To the Editor of the Tiskilwa Bureau Valley Chief

RE: Heroes - Police

Dear Sir:

We can no longer tolerate your recalcitrant snobbery of our exemplary community. The rag you print virtually bubbles with mindless trivia regarding the happenings of your city while the wholesome events and enviable citizens of Blandtrap go wanting for recognition.

Officer Monk is retiring today. There won't be a band playing or banners waving in his honor but his selfless service to this village will be sorely missed. A dinner will soon be held to recognize his service. Others will testify to the value of his service to Blandtrap while he remains silent. That is his way.

I look forward to the dinner and hope I am invited or allowed to speak some words in gratitude. It is unlikely I will be asked. Competition for time on the microphone is fierce and the best speakers and closest friends and colleagues will prevail. To his credit, Officer Monk's quiet humility along side his confidence and his ability to keep the peace made for a powerful representative of the law.

The invited speakers will, no doubt, be more visible pillars of the community than Officer Monk, but none more significant. The mayor, the county road commissioner, and the superintendent of schools will headline the event while the supervisor of parks, a clever part-time preacher and a local character with whimsical stories will be added for spice. All will be dressed formally and only formal and proper behavior will be tolerated. Not one of these fellows, at one point or another in their misspent youth had escaped being dragged by the scruff of the neck by Officer Monk. He had taken them home to their parents, behind some garage for a good talking to, or downtown for more formal discipline. Most of Blandtrap never knew of their youthful behavior. Officer Monk was discrete, even able to avoid, on most occasions, the relentless village grape vine. Each speaker hoped secretly he would not choose tonight to loosen his tongue about their indiscretions.

The ignorant make mistakes because they don't know better. They've never been taught. There's no shame in ignorance, as long as it is not a permanent or recurring condition. Most of the ignorant will not remain in that situation because embarrassment energizes them to seek knowledge which is nearly all that is needed to acquire it. Wisdom often follows knowledge.

Morons differ from the ignorant by their actions; they seek their own pleasure and comfort rather than knowledge and wisdom. Unfortunately, a man's reputation, for years at a time, can rest in the hands of morons. So it was when Officer Monk was young and new to the force.

First assignments on a police force tend to be similar to first assignments on any job. Tedious and mind-numbingly boring tasks at odd hours fill the list of things to do each day. The worst of these details was herding drunks safely out of town and checking doors in the business district.

It had been a bad day all around. Officer Monk had worked late the night before and had to get up early to give a short talk to a Cub Scout den meeting. Grumpy when he awoke, he said something inappropriate to his wife. She immediately retaliated with more colorful language. Escalation to a full fledged argument was certain but it had to wait since he'd overslept. He had an unpleasant morning with the promise of an uncomfortable evening. It's amazing how we reap what we sow, sometimes before the seed hits the ground.

When he stopped by the police station to pick up the hand outs for the scouts, the chief cornered him and chewed him out for filling out some paperwork incorrectly. He was feeling like a kicked puppy when he arrived at the Cub Scout den meeting. The Feiden kid was there. Officer Monk hadn't been on the force but a couple of weeks and the Feiden kid was the only Blandtrap student he knew by name.

Ken Feiden was a handful with his mom and dad at each side. Unbridled, he was a living, breathing monster in miniature. Hosts would often amend his invitation to include a note to his parents: "if you are unable to escort your child, please send the whip and chair needed to control him." The Feiden boy interrupted, poked others, screamed twice for no apparent reason, ran around often, and generally made a nuisance of himself until Officer Monk was visibly shaken.

He finished the talk as best he could, not always in a coherent manner. The fifteen minute talk was too long for the audience. He had the attention of most for the first five minutes, except for those poked and prodded by the Feiden lad. The parents were paying attention for maybe ten minutes before they had to devote all their attention to crowd control. He finished the scripted presentation and returned to the police station to rewrite and file the reports he had done the night before, completing the mundane task just in time to make the rounds checking doors on the businesses around Village Square.

Walking out the door, he overheard an alert from the County Sheriff come over the radio. Thieves had hit small businesses in the area. Downtown businesses as close as Butte Crossing and Bureau had been robbed. He took notes by hand and typed them up as a formal notice. Not adept at office tasks, the eighth attempt got the job done with only one erasure.

It was late, now, and overcast. No stars or moon were shining to provide additional light to the scant street lights and night lights inside businesses. Village Square was better lit than the businesses surrounding it. The door to Mrs. Clariette's Millinery was unlocked but she preferred it that way. Regularly forgetting her own set of keys, she had grown too old to make unnecessary trips home so she left it unlocked whenever she departed. She could remember she had given a key to someone just for these situations, but she could not remember who had it. In fact, she had given a key to nearly everyone. She had keys made so regularly that Hugginbough Hardware and Lumber kept her master permanently mounted in the key guide. It was only briefly removed to serve some less regular customer.

Older fellows, at least some of us, still looked on Officer Monk with a suspicious eye. He had figured out every odd occurrence in Blandtrap with one exception. He had never identified the Bagpipe player. When questioned directly about the failure Monk would doubletalk, stammer, and change the subject. It led you to believe he was somewhere between complete confusion and admiration for the perpetrator. "He's a slippery devil." Officer Monk would say about the mysterious musician. "I've got some plaster casts of shoe prints but I've never been able to make a match.

He said it in a convincing demeanor so the younger men believed what he said. Clovis' father, Stu, Ray Solomon, and I think we can see through the masquerade. Officer Monk knew more than he was telling. If the bagpipe player were a thief or a murderer, he would be in custody by now. As a local character, Officer Monk allows the musician to roam free as long as he causes no one harm other than fertilizing overactive imaginations.

One day a work crew from the county jail was doing some curb work on Village Square. Blandtrap welcomes workers from County Jail. It provides economy for village improvement projects and there is a general consensus of 'there but for the grace of God go I.' Granted, few of us would shoplift, extort, or strike our wives under any circumstances, but we understand how the weak willed and faithless could lapse into that behavior. Also, we are aware of an evil that would seek to commit these crimes without remorse and with full knowledge that the behavior is wrong and an affront to man and God.

Before they loaded inmates into the bus to drive them back to jail, a guard called Officer Monk aside and handed him an item. He said one of the prisoners who was getting out the next week had reformed.

The inmate confessed he didn't feel right leaving town with a key to the hat shop. It had been offered to him without coercion. To avoid distraction and keep to his schedule, he unthinkingly took it, placing it in his pocket. He accepted the key with the best of intentions, still, guilt haunted him.

Mrs. Clariette had given the incarcerated man one of her many spare keys 'just for good measure.' Her habit of handing anyone and everyone a key to her shop had to stop. The Chief pulled her aside at the next opportunity strongly recommending she leave the door unlocked during the day. He would lock the door during evening rounds. It was better for every merchant on Village Square to keep an eye on her shop rather than every passerby carry a key in their pocket. The store would be more secure for her and much less trouble for everyone else if she cooperated with his idea.

Every night Officer Monk would walk Village Square checking doors. It was rare to find any door, other than Mrs. Clariette's door, open. He would secure the unlocked doors after investigating to see if anyone was in the store.

If he was in error and the door left open for some reason, he would account for his actions in the morning. It was their ritual. It was prudent to secure a business under these circumstances. He could always apologize later.

One night, he proceeded around Village Square door by door in his usual manner. Nothing was out of the ordinary until he reached Jane's Dress Shop. The name had been changed to just Jane's. She had made it much more than just a dress shop. Any conceivable accessory was also on display. Folks didn't feel comfortable calling it a dress shop any more. The name on the sign was never changed but the ladies just call it 'Jane's.' It was recognition of achievement.

The door to Jane's shop was unlocked and slightly off the stop so the latch hadn't fastened. New to the village, Officer Monk hadn't had a chance to meet Jane, but her reputation was she paid attention to details. It was out of character for a meticulous person to neglect such an important matter. Reaching for the knob, he heard a noise from inside the shop. Thoughts of recent thefts in the area raced through his sleep-deprived, coffee-jazzed brain and he responded accordingly. All his natural ability and police training merged in his mind to focus on the crime before him.

Opening the door and entering without a sound, he crouched behind a display table, listening intently for a clue to what was going down. Road noise from a passing vehicle caused him to worry he would be detected because of the open door. With belt buckle scraping the floor, he crawled back to the door and closed it, causing only a muffled click. It could have been enough to give him up. Crawling back to the display table on his hands and stomach, sharp pains shot through his hands and belly, distracting him. Thereafter, any time the subject of new clothes came up he would caution people to be careful with those tiny pins that come in packaged clothing.

He could see a light in the office and could hear rustling noises as he crept closer. Sure that Jane's records were being ransacked or her cash receipts pilfered, he thought carefully, reviewing the rules of his training, and cautiously drew his pistol. Protocol suggested he find an advantageous position and call to the thieves to surrender. He wasn't really sure, after all, how many there were. Backup would have been prudent but he was too engaged to retreat.

The office door must have only been cracked a bit since the light was so dim. He snuck around the corner by the dressing rooms where he had a clear view of the office and had easy access to the back door if a quick retreat was the best course of action. It was a complete plan allowing for reasonable contingencies.

Muscles taut, he moved toward his ideal position, kicking over a short earring display sending the product skittering and clanging across the floor. Officer Monk jumped to the side, seeking cover when he clearly saw a man holding a revolver. Responding to imminent threat to his life, he raised his pistol and identified himself to the perpetrator, "Police! Drop your weapon and put your hands up!"

Everything was happening at the speed of light and in slow motion at the same time. The thief didn't heed the warning and continued to raise his hand gun, pointing it at Officer Monk. He had no choice. To protect himself he fired his pistol at the thief.

Shards of glass were flying everywhere and a flash of light briefly blinded the officer as the office door flew open. Jane ran out shouting, "Don't shoot. Don't shoot." She was shaking with fear, yet relieved to see Officer Monk. "What happened?" Jane asked when words returned to her.

Her answer was slow in coming. Officer Monk wasn't sure of the events. Clearly there was no one other than Jane and he in the store. On the wall next to the office door were the remnants, screws and glass shards, of a full length mirror. As he had approached the office he had seen his reflection raise a pistol. In the dim light and confusion, he fired on what he believed was someone drawing down on him and he responded in kind. As bad as it was going to sound, he had shot himself.

The chief back then didn't leave loose ends and wouldn't let matters alone. He made measurements. Officer Monk was forced to reenact the incident several times, reliving the humiliation. He had to reimburse Jane for the shattered mirror out of his own pocket. The official findings of the chief's investigation were never made public, but he shared the events among fellow officers. What the chief found was that not only had Officer Monk shot himself, from the trajectory of the bullet and the location of the slug in the wall, he had quite likely killed himself.

Most of the town understood Monk's actions when they heard the whole story. Jane expressed her gratitude to the officer with a bundt cake - her prized Milky Way bundt cake. Morons continue to pass on the story as part of their oral tradition. The much embellished version is passed from idiot to simpleton, losing the point that Officer Monk was willing to risk his own life to protect the village.

The rest of the villagers remember other, more endearing interaction with Officer Monk. I recall a confused teen, a senior in high school and not as mature as the other boys, making some poor decisions. The preacher's daughter was sweet on him for a moment. She had recently become a flagrant flirt but hadn't acquired a reputation yet. Rumors about her were just beginning to float.

I suppose he relented to the invisible pressure young men hold inside or perceive from the outside. Young women have a similar pressure, but it is different. In retrospect, he couldn't figure out what he was trying to prove by pursuing that girl, he only knew it was wrong and he didn't care. Looking back with eyes of acquired wisdom he could see that his goal was simply too expensive, too wasteful. What was lost in pursuit was more valuable than what was gained in conquest.

It was after one of those youth group meetings they slipped away alone. He was driving that night and, due to rain, he drove many who would have, in better weather, walked to their homes. Arranging the route so the preacher's daughter would be the last passenger, they were alone in the car. She said she was game for a ride in the country so they scooted out of the village and up Lusty Hill. Cutting across to Roller Coaster Road, he turned down an isolated road. Since no one lived on the road, it had been labeled with a number rather than given a name.

He parked the car alongside the road. One thing lead to another like they tend to do when people, young or old, put themselves into that situation. The outcome wasn't what you would think. They were both innocent and new to the game. Neither of them had seen the roadmap; and they lacked consensus on a destination. He wanted to prove what a man he was while she wanted to defy and embarrass her parents. Their hearts and minds weren't on the trip.

They were on their third attempt to get started. Nothing either of them tried got traction. They had no interest in each other in that way and it dampened enthusiasm. They were working through the usual fundamentals. The direction of the head tilt when you kiss should be natural and when it must be discussed, it leads to a lack of spontaneity. He was very right handed. When in a car and facing a passenger, one arm, the right arm for the driver, is crushed against the back of the seat. An uncoordinated teen like he was, it was only a matter of time before he was going to poke a few eyes trying to use only the left hand. As she was wiping her eye, burning from whatever he had been attempting to do, waiting for the sting to subside, red and blue lights flashing behind their car broke whatever mood they had been working so hard to initiate.

A rap on the window with his flashlight and a gesture to follow him back to the police car got him out of the driver's seat and into his cruiser. "So…you think you're going to marry this girl?" He asked abruptly with that gruff voice of his.

"No, sir," He replied, "I haven't given much thought to marriage, really."

"Then why are you out here fooling around with a girl who is going to be someone else's wife?" The words stung at his heart.

"She's not married, sir." He was confused by the question.

"Not now, lad, but do you suppose she will ever marry? Please try to keep up with the conversation." Officer Monk was on the trail of something but the young man hadn't caught the scent of it yet.

"Sure…I mean…I suppose she will." He still wasn't getting it. He could tell the officer was getting impatient, but he wasn't as quick a lad as he was pretending to be as an adult.

"When she does marry, you will have fooled around with some other man's wife." If this didn't work he would have to start over, maybe with pictures.

The lad got it and Monk could see the light go on in his head. He wasn't through, "Do you suppose some other sweaty, pimple-faced teenager is out defiling the woman you will eventually marry?" He wanted the kid to see consequence to his actions. It was beginning to work.

The idea of some kid fooling around with his wife bothered him in some odd way. He didn't have a wife; He didn't have a girlfriend for that matter. But still, it dug at him.

Officer Monk left him in the car and went to talk to the girl alone. The boy didn't know what the officer said to the girl. Whatever it was, she was crying uncontrollably as he followed them back to her house. Monk rested, standing at his car, while the boy went in the house with the girl.

She ran upstairs to her room, still sobbing, leaving him in the parlor with the preacher. Never has anything been more difficult than to explain to the preacher what he and the preacher's daughter were about to do and what his intentions had been.

The preacher had a red face naturally which turned maroon when he was angered. The boy had heard several sermons on this very subject. Once the preacher got going, he delivered a montage of those discourses, complete with scripture references and a graphic description of hell. When he was through, he dismissed the boy without the usual hymn. The boy was surprised he was able to leave untouched. A lot of people who preach to turn the other cheek also throw a mean right hook.

As he walked down the porch steps, Officer Monk slid off the hood of his car where he had been napping, tipped his hat, and drove away. Pulling away from the preacher's house, the lad knew he had to face the music at home. He could see the preacher on the phone as he pulled out into the street, knowing his parents were on the receiver at the other end of the line.

I have heard Brimstone tell that story twice, so far. Both times he used the tale as the reason he chose ministry as his profession. That kind of impact on a young man was typical for Officer Monk. All of us growing up in Blandtrap had an experience with Officer Monk and each different from the other.

My experience with Officer Monk was much different than other stories I had heard. Just after starting high school, I started to run with some of the tougher guys on the football team. I wasn't a good player but they were. Most of them were older and drove cars. A couple of them had a driver's license. We had some merry chases with the officer and we had some close calls with a few ditches and several sharp curves. We always seemed to get away. When the driver would begin to drive beyond his ability, it seemed Officer Monk broke off the chase.

One night when I was riding with the guys, they stopped the car behind the dime store. The others got out so I did too. Not knowing what they were up to and not being smart enough to think it through, I stood there as the other three started taking the screws out of the rear window of the store.

I had started to back away as the enormity of what was about to happen seeped through my thick skull. About a half a block down the alley, a spotlight from Officer Monk's cruiser caught the other three dead to rights. Nobody ran, Monk had the alley blocked. The guys didn't run because they were familiar with the drill, knowing running would only add to their troubles. I didn't run because I was frozen with fear.

He put them in the cruiser and I couldn't hear what they said. A lifetime later, so it seemed, Officer Monk closed the door and walked over to me. "They told me you didn't know what they were up to. I'm not sure I believe them. It is so rare they would attempt an act of kindness or justice. I'm going to let you go this time. Don't let it happen again. If it does, I don't care what the others say; I'll run you in and charge you with the rest of them."

"Thank you, sir." I choked out the words, shaking a bit.

"You really ought to think about getting some better friends. If you can't do that, then you should get some smarter friends because these clowns sleep on my cots more than they do in their own beds." He advised me frankly. "Get out of here. You're free to go."

I remained at attention. "Can we keep this just between us, sir?"

"Yep," He said. "It's just between you, me, and your daddy."

I was disappointed I wouldn't get off Scott free. I would have to dance to the music when I got home. That was the last day I spent any time at all with those guys. I didn't miss them and, as far as I know, they didn't miss my company either.

So you can plainly see, if you would only open your eyes to what surrounds you and widen your scope of interest to include the obvious, you would realize the wealth of upright citizens and even heroes who walk the streets of our village. Blandtrap is full of worthy examples. You should take note of them and share your knowledge with your readership.

Respectfully Submitted,

Harry Ellis

March

Lifted from among the likely possessions of Calvin Farnsworth:

If you were to really relax while decorating a breath mint with diagonal lines to use as an heirloom, wouldn't that be…

...a kicked back ric-a-rac Tic Tac knickknack?

Harry Ellis

238 Persimmon Street

Blandtrap

To the Editor of the Tiskilwa Bureau Valley Chief

RE: Planning the Garden

Dear Sir:

I see advertisements for garden stores have begun to appear in your pages. I find I am quite behind my time. The page of the calendar has changed to March and I have not planned my garden. The seed catalogues have been haunting the horizontal surfaces of my home since January, but I have done nothing but breeze through, gazing at the pictures and dreamily planning the gardens of Solomon, without the consideration of my meager barren beds.

You have not yet announced the garden competition you sponsor each year. Blandtrap gardeners hope you will expand the competition beyond your city limits to include our village. Several local gardeners, based on pictures of the past winning gardens, think they have more than an even shot at capturing first prize. The widows in particular are chomping at the bit to go head to head against city gardeners. I should warn you, they are quite confident in their abilities.

Should you allow them into the contest and send your representative judge their work, you might want to print the milk cartons before they leave because once the widows get a hold of an eager ear, they will not let go of it until it falls from the head. Each widow has a family history, deceased husband's shortcomings, and social etiquette requirements engineered into each bed of blooming splendor.

Explanations of their gardens are complete with side-trips to the countries of their predecessors replete with hardships they overcame in immigration and assimilation. I am sure each interview will take days rather than minutes to compete even if only the most basic details are elicited. No doubt, you would consider it an unfair advantage to have those familiar with the soil compete against city folk just as it would be unfair to have country folk compete against city folk in a pick pocket competition.

We in the country would consider it cheating to start with plant stock rather than seed or bulb, or the occasional cutting. Starting with a seedling or more mature plant would be like boasting about building a farm implement having started with a tractor. It was already a farm implement when you began! I have four raised beds for vegetables in the back yard. Two small beds and a large one in the front yard for flowers and three modest beds in the back. Those are in addition to the two peonies at the sides, and the rhubarb near the alley.

The back yard has full sun, while the front yard is shaded much of the day. The catalogues give information on each plant, such as 'part to full sun.' The key is knowing what to do with the information. Put a fern in full sunlight and it will fry. You might as well plant it on a stone. With regard to sun, believe what catalogues tell you.

Information provided by the seed companies begins with a photo to lure you in, then a bit of text regarding when and how long it blooms. As you read you make the decision that you would like to feature this blossom and design the entire yard to draw attention to its elegance. In the last ad you read, the flower won't grow north of Key West and, short of building a biodome, it cannot thrive in the type of soil found in your yard. That type of key information should be foremost in the ad.

It is always difficult for me to gauge the density of planting. Articles often say to plant large species thirty inches apart. A regular result of that strategy is that I have one inch of plant to tend and twenty-nine inches of vigorously persistent weeds to battle. It seems somehow unfair to give more ground to the enemy then to my allies. Yet, when I plant too closely, the plants become weeds unto themselves. They never fully develop and whether fruit or flower, are a disappointment. It was urgent that the early crops get in the soil immediately. Lettuce, greens, peas, and radishes could withstand a decent frost. Since it appeared to be an early spring this year, time was wasting away. I got up early and headed to the Seed Shack, but somehow found myself with coffee in my hand, sitting in Plowboy Diner a few minutes later. The gang was beginning to gather.

Stu and Clovis' father came in first and I casually mentioned my sloth in planning the garden and the dilemma I now faced. They were sympathetic, but offered no suggestions. The conversation moved to the topic of weather. Suddenly, the door of the diner swung open and an imposing image occupied the doorway. He moved slowly but with purpose past the counter, motioning to tip the hat he would have been wearing had he not removed it as he entered. Turning toward the dining room he straightened himself so he could get a better view of the assembled.

We all wanted to grab our jackets and run, but we were like frogs caught in the beam of a flashlight. Frozen by some involuntary primal reaction to fear, we sat there, trying to be inconspicuous. We could see him mentally weighing his options as his eyes scanned across the diner and, with horror in our hearts, we saw his face light up when they settled on our table. He was on his way over.

It was Brimstone, Pastor Brimstone and we all knew why he was there: writer's block. Everyone was racking their brain thinking of a credible excuse to make a hasty exit. Lies don't come easy when you're staring in the preacher's face and Brimstone was aware of that fact. He challenged each excuse tossed his way, so your reason better be good and well supported. "I believe my dog is loose," Stu said, rising to put on his jacket. "Managed to dig himself out of your garden, did he?"

Brimstone was on the hunt. "You buried that dog more than a year ago. If he's running loose now you either need to bury him deeper or talk to the vet about the conclusive symptoms of death. Sit down, Stu."

Clovis' father had begun to rise as well, but when he saw how Brimstone nailed Stu back in his seat, he decided to stay peacefully. He sat back in his chair and braced himself for the worst. Brimstone had busted him on his fake deaf act a few months back.

"What are you boys up to today?" The preacher grilled. Stu and Clovis' father shot pointed fingers toward me and said in unison, "Harry's planning his garden."

Brimstone's face broadened into a grin. I could see the cogs beginning to turn. "Planning…planting… gardens; all good topics for a sermon." He said, "Spring… death of a seed and life through the plant." Everyone else noticed Brimstone mull over the possibilities, too, and it was somewhat of a relief to all. The preacher wasn't done yet; we had learned from experience. He still needed examples to "personalize" his message to the congregation.

We never went to the extreme of following Brimstone to get some dirt on him, but we often wished we held some knowledge about him that was not that flattering to use as a bargaining chip to leave us alone.

We thought we had him once. We had been bowling in Butte Crossing and were driving through downtown when we saw Brimstone enter the back door of Skinny's Tap, a local watering hole there. We immediately pulled into a parking space wondering if we should investigate further or whether the present information was sufficient for our purposes.

We were getting our stories straight. This type of expose' can come back to bite you if you're not careful. As soon as you tell a person "I saw Preacher Brimstone go in Skinny's Tap," they're going to want to know what you were doing in Skinny's Tap to witness the event. It all as to be done carefully and the whole thing structured just right.

Rumor has to be constructed carefully. If it is done hastily, it will come out as either mean or less interesting than the actual event. If the story is pieced together with the mind, it can be led in the most unusual direction. Maybelle Oufsbacher is a master craftsman of rumor, while I'm not sure if I do it correctly. Not long after we had gotten under way, the car darkened and a large face wearing an even larger hat occupied the open window. It was Brimstone! "What are you boys doing in Butte Crossing this time of night? Do your wives know where you are?" We were all caught off guard and suddenly became aware of our surroundings. Simeon Swagg, who had battled the bottle to a bloody victory, piped up from the back seat. "Spend a lot of time at the local establishments, do you Preacher?" Brimstone stuck a pin in our balloon as those without a guilty conscience often do. "I'll see you inside," Brimstone said to the pastor of the Lutheran Church in Blandtrap as he passed by our car, nodding to us. Then Brimstone directed his attention toward the four of us. "If you have nothing better to do, and that certainly appears to be the case, you're welcome to join us."

Our collective response was a jumble of excuses:"I've got to get home," "Any other time I'd say yes," "My wife is expecting me," and "I believe my house was on fire when I left. (Some of us don't lie as well as others.) "Come on Brimstone!" arose a shout from across the street. When we jerked our heads we saw two priests standing on the sidewalk, waiting for Brimstone. "We've got all the time in the world, but the boss," he said pointing and looking up, "can be strict regarding these matters." "Very well, then. You boys enjoy the rest of the evening." And Brimstone was gone. We drove home that night in relative silence. We had been disappointed on the lanes by a third game, tenth frame comeback mounted by our opponents, then again by the missed opportunity to best Brimstone.

In the restaurant, Brimstone was still digging for examples. He poked us with questions and prodded us with inquiries hoping for something he could capture for a sermon would pop out. Each of us tried to be as vague and evasive as we knew how but we were not skilled in the art. He kept beating his sword against our shields until one of us must have said something unintentional. We saw Brimstone's face light up and he lit off.

We didn't know what had been said or who said it. We would all be uncomfortable until we knew what it was Brimstone had extracted and how he was going to reduce it to use in a sermon. From past practice, we were aware he wouldn't spill the beans until he blabbed it during church on Sunday. The only way to find out what he was up to was to fill a pew and face the music.

Stu and Clovis' father tried to reintroduce weather as the topic of conversation. It is, after all, the building block upon which men construct nearly all communication. "Ouch!" is probably a close second, but weather wins the race at the wire.

I was insistent, though, that they help me with this garden planning business. Clovis' father is a farmer. He grows cash crops like corn and soy beans. He doesn't have time anymore for vegetable gardens. In years past he would put in some vegetables for the cannery in Princeville, but it had been decades since that venture was profitable.

Indeed, few farmers bother with vegetables even for their own consumption. Farm kids today are unfamiliar with the traditional garden patch.

In the city, children are bussed to zoos to see cows, pigs, and chickens because they rarely encounter these species in the streets. It has nearly become the case with farm children today, who must be taken to the grocer to be shown tomatoes, onions, and garlic. They are surprised to see where the sauce on their pasta is derived. They must be taught that apples don't grow in piles on tables indoors like they see in the produce section. It is the passing of an era, a loss of tradition.

"Look, Harry," Clovis father began with intent to put the matter to rest in short order, "It's still early so plant the field greens, peas, broccoli, and onions. You should have planted the garlic last fall. Potatoes are planted on Good Friday and that's about all you can safely do until the middle of May."

Knowing Stu as well as I do, I recognized the mistake Clovis' father had made. He mentioned raising potatoes and onions. Stu was a fine citizen, dedicated to the community. He was a man of God, in his own way. You could even call him a patriot for his service to this country. Stu was a good husband, a fine father, and about to be a grandfather. He had always been a good friend to me and others, but foremost, before any of these other noble traits, Stu was cheap.

Stu had the reputation of squeezing a nickel until the buffalo screamed. It didn't negate his other good qualities; rather, it enveloped them, forcing you to deal with the matter to get to the reward of his acquaintance much like you have to fight through a hive's worth of swarming bees to get to the honeycomb.

"Why in the world would anyone plant onions and potatoes?" Stu was incredulous, "Few vegetables are cheaper to buy than onions and potatoes. The onion bulbs and the seed potatoes cost almost as much a buying the produce. Why, it must cost twenty beads of sweat per plate of hash browns to grow these cheap crops!"

Stu was prone to using unconventional units of measure without warning. We were used to it, but it continued to disturb Calvin Farnsworth. Calvin tended to record these units of measure and examine them closely at his Institute for Idle Science. Because of Calvin's response and the explanation that inevitably followed, Stu had recently refrained from colorful phrases.

Calvin would first confirm what he thought he had heard, then meticulously write it in his notebook and reconfirm his record. Calvin would wander to the library to see if these units were unique. If the term proved to be unique and had even the most remote applicability to a real situation, he would initiate a letter writing campaign to scientific publishing houses encouraging and eventually demanding they include the term in their lists of standard units of measure. Understandably, he met resistance in the acceptance of these new terms.

Calvin was pleasantly surprised when one scientific publishing house wrote back with interest in the unit 'obscenities per refrain' as applied to gangsta rap music. They wanted to know if it should be included under the English or Metric Systems. Calvin believed that gangsta rap crossed these lines and would be applicable in either system. They also wanted to know if this new unit of measure was related to their existing unit 'station changes per measure of music.' It was observed that for the unit to be used universally, all time signatures must be converted to 4/4 time.

The rest of us could see it, but sarcasm was wasted on Calvin. He jumped on the questions they asked, applying logic and reason interchangeably with enthusiasm and zeal. He worked non-stop and after two days Hugginbough and I saw him staggering from exhaustion toward the library.

We dragged him into the diner and made him eat a decent meal. Motioning to Frank, we gave him some 'doctored' tea. Frank slipped him about three fingers of Old Granddad from a bottle he kept under the counter in case of snake bite. It is remarkable how the frequency of snake bite increases as the temperature drops below freezing. If only the fish would bite with the same frequency as snakes, Blandtrap would be a resort destination.

Hugginbough took Calvin home and put him away for the day. He had trouble holding his liquor and fell off to sleep almost immediately. We wouldn't hear from Farnsworth again for a few days.

Stu finished his tirade while Clovis' father and I planned the rest of the day in our minds. If Stu had been suddenly struck with laryngitis, either of us could have flawlessly finished his rant for him, so familiar with the old saw we were. Since he didn't need us for this lecture, we waited patiently for his next breath so we could excuse ourselves and get out of there.

On to the hardware store, I went to the seed section to select my purchase. Late in the season as it was, the options were few. I chose some mesculun mix, red bib lettuce, sugar snap peas (edible pod), and radishes. I paid Tommy, asking how school was going and if his parents were doing well. After receiving my change and a thumbs-up to both inquiries, I dismissed myself.

At home, I diagramed the garden space and decided where each crop would be seeded. Consulting my limited reference library, I determined which patch needed what fertilizer, checking inventory to see if it could be accomplished with existing inventory. All that was left was to wait for the soil to dry to the point where I could work it productively.

So you see, in Blandtrap we are complete. Your advertisements fall short of the allurement necessary to drag us to the city when Hugginbough's Hardware and Lumber provides all the resource we need to make our lawns bloom. The assistance of your city is not needed here.

Respectfully Submitted,

Harry Ellis

Harry Ellis

238 Persimmon Street

Blandtrap

To the Editor of the Tiskilwa Bureau Valley Chief

RE: Institute for Idle Science – Jelly Side Down

Dear Sir:

High teas, celebrity auctions, and masquerade balls are laid end to end in articles on your pages, all to raise money in the name of medical research. You would have us believe we would all be lost to disease if it weren't for a cranberry scone, the mayor hired to wash your windows, or a debutant behind a Cinderella costume.

Must you continue to bore us with details of your medical research facility for which you ceaselessly raise funds? Medical research is not the only research that can impact the quality and quantity of life. We have within the village limits, a person dedicated to searching the corners of science for elusive laws of science and hidden phenomenon that can change the very way people live.

Calvin Farnsworth has the heart of a scientist and he may be, at any given moment, testing one rare theory or another. I have always considered myself an educated man and find it stimulating to pursue the philosophy of science with persons such as Calvin. He is unique among scientists of this generation.

Many pursue the hard sciences such as Chemistry, Biology, Physics, or Medicine. Others favor the social sciences of Psychology, Sociology, or Anthropology. Still others are inspired by the Humanities or History

105

or Economics. Calvin, however, ventured into the realm of science he prefers to call Idle Science.

"There is a vast warehouse of knowledge that is untapped," he would say, "Sure, these theories, applied individually, produce benefit in a single application, but what marvelous revelations of wisdom must be found from combining these seldom-used theories. For instance, the Gas Law and Bernoulli's Law are brilliant observations in their own right, but combining them has given us the gift of flight and travel in space.

Idle Science, as Calvin chooses to define the field, includes what can best be described as adages and bits of wisdom from the collective wisdom of many generations. The science is to combine them in unique and imaginative ways. Laws of Science, as Calvin would call them, like "A stitch in time saves nine" comprised the discipline. He called it Idle Science because he thought these laws were underused and not living up to their full potential, depriving mankind of the richer life that would be possible with widespread application of their principles.

Calvin didn't limit his service to community to his work at the Institute for Idle Science. He chronicled every event in Blandtrap. He would document participants in parades, band members playing in concerts in Village Square, and winners of the Labor Day Hog Roast and Quilt Show. He kept his records in the basement of the library.

Villagers refer to the collection of records as the archives of Blandtrap. The information has proved invaluable on several occasions. Old people need to have their memories reset once in a while and more than one bet has been settled by rummaging through records in the archives.

Calvin didn't let past failure haunt current experiments. He had learned much by subscribing to Thomas Edison's philosophy, which was to remain enthusiastic in the face of apparent failure. If it is knowledge that you seek, you will always find it. It may not be the knowledge you were seeking, but it will be knowledge nonetheless.

The scars and humiliation of failure, however, live on in others who remember disappointment and keep track of blame. In hindsight, he should have seen the problems associated with the "Monkey see, monkey do / A watched pot never boils" experiment. With time comes forgiveness. Or, is it forgetfulness? Either way, relief is the result.

Calvin's picture still hangs in the primate building and every new trainee is shown the photograph and told to burn the likeness into their memory. The matter seems to be largely smoothed over, now, and he has been granted limited and conditional access to the zoo again.

In his one and only visit to the primate house since the incident he apologized to the offended apes. It was a tense meeting to be sure. The other monkeys were agitated at Calvin's presence. Obviously, the ugly experience had been shared with their roommates. Close quarters like they have in the monkey house and with little else to do other than pick lice, I imagine there are almost no secrets among them. A trauma like they endured must come up regularly in daily conversation.

It was much like a poor man visiting the wealthy parents of his fiancé for the first time and realizing the relationship had no chance of success. Calvin would never be allowed access to research animals again. He would have to restrict research activities to humans; a subject species he felt was inferior to all others for the purposes of science.

Camaraderie, in spite of the pain of the event, developed between researcher and subject. After the initial shock of seeing Calvin again, the monkeys calmed and the two monkeys involved came close to Calvin in a gesture of truce.

Monkey See, who had been injured the most, was first to make up to Calvin. Monkey Do took longer to warm to him. Monkey See didn't know what hit him, but Monkey Do saw the whole chain of events coming at him and couldn't get out of the way in time. It was more than Monkey Do had grown to expect in his captive environment. Lulled into complacency, never having to forage for food or hunt for safe shelter he was off his game, his reactions dulled. In the wild, he thought, his reflexes would have been honed to the point where that boiling pot would have missed him entirely.

Calvin and the monkeys spent their last few moments together comparing scars, exchanging excuses for the accident, and begging forgiveness. They parted in silence, but with a new understanding of each other's pain.

Yesterday I had a chance to chat with Calvin as I was trolling for coffee at Plowboy Diner. "What's on the front burner at the Institute?" I asked. He has a laboratory and conducts experiments from time to time to prove or disprove his theories. The laboratory and those who have participated in the research are referred to as the Institute for Idle Science. I am proud to be adjunct to the Institute; however I am presently without official title. Continued cooperation on experiments such as this will remedy the oversight, I hope.

Platitudes and sayings do not hold the same place in Calvin's world as they do in larger society. Sayings are fuel for research, not modes of communication. They are lost on him. "The burners are arranged from left to right across the lab bench. I'm not sure which burner you're referring to when you say the 'front burner.' I could measure, I suppose. One burner is probably ever so slightly nearer the edge of the counter maybe a degree or two hotter than the others." Calvin began rummaging for a ruler and thermometer.

"No, Calvin," I said, "What is your most current experiment." Getting Calvin back on track sometimes took extraordinary effort. Once he commenced collecting data he wouldn't come up for air until his notebook was full.

I wrested his attention from burners and returned his focus to my question. "Right now we're working on the interaction of two Idle Laws of Science: The first idle law is "the bread always falls jelly-side down; and the second law is that something is always found in the last place you look for it. We hope to show that if you look for the jelly-side of the bread to land face-down, and since there are only two alternatives, then the bread will necessarily land jelly-side up, because jelly-side down is the last place you could possibly look for it."

It all made sense to Calvin, yet my head was still reeling from the twists of logic. I mustered a weak response, "How unique! When will experiments begin?"

"This afternoon," He informed me. "Care to observe? I can occasionally use another hand, you know." He was quite adamant about openness. He had no professional secrets and found independent observers were useful in defending his data. With nothing to hide, he swore that his research was not for his personal profit but for the benefit of all humanity. Truly he had Nobel Prize intentions if only he could discover something meaningful to man.

When I arrived yesterday afternoon, Calvin was well into the research. He was running behind schedule so my late arrival hadn't held him up. He brought me up to speed on the experiment while we drove to the daycare center.

"Early experiments had to be refined as a result of flaws in procedure. Originally I used a machine to drop the bread and obtained some pretty disappointing data – no correlation of the two laws. That's when I realized my error. The machine was dropping the bread! The machine could not expect the bread to fall jelly-side down. It was a machine. It could expect nothing! The data simply had to be tossed out. This afternoon I hope to repeat the experiment with human subjects."

Talking with Calvin often made my mind feel seasick and long for dry land upon which to take a solid stance. He told me about the various groups of participants he had tried. The elderly had been his first choice. Most of his subjects had complained that they weren't allowed to eat jelly. When he tried to explain that he just wanted them to drop the bread, not eat it, he was met with glares of disdain.

His explanation of why he wanted them to drop the bread didn't soften the resolve of the wiser minds of the nursing home. Hours of begging and cajoling non-responsive residents bore no fruit. Eventually it resulted in him abandoning the elderly as subjects for the study. They would not throw perfectly good food on the floor to satisfy his whim. It violated their frugal upbringing. Waste was only justified in a life or death situation.

The next group he tried was working people. After distributing the bread and jelly to the first two subjects, he had to resist the participants' repeated requests for a BLT, salami on rye, or some other deli delectable.

After, once again, reviewing parameters of the study with the subjects and stressing the necessity of using jelly, they proceeded once more with the research.

Everyone was in their place and had their bread with strawberry jam. One of the subjects pointed out that they didn't have bread and jelly; rather, she had bread and jam. Calvin winced at the observation. It was out of character for him to overlook an important detail like this. He seemed a bit shaken by the dilemma and not just a little bit disappointed in himself for the oversight.

He admitted he had never heard the adage "the bread always lands jam-side down." He set about to rectify the deficiency. By the time he returned from the IGA with the jelly, all subjects had wandered off to other, more pressing responsibilities, so he had to eliminate working people from the study.

The third group he tried was teenagers. Calvin got caught in a long slow line at the grocery buying ample supplies of bread and jelly in advance to avoid the problems he had encountered the last time he left participants alone. Teens, though, had come hungry as they often do. Irresponsible in many duties, they may be but when they know food is to be eaten, they attend to the job with due diligence.

While they were waiting for Calvin to show, one of the teen girls mentioned it was South American month at Jose Wong's Ye Olde Fashioned Creole Chuckwagon Smorgasbord Buffet. The boys were on board immediately because the venture promised the two things they loved most in life: girls and food. They were especially fond of the 'all you can eat' aspect of the restaurant.

A tall teen boy who played on the basketball team said 'all you can eat' was deceptive advertising. Every time he went to a buffet, the restaurant closed before he could eat all he could. Judging by how fast he was growing I supposed it was true.

Thinking Calvin was a no show; they got to talking and decided they would prefer tacos to bread and jelly. He arrived to find an empty hall because the teens had set out in search of a better menu. That's the way with youth; always looking for greener pastures.

A fourth group of elementary school children, was overlooked because their mothers were too busy to bring them. Between soccer, dance classes, Sunday school, and martial arts training, a jelly eating session could not be wedged into an already overbooked schedule. It also seemed to the mothers that the additional laundry from all that jelly would be much more of a hardship to them than any benefit the research could bring to humanity.

A fifth group of children, comprised of day care kids, was where Calvin was hanging his hat today. He was hoping to overcome the problems of previous experimental runs and gather some good data. Good data is the backbone of good science and as rare as hen's teeth.

Calvin and I were greeted with cheers as we arrived in the classroom. The teachers, anticipating the bread and jelly, had delayed snack time until our arrival. I keenly observed that hunger didn't help the research, even in the smallest way. As fast as Calvin could spread the jelly on the bread, it was ravenously consumed. If you could manage to force a child to drop the bread and jelly, another child would snatch it out of the air before it could hit the floor.

"This is better'n crackers!" The children were shouting. Calvin wrote off to coincidence that the children's hunger subsided at precisely the same moment as he ran out of bread and jelly. The children had put an unreasonable demand on his inventory.

One of the most endearing characteristics of a small child is their willingness to share every intimate detail of their home life with only minimal prompting, whether they understand what is really going on or not. You can get information from a child that only a fly on the wall would ever see.

As he dashed out to restock the research supplies, I couldn't help thinking that something like this current snag could have been anticipated.

Returning quickly with bread and jelly he thought he was back in business. But when the children saw a picture of a boysenberry on the label, the all shouted, "What is this stuff made of?"

"Boysenberries." He answered.

"Eeuuww! What's that?" they chorused.

Calvin seemed stunned by the question. A few minutes ago they would have eaten sand from a dirty sock, yet now they seemed fussy. Calvin carefully explained what boysenberries were and assured them that boysenberries were wholly healthy and nutritious, and entirely suitable for making jelly.

With children one must use strategy to get them to cooperate and the tack Calvin chose was unlikely to garner their support. Had he pretended Boysenberries were a delicious, forbidden fruit and made them vow never to tell their parents he had given them a taste, they would have followed him to the ends of the earth.

A better description would have served him well. Healthy and nutritious is how you describe cooked spinach because it is so foul. When encouraging them to eat, healthy and nutritious are not persuasive words to small children.

That was all it took to lose the respect of the wee ones. Mutiny ran rampant and most children refused to play along unless they had grape jelly. Only grape would do. In an effort to salvage the project, I called Edith and she assured me she had an unopened jar of grape jelly in the pantry.

Calvin was off again and would be satisfied by nothing but grape jelly. By the time he returned it was nap-time, further delaying the experiment. As children awakened from their slumber somewhat grumpy, they needed encouragement to cooperate.

Back to work he went with his shoulder to the wheel, so to speak, and jellied bread with nimble fingers seldom seen, except on court recorders and pickpockets. The jellied bread was in the hand of each child and he was ready to begin. It took a few moments for Calvin to organize his paperwork to properly record his observations. That, unfortunately, was adequate time for the children to get jelly smudged not only all over themselves, but to get enough smeared all over the bread as to make it uncertain which side was "jellied" and which side was "clean.".

The children became so messy they had to be washed. Faces and hands were easy enough to scrub, but clothing was another matter. Being the end of the day, parents began to arrive to retrieve their children and they were not pleased to find their little ones glued to one another with grape jelly. The hopelessly stained clothes and the lateness of the hour caused the parents to be unwilling to let Calvin distribute still more jelly.

This group, in the end, also had to be scuttled and it forced Calvin to postpone the experiment until protocol could be sufficiently enhanced to allow its completion. He placed his meticulous and quite sticky notes in the Archives of Idle Science and vowed to revisit the matter when circumstances improved or when villagers became more sophisticated and would be willing to put the rigors of science ahead of personal comfort.

Although frustrated, he was not humbled. Calvin was still insisting his hypothesis had merit and these two Laws of Science were mysteriously and irreversibly connected. Whether it was dedication to science or stubbornness, he was sure he was right.

So you can see that although all the research at the Institute for Idle Science is not successful, the search for deep knowledge and understanding continues. Discovery is not limited to ivory walled academic buildings or metal and glass hospitals. It occurs out among the real people and the hustle and clamor of your city is simply unnecessary to the process.

Respectfully Submitted,

HarryEllis

Harry Ellis

238 Persimmon Street

Blandtrap

To the Editor of the Tiskilwa Bureau Valley Chief

RE: The Bag

Dear Sir:

I regret I am unable to report on the affairs of Blandtrap this week as I am traveling and not in contact with my usual sources. We, Edith and I, are in Columbus, Ohio visiting friends. I am forwarding you a copy of a letter which will explain the difficulties I am having here:

To the Publishers of "The Bag"

Dear Bag People:

I am accustomed to receiving a copy of "The Bag" in Blandtrap, my home town which is a good distance from this locale. As you know, the bag contains advertisements from local grocery stores, other food establishments, and the occasional odd ad from unrelated businesses. While mining these documents for weekly specials and exceptional bargains is no longer a necessary adjunct to our budget, I find it relaxing to peruse these pages and it has become a part of my weekly routine.

You can only imagine my dismay when, on the usual day of delivery, the residence I am visiting was overlooked in the

114

normal distribution of "The Bag." I set about to remedy the deficiency and, perhaps, discern the reasons for the slight.

I looked to my own shortcomings first as I am not one to point fingers at others until I am sure no responsibility rests on my shoulders. I could recall no error in etiquette or misstep in manners. If there was a more formal aspect to the protocol of receiving my "bag" I am unaware of it. In Blandtrap we sit at home and it appears at a regular time each week. Citizens play no role, real or ceremonial, in its delivery.

I went to the mailbox thinking that it may have fallen to the ground, but that was not the case. Neither had it blown away because no wind was in the vicinity. A search behind the mailbox, under a nearby pine tree, and in the neighbor's bushes was also unsuccessful in revealing its whereabouts.

As I was searching his bushes, I came upon, rather suddenly, the neighbor himself. We both were a bit startled at the experience, but, since it was his yard and not mine, I suppose he won that contest. Politely, yet quite firmly, he inquired as to what I was doing in his yard. My host had not introduced me around the neighborhood nor announced my coming so we were strangers, the neighbor and I. Excited and more than a bit embarrassed, I offered my story hurriedly.

My explanation didn't wholly satisfy him. I assured him I meant neither his shrubbery nor his person harm. Failing to win him over, I was convinced he was not comforted by my words. Initiating a retreat, the neighbor puttered about his car and yard and, in general, kept an eye on me all the while as I returned to my friends' home.

Realizing I was incapable of making him feel at ease, I tried to put him out of my mind as I resumed my search. I took a position in the middle of the street to get a better perspective on the neighborhood. From that vantage point I could clearly see that all the other houses had received their deliveries of your advertisements. Bags were hanging from curbside mailboxes or door handles on all the other houses. None were absent except for my temporary abode. This was perplexing and I paused to ponder its profundities.

Perhaps I tarried a bit too long. Jolted into awareness by the honking of car horns, I found behind me was a string of autos with drivers in varying stages of aggravation. They were trying to get past me, but we couldn't seem to get it orchestrated. When they played harmony, I sang the canticle. If I went left the cars were already there. If I tried going to the right, so did they. The honking and veering continued until an opportunity arose for escape. I timidly shrank from the roadway finding the sidewalk a much friendlier footpath.

Another neighbor, also from across the street, had wandered out into his driveway and must have been enjoying the floorshow. He shouted to the first neighbor from a few houses away, "Hey Larry! Look, it's Dances with Chevys." No doubt it was a reference to a nearly popular movie.

Larry, after convulsing for a while, headed over to the other neighbor for more conversation, probably at my expense, so I moved on in the opposite direction. Nothing against the chaps, I'm sure they were nice enough folks. I, however, was otherwise engaged with the search with no time to spare for their foolishness.

The walk up the street gave me time to think through the matter. The real problem was not that "The Bag" wasn't delivered, but that I didn't have one! This disease was easier to cure. I made a careful diagnosis and proceeded with the recommended treatment.

A lady was walking her dog and I approached her hopefully, "Hello ma'am. I was wondering if you knew where I could get one of those "Bags?" I gestured toward a nearby mailbox with its suspended booty.

"They leave 'em on yer house," was her retort.

"Of course I know they deliver them, but my host was not included in the route today." Personally, I was offended she thought me so backward as not to know that. Not knowing the kind of person she normally encountered in the neighborhood, I didn't want to be hasty in judging her.

"Ya didn't tick 'er off did ya?" She continued, "If ya tick 'er off she'll skip ya fer sure."

It was an unplowed field to this farmer. How in the world could you "tick off" the delivery people? First, they are like ghosts. No one ever sees them. "The Bag" hanging on your property is the only evidence we have that they really exist. You get up and get dressed in the morning, got to church, and when you return, the "Bag Ghosts" have decorated the neighborhood with their own style of plastic and paper waving in the breeze. Anyone else guilty of the same crime would be arrested for littering. "The Bag" people must be exempt from this regulation.

Second, these are delivery people. Delivery people are not famous for being thin skinned. The most grievous slight to them must be the periodic "no thank you." Offending them seemed impossible although Edith contends I have a gift for it.

"No, I didn't offend her. I don't even know the lady." I protested. It's not my habit to insult strangers. Ire was rising in my blood and I gave serious consideration to changing my position on that point.

My agitation must have been showing more than I intended. Her dog, which had been sniffing about the lawn, began to show an interest in me and came closer to explore. My pulling away to avoid confrontation with the creature caught the lady's attention.

"He doesn't bite!" She snarled. I doubted I could say the same of her.

"That may be ma'am," I cautioned, "But he keeps lifting his leg like he's going to kick me."

Levity got me nowhere. Neither did borrowed jokes. At this the lady reddened deeply and the dog was quick to sense it. He set out, not unlike a master tailor, to alter my trousers. With teeth and paw he was an expert. By the time I escaped his attack he had the stitches out of the cuff and shredded a bit of it to boot. Up the street and around the corner I went seeking refuge. I could hear the dog barking and the lady shouting behind me, but their troubles were no longer mine and my escape was clean.

Clear of canine calamities, I paused again to reflect. Was I thinking of this all wrong? Everyone else got a bag except for me. Still, did I deserve a "Bag?" Did they owe me a "Bag?" I was unsure of the answer or whether I liked the consequences a likely answer might bring, when, I noticed the apartment building across the street from were I was standing.

The panorama of the street included several apartment buildings. Each apartment had a "Bag" hanging from the mailbox cluster in the small cul-de-sac. Could all of these apartments be occupied? Surely there was at least one vacant apartment among them. If I could locate a vacant residence, I could take that "Bag"; then I would have one, and no one else would be a loser for it. If I didn't take it, it would eventually blow off and paper would be strewn over the grounds. Maintenance would have to pick it up in response to tenant complaints. I was actually doing a good deed by taking "The Bag." It was a favor to residents and to management.

I was careful to identify a vacant apartment. Second from the left was the nearest one I saw. Not wanting to take chances with this venture, my recent record being what it was, I went closer to confirm my supposition. This had to be the one. No curtains adorned the windows. With my nose pressed against the window I confirmed no furniture cluttered the living room. I was confident in my selection and walked, maybe even strutted a little, to the cluster of mailboxes to claim my prize. A reward is due the victor and I would claim my prize.

This is where things began to get sticky again. While the apartments each had a prominent, clearly visible house number displayed by the door, mailboxes were labeled with letters of the alphabet. This type of inconsistency is something that always raises the hair on the back of my neck. I made a mental note to write to the apartment owner and the Post Office demanding they resolve the incongruity. That would have to wait for another day because it didn't serve me in my present situation.

I applied logic to the solution of my dilemma. The apartments were numbered consecutively, left to right in increasing numeric order. Mailboxes were lettered consecutively, left to right in increasing alphabetic order. Therefore, the apartment that is second from the left in the building must necessarily be the mailbox second from the left in the array of mailboxes! This was flawless logic, so I removed "The Bag" from the second mailbox from the left and began to withdraw its contents.

I heard a car pull into the parking space next to the mailbox cluster, but paid no attention to it, being preoccupied with brightly colored flyers and other ads. They can be quite festive, particularly during holiday season.

"Excuse me! Just what do you think you are doing?" a gruff voice boomed from behind me. Although I wasn't facing him, I could tell he was right behind me. He was closer than I would have preferred.

"Just thumbing through the ads," I said absentmindedly while turning over a particularly interesting promotional brochure. The store was touting some excellent values. Edith would have been interested so I knew shopping would be added to our agenda.

"We saw you take our "Bag." His voice almost sounded combative as he accused me of theft. "Please give it back and leave immediately or I'm going to call the police!"

Now that he had my attention, I turned to observe a man standing next to his car, confused and angry, with his wife inside worried and scared.

"Don't be silly," I said, "This mailbox belongs to this vacant apartment." I feebly gestured toward the second apartment from the left. I, too, was surprised and my hand waving may have looked as if I was motioning into space. My behavior could have given the startled residents the idea I was not entirely in my right mind.

"You are wrong, sir. This is our mailbox and we can prove it if we must. But, if you thought it was for a vacant apartment then you most assuredly knew it was not yours and you took it anyway. That, sir, makes you a thief!" His timbre was in crescendo as he spoke.

The logic he used seemed impenetrable, yet I foolishly insisted on trying to poke a hole in it. Starting to explain my problem and the apparently flawed conclusion that lead me to select their particular mailbox, I stammered and hesitated as I went. My mother told me the guilty stammer to give them time to think up a lie. I tried to be sincere in case the man's mother had given him the same advice as mine. This fellow wasn't buying my line, though, and while I was still relaying my account of the events he nodded to his wife and she began dialing her cell phone. Perceiving she was calling the authorities, I cut my story short, pushed the bag in the man's hand, and paddled-on down the sidewalk, making better time than I had in recent memory.

Safely out of sight of the grumpy man and his snitching wife, I slowed to a more comfortable pace. Due to my inadequacies in securing "The Bag," I resigned myself to the task of driving to each of the stores and obtaining a copy of their ads in person. It would be a time-consuming job, but it would be much safer than alternatives I had chosen so far.

Continuing my stroll toward the home of my host, memory was jogged when I caught a glimpse of Larry and the other neighbor sitting in chairs in the driveway chatting away. I imagined they were waiting for my return to make sport of me once more. Wishing to avoid further embarrassment, I retraced my steps until I could see my host's house, from the back, through the yard of the neighbor behind them. A circuitous route for sure, but it gave me a level of privacy I had grown to crave that day.

Cutting through their yard, I made my way to the fence and threw one leg over. As I pulled the trailing leg into my host yard I heard a pronounced tearing sound and felt a stabbing pain in my inner thigh. Pressing on to the house and wishing I could awaken from this nightmare, I saw a piece of my trousers and, what I believed to be a slab of my flesh, proudly displayed on the fence, like they were a trophy. With an ache as my companion, retreat to my new found domicile was my only desire and safe haven in that stormy port was my solitary goal.

I hope this was an unintentional lapse in the quality of your distribution. I can't help but think you somehow responsible for the trespassing, traffic jams, animal attacks, petty thefts, and maiming that have haunted this neighborhood today. All of it was a result of simply overlooking an innocent resident in the normal circulation of your product. Prudence in duty and attention to detail will resolve your deficient service. I fear my plight will remain with me and my hope to ease my suffering will be in vain.

I will leave the matter to stand where it is, but I assure you, if the oversight is repeated, I am prepared to complain in a more public forum and more often, if necessary.

Bitterly Disappointed,

Harry Ellis

I have telephoned the scoundrels with daily regularity and they seem unwilling to respond. So, as you can plainly see, I not only am out of town, but I find myself out of sorts as well. With the application of persistence bordering on dogged tenacity, I can resolve this matter. I have issued thinly veiled threats which I predict will yield the desired result.

Through messages I have informed them I have acquaintances in the press. We have had our differences in the past, but in a jam, I am sure you will cooperate to right this injustice. An ally of your stature could, if properly motivated and willing to apply their influence, relieve my present suffering. I leave it to you whether you will come to the aid of your most regular correspondent or whether you will turn a blind eye to this pressing need.

Respectfully Submitted,

Harry Ellis

Harry Ellis

238 Persimmon Street

Blandtrap

To the Editor of the Tiskilwa Bureau Valley Chief

RE: Mowing the Lawn

Dear Sir:

Since you seem to think that "nothing ever happens in that one-horse town," and all we do is "sit around watching the grass grow," I have decided to humor you. Now that the weather has improved to warmer temperatures, lawns are indeed growing again.

The last Burnett boy is grown and off to college, so a void has been created in the lawn labor market. I will have to train another young lad in the fine art of lawn mowing in order to fill the vacancy. Not everyone has the patience and experience to effectively train a young man in the fine art of properly tending and manicuring my beautiful lawn.

I trained the first Burnett boy several years ago. They passed the tradition down through the family, from older brother to younger, until the third and last Burnett boy completed the family destiny last fall. I imagine the ivy walls of some institute of higher learning may, right now, being enriched with the wisdom I taught these children. How blessed these institutions must be and how rewarding it feels to have enriched higher education in this way.

Although I take pride in my lawn, my general opinion of grass is grim. Lawn grass is one of the least enjoyable of God's creations.

Its primary function seems to be holding dirt to the surface of the planet. Aside from that, I don't see much use for it. Like it does with hammers and houses, gravity normally keeps dirt from flying about unless drought or senseless humans intervene.

In other inclement weather, grass does seem to help hold the dirt down like during strong wind and heavy rain when gravity has trouble doing its best work. Other vegetation, however, performs the job as admirably as grass and does it with more form, style, color, and significantly less work, in the long run, than grass demands.

When frequently watered, regularly fertilized, occasionally weeded, constantly and meticulously manicured, grass appears green and flat. In my book that is not a spectacular accomplishment. It seems like a lot of work for the same appearance that a good coat of latex could do on concrete. Other botanical options offer more variety. Ivy, wildflowers, bulbs, and other flora deliver color and contour, yet we insist on grass. A consequence is that we must mow. I firmly believe it is a penalty we must suffer for settling for the mediocre.

In earlier years I mowed the lawn myself. Now I find myself using the same tool to perform many household tasks such as mowing, snow shoveling, tree trimming, and other tasks. Only one tool has the versatility to master all these chores - a checkbook.

With a single swipe of a pen, my signature can move a stack of bricks from an inconvenient location in my yard to another. Jotting on paper can repair my car without any other participation on my part. I don't need a box of tools or a repair manual. The checkbook seldom comes up during a discussion of favorite tools when it should be first on the list. Many men try to juggle a lack of knowledge, a lack of ability, and a lack of desire in order to finish a job they don't want to do. It is foolish when an easier route is staring them in the face or pocketbook as it were. Why, the checkbook is right up there with fire and the wheel as tools that have changed the course of lives, at least it has mine.

I awoke this morning mentally engineering the task before me. Kissing Edith as she slept, I took my leave and headed for the diner for breakfast. A meeting with the village brain trust could only make my job easier. It is important, if civilization is to advance at all, that we learn not only from our own mistakes but those of others as well. So I headed for the diner which has, lately, become a retreat for those who make mistakes.

"How's your boy, Seth?" I asked as I slid into my usual chair. Stu was there too but he was uncharacteristically quiet. He must have been in one of his contemplative moods where he examines and challenges his beliefs and his understanding of life. I was grateful he was not trying to drag me into the mental melee.

Owning the Hardware Store and Lumber Yard brought Seth financial security but it hadn't helped him raise his children. His daughter was best friends with the Beeman girls and Eliza had spent a lot of time at their home. When those two girls got together they would drag out fashion magazines and gossip rags, thumbing through their pages lusting after the beauty and possessions of the perfect people featured within. Magazine envy has become the standard by which degrees of coveting are measured. Folly was not restricted to his daughter.

Seth's son tended to skate through life. As a young boy he worked at the Hardware Store and Lumber Yard but never very hard. Working at his own pace rather than one that got the job done on time; he kept plodding along, more out of duty to his father than anything resembling a work ethic. The boy came to work late and left early, often without letting Seth know and leaving the store unattended. Responsibility was a foreign word to him.

Seth kept forcing his son to come to work until he hired Tommy Hunter to help with a big order one Saturday afternoon. Seth didn't know what he had been missing until he stood shoulder to shoulder with Tommy, never slowing or asking for a break until the work was finished.

"You know how my son is…ungrateful and demanding. He can hardly hold a job because, you now, he's awful busy. He sits and calculates, planning a way to earn vast sums without lifting a finger. Every scheme he imagines involves something immoral if not illegal. He's too lazy to put any effort into a job. I'd feel better about him if he showed the initiative to get a gun and knock over a liquor store like any enterprising crook would do.

I imagine he's mainly waiting for us to die so he can get his hands on our money," Seth moaned. It was a familiar theme for my good friend.

"We never know when we are going leave this earth. It makes preparation for the event more difficult." Stu lamented. He'd been feeling kind of down lately and his conversation was starting to depress me.

Pretending not to hear Stu, I played along with Seth, "What makes him think he's getting any of it? He hasn't seen a cent since he finished college. Is he working at all?"

"College! The pursuit of knowledge is a noble cause," Stu reflected, "but what can we really learn? What can we truly know with any certainty?"

There being no future in following Stu's train of thought, Seth and I continued our conversation without Stu's participation. "Not so's you'd notice. He's doing something that involves interviews over the phone. It doesn't sound like much of a job to me, but I suppose it suits him well. He's always poking his nose into other people's business. It only stands to reason he would be qualified to get nosey with strangers. It's ideal for him in many respects. Since the work is over the phone he hardly has to move in order to do his job. He is not only adept at it but well practiced in the procedure."

Seth seemed to be getting as depressed as Stu at this turn of the conversation, so I tried to steer the ship to cheerier waters. "Will you see him for the Holidays?"

"I suppose so. You can hardly keep him away. He'll show up some time around Halloween and stay until the New Year when

I overrule his mother and throw him into the street. When the kids were little I used to dream about how wonderful it would be when they grew up, got married, had children, and came to visit. I thought they would be a helping hand around the house and grant the pleasure of grandchildren. It didn't work out that way. Now when I see them coming up the street I'm struck with panic the way I would be if I saw a plague of locusts coming over the horizon. You know how we had that business windfall this year?"

"I think so," I answered. I didn't really remember, but Seth was always having a windfall. It surprised him when he made good money on a job. Given his hard work and caring attitude toward clients, no one else was surprised when it happened. He was good with business and knew how to tend the money he had. I would be surprised if he only had one windfall in the last twelve months. He didn't usually brag about business successes.

"Well, the boy found out about it and every time I've seen him since then he keeps sayin' how its going be a good Christmas for him this year. Says he's lookin' forward to some pretty expensive gifts, maybe even something he can drive. He makes no mention of the gift he is getting for his mother or sister. He can't see past his own desires."

"Wow, it's closer to last Christmas than next, he looks pretty far into the future for someone with no plans at all. Assuming he loses this job and he doesn't find other work by then, he could be living at your house again by then. Do you have any plans for what you're getting him this year?"

Seth sat back and scratched his flat stomach, "I hate to disappoint him entirely, so I'm getting him a fully stocked nail bag and a hammer. Let him drive spikes until his greed cools down."

He rose from his seat still grinning from ear to ear and quite full of himself. Stu followed him muttering under his breath. The cashier chatted with them both for a bit. Eventually Stu pointed toward me, grinned real big, and nodded in my direction. I knew what he was doing. When I went to leave, the cashier gave me the present Stu had left for me. If it pulled Stu out of his funk it was worth a few dollars out of my pocket.

Paying both our checks and leaving a tip, I headed for the hardware store to check on the mower blade I was having sharpened. I could have asked Seth about the matter while we were still seated at the diner but we prefer to keep a fence between our personal and professional relationships.

I had to get home early today because I had to train the new young lad in the fine art of lawn sculpture. Intending to teach him the intricacies of trimming close to objects, show him how to avoid clipping protruding roots, and demonstrate techniques to ensure an enviable lawn, it promised to be a full day. What a fortunate child, this new employee, to receive the benefit of my vast experience. Training the young is truly a noble task and one I take most seriously.

"I'm here to cut your grass," shouted a voice that pierced my ponderings.

The Lawson boy had arrived. I sized him up: A normal looking boy by my estimate. He possessed a bit more in the ear department than necessary, or even practical for that matter. Like most boys, I imagined that his large ears were like fins on old cars - more for show than for any useful purpose. I was determined not to embarrass the boy with talk of his giant ears but they were difficult to overlook, or see past for that matter. I suppose they could be helpful to him if he used them like a cat's whiskers to let him know how close he was mowing next to houses and trees. It would be up to the boy to determine whether his deformity would be a blessing or a curse. From time to time, we all have those decisions to make.

I decided to carefully preface my instruction by explaining to the boy the responsibility that comes with holding a job and, particularly, the additional honor of having been selected by me. Out of all the young men in Blandtrap, he was the only one who survived my screening process. He was also the only one who responded to my inquiries but that was another matter altogether.

"Mowing is a privilege, not a right." At hearing this, his eyes appeared to get a little loose in their sockets because they tended to roll back. It recurred each time I spoke. The ear deformity should be enough for any young man to bear; it's a shame he has the eye infirmity to accompany it. I hope he saves some of the money from the mowing to tend to this malady. Medicine is a marvel today yet I thought they could have found a cure for this particular affliction by now.

I had spent the afternoon mulling it over so I knew exactly what I wanted to tell him. "I think you'll find mowing a profitable, skill-building experience. You will learn principles and skills that will serve you well throughout your life. Let's begin your tutelage with a lesson on how the mower works."

"Ya clamp the handle down; pull the cord an' it starts, right?" He snapped.

"Well, yes, in a nut shell, I suppose that describes starting the mower, but there is much to do before you start the mower." I interjected. The boy was cheekier than I anticipated. That attitude lengthens learning time and complicates instruction.

"Yeah," He returned, "Ya check to make sure the blades are sharp and secure, that the spark plug wire is attached, and that it has enough oil and gas, right?"

"Yes, Yes. All that is important, however, before you begin mowing you..."

He cut me off in mid sentence. I began to reexamine the boy. At first it seemed his ears were too big, but their size belied their scant ability to hear. He could benefit from more efficient, rather than larger ears. Every time the ears should be listening, his mouth moves. Perhaps he suffers from a nervous disorder of some kind, you know, not wired right or something. I must have overlooked the obvious. It was becoming apparent that his mouth must have been much larger than I had originally observed, well proportioned with the size of his ears, I guess. Things like that are often more balanced than we realize.

Pushing ahead with my instruction and trying to ignore the boy's poor manners, "When you come to the raised flower beds in the back yard you will need to trim carefully around them. Of course it shouldn't be, but what should you do when you are mowing around the thyme and some of it is drooping over the bed?"

"Make pesto?" His sarcasm was biting.

"No, that is made with basil." I reminded him.

"Stuffing, then," the boy shot back. He was showing his impatience; still, he knew more about the kitchen than I would have guessed. "Exactly how long is this cooking lesson going to last? I've got another lawn to mow after this one and it's getting late."

"Lift it, lad! Lift it and mow on." I was visibly agitated and the boy knew it but I was determined to finish my instruction. I couldn't have this young, deformed, smart-alecky kid go about the job without knowing the proper way to do it. It wouldn't be safe. It wouldn't be right.

"I think I'm ready to start now, if that's OK with you." The boy was wisely retreating into a more polite tone. I thought it best to let him do so since I wasn't faring well in the war of words. I decided to let him make his own bed.

"Let's get at it then," I said. "And I'll examine the yard to see if any weeding is needed."

Ah, weeding. That is the atomic bomb of the yard owner. The mower may best the yard owner in many ways, but weeding was the trump card. Always paying just enough money to make the yard mower crazy not to do the work, even though the work of crawling around on your hands and knees looking for foreign grasses is the most demeaning job a kid can do, it's the cash that makes him crawl and cash that builds character. It can be fashioned in no other way in a young boy than by performing monotonous, tedious, and demeaning tasks for an unreasonable employer. It is both an omen and good practice.

The despised first job is what turns a boy's mind from folly to what ever it will take to never have to do that kind of work again. Nothing else can replace experience. The unfortunate who are pampered and are given first jobs they enjoy often find themselves later in life with work that strains and stresses their minds and bodies to their own detriment. A wretched first work experience would have taught them to avoid work damaging to body and soul. In this matter, the blessed are the less fortunate.

I have retreated inside and left the boy to make his own mistakes. I'll look in on him to see how he performs and keep you informed. So, yes, we do watch the grass grow in Blandtrap, but there is precious little sitting around while it happens!

Respectfully Submitted,

Harry Ellis

April

Plucked from a pigeon hole in the desk of Calvin Farnsworth:

If you were to offend God while easily hiding an acne scar, wouldn't that be...

...a sinful simple pimple dimple?

Harry Ellis

238 Persimmon Street

Blandtrap

To the Editor of the Tiskilwa Bureau Valley Chief

RE: April Fools Day

Dear Sir:

We are a more sober people in Blandtrap than you in the city. Rumors run rampant each year regarding the nonsense that goes on in your community on April Fools Day. Your paper's pages are void of stories documenting these misadventures and childish pranks we hear about. It is, no doubt, some pathetic attempt to preserve the modest portion of dignity you pretend to possess.

Yesterday was that day you pranksters in the city revere above all other days of the year. I am sure your day was filled with practical jokes played on unsuspecting saps and levity at the expense of the innocent. That kind of childish behavior is not tolerated among the adults of Blandtrap. We prefer to live a reserved, courteous life, thinking of the welfare of others before our own base amusement.

My day couldn't have been more ordinary, except for a series of unfortunate accidents. It was just another day. The sun rose and it set. Between these events we went about the business of life. Going to work, comforting the mournful, and caring for family consumed our day.

When I arrived at the Plowboy diner the usual characters were present. On the average, I beat them to the diner by about fifteen

135

minutes but yesterday they must have been early birds. I grabbed my cup of coffee and landed at the big table. If you're late you have to sit behind the worst scoundrels while the prompt hold down a proper place at the table. Conversation was still on the weather, so I hadn't missed much. I joined in as I do every day.

Upending the sugar dispenser to sweeten my beverage, the lid dislodged, filling my cup with sugar. I commented that Frank, the partner in the diner business that tended to the dining room, had been slipping lately. He was well into his eighties and, everyone recognized, was going to start heading downhill soon. Indeed, it had been suggested if someone was to hold a level to him, it would show him off by more than half a bubble. It was sad, really. I motioned to the waitress and she came to my assistance. We cleaned the mess together and I begged her not to ridicule Frank. This type of oversight was bound to start happening with increased regularity, so it couldn't really be his fault.

I put in my order and got back to the topic at hand, which was still the weather. It should have moved on to crops by then but they were stuck in a rut. It was as if they were distracted by something. My fried eggs and hash browns arrived almost instantly. It was the practice of the diner that Frank cooked without salt in anything he prepared because so many of the older folks needed to limit sodium intake. A simple courtesy to the aged and a minor inconvenience to the rest of us, it had become a tradition. Before tasting my order I gave the hash browns a light dusting of pepper and more than a little salt to make up the deficiency.

The first bite of breakfast often sets the mood for the entire day and I was looking forward to a good day. With a healthy forkful in my mouth, I sensed something was wrong. The flavor wasn't what I had expected. It was….sweet! Without thinking I spit out the potatoes onto my plate, in spite of the consequences of drawing attention to myself. More reflex than response, my behavior, I fear, was dramatic given the setting.

"Are you choking?" Stu leaned in close to see how I was doing.

Clovis' father said to his son, "Get ready to Heimlich, Clovis. He looks like he's in trouble.

The mere thought of the hulking Clovis wrapping his huge, muscular arms around me to perform the Heimlich maneuver on me was more objectionable than the sweetened potatoes. Being caught in a Clovis bear hug and shaken like a rag doll was legitimate cause for concern. An immediate response was necessary to avoid peril.

I motioned as if to say I was not in distress and reached for my glass of water. Simeon Swagg snatched the glass before my fingers could entwine and secure the vessel. Talking to Clovis' father rather than me, said "Better not let him drink. It could cause the object to lodge farther down the throat."

Hugginbough rose and started for the counter. "I'll call the emergency squad, just in case."

It was as if I was watching my life in slow motion like what happens when you are in an accident, except nothing bad was happening to me; unless, of course, Clovis got his hooks on me. Simeon began pulling me up from my seat and the Townsend fellow, Lauretta's husband, had my other side. I felt weightless yet I knew I wasn't in space.

"Really, guys, I'm fine." I tried to assure them to no avail.

"He's ranting now." Simeon told the crowd attending me, "It's worse than we thought." They headed me toward the door. Clovis ran ahead to get the door for my rescuers.

I wrenched myself free of both men and grabbed Simeon's face in my hands so I could control it and get his undivided attention. "I'm OK, Simeon! I'm not choking! I'm OK!"

Breathing a sigh of relief, Simeon noticed my recovery. "He's better, guys." He yelled to the mob that had stopped listening to me long ago. "Our efforts have worked!"

"That was close. Don't scare us like that, Harry." Stu said. He seemed a little shaken but a grin might have been hiding beneath. It's nice to know your friends care for you and are willing to do whatever it takes to ensure your welfare. It's comforting and flattering at the same time.

"Put the phone down, Hugginbough. It looks like he's going to recover." Clovis' father shouted across the diner. Hugginbough said a few closing words to the party on the line and returned to the table smiling. "It's good to see you in good health again." He patted me on the back.

"If you chewed your food more," Clovis' father tried to educate me, "you'll be less likely to choke. The same thing happens to some or our heifers."

The best course of action, I guessed, was to act as if they were right about what had happened. I'm not sure I had my wits about me yet, anyway. Sitting quietly, I just listened to the conversation; nodding in agreement when I favored a statement and showing no reaction when I opposed the view.

"That was pretty good, wasn't it, guys?" Clovis said to the others. It was not clear to me what he meant by the comment, but that was normal with Clovis. No one responded to Clovis, returning to the conversation at hand. I was surprised they returned to the topic of weather again. Seldom does the weather come up more than once, except during the worst of storms. I sat through it once more, though, afraid to voice my opinion and uncertain whether it would be misunderstood and incite panic once more.

The waitress stopped by the table, eventually, and asked if I wanted another plate of food. I declined the offer, not wanting to take another ride on the merry-go-round. I mentioned to the waitress that Frank' behavior was slipping and he might need closer watching. "He's put sugar in the salt shakers by mistake." I told her and motioned to the salt shaker on the table. "You probably want to take that with you."

"Take what with me?" She questioned with a puzzled expression.

"The salt shaker." I said turning to the table. I couldn't find the salt shaker anywhere on the table. "It's around here someplace; I used it just a moment ago."

I was trying to fly under the radar, but the waitress blurted out to the table, "You boys seen the salt shaker? Harry wants to use it."

"Harry, you might not want to use so much salt. Didn't we just have a talk about that? No, it was about choking wasn't it? Well, salt's not good for you either. You've got to be careful about things like this." Clovis' father was getting wound up. I never knew how long it would last when he got that way. He had continued for days on previous occasions.

Trying to interrupt him, "What I was trying to tell the waitress…" Raising my voice to get their attention, I tried to out-shout Clovis' father. It was unusual to have this kind of trouble being heard, or being understood, either. "The salt shaker had sugar in it. I don't want anyone else to ruin their meal the way I did."

"Sugar?", Stu said, still half in the discussion of weather with Clovis. "Get Harry some sugar." He said shouting past me to Hugginbough.

"Which is it, salt or sugar?" Hugginbough asked Stu. It was as if I wasn't present.

"He had salt that tasted like sugar but he didn't care for it so now he wants sugar. I don't know why, just give it to him. He's getting kind of fussy." Stu returned.

"Harry can have my sugar." Ward Doubet offered from a nearby table where he had been sitting with Remo Astapacas. Remo was not a regular at the diner, only an occasional patron. Being a loner, he would normally have sat at a table farther away from us, as there was tension between Remo and Simeon.

Each fancied themselves a card shark. Euchre was the game. They had only met twice, each winning one match. Pride can be destructive when it gets a hold on a man, but it can become dangerous when it comes between strong competitors. They wisely kept their distance from one another until they could prove themselves in competition.

I had noticed Ward had been hanging off the edge of his table with one ear in our conversation and the other in his own. He had a bit of a smirk on his face like he gets when he is conjuring up a new joke. He had probably tried it out on Remo. I was looking forward to hearing the new yarn but was otherwise occupied.

"I don't want sugar, I want the salt shaker." I said slowly and clearly enunciating each word.

"Be reasonable, Harry. If you think the salt tastes like sugar, just use the sugar. If you can't tell the difference, then why use anything at all?" Ward pleaded.

The waitress had slipped away in the confusion. I'm sure she had orders up and empty coffee cups to fill.

"I don't want sugar! I want the salt shaker! I want to give it to the waitress!" I was red in the face and while I paused a moment for air.

The waitress shouted from behind the counter, "Don't worry about me," holding up a tray full of salt shakers, "I've got plenty of salt shakers. Harry, go ahead and keep yours."

It was unquestionably time to give up the helm. No longer able to steer the ship of my intentions, I was going to have to tie off and ride the seas until I washed up on a beach somewhere. My own efforts were futile and it was time to try something else. Raising anchor and sail, I shifted to another course.

"How are tractor sales going, given the weather we've been having?" I directed the inquiry to Ward who was unable to ignore a question regarding his business. I was attempting to change the subject.

He wasn't prepared for the question so it took him about half an hour to answer it. With notice, Ward could have gone the whole hour. His dissertation had a calming influence on the group of men. Everyone sat down and it became a more typical scene. A great relief to me not to be the center of attention, I strove again to fade into the woodwork.

When the waitress made her next visit, I eschewed solid food holding onto my precious coffee cup. I would drink it black, with no sugar, today, unable to predict the product in the dispenser. There was no sense in kicking the beehive again. You never know what or how many will fly out to attack you.

I fell in line in the conversation by using inane gestures of agreement and guttural noises of participation. It wouldn't do to start talking yet, not until I could guess the outcome. Unfolding and refolding a piece of paper, Stu kept glancing at the message captured on it. He held it tightly in his hand and it caught my curiosity. "What have you got there, Stu?" I asked after a long lag time of pondering what might result from my inquiry.

"You know that family from the Philippines that moved here a few weeks ago?" Stu asked.

I didn't remember even a shred of information about a family from the Philippines moving to Blandtrap but I tend to keep to myself, not involving myself in other people's business so it would be easy for me to miss an item of gossip like that. I nodded my head as if I had heard about it. It is often better to assume the facts in evidence rather than subject yourself to the explanation of the details.

Stu seemed to be energized when I said I had heard of them. He raised the paper and waved it around. He didn't speak for a while but I could tell he was thinking. I believed he was trying to recall a name that was hard to pronounce or a minute detail crucial to understanding the story.

Finally, it began to spill out of him. "They are going to open a martial arts studio above the notions store." Stu spoke at a measured pace. "The space has been vacant for years, so, I guess, they probably got a good deal on the rent. It's mostly open space up there."

"On the face of it, a good match might be hiding there. The notions store and a karate dojo in the same building sounds odd, but it could work. The mostly older ladies who frequent the notions store come early in the day and are back home by mid-afternoon. The store closes at 4:00 PM. The karate clients are mainly school kids who take instruction after the 3:00 dismissal of classes. The notions customers will be gone by the time the karate kids show up. One won't bother the other." I keenly observed.

"It will give the young boys something to do after school besides chasing the young girls." Remo leapt in. Remo had four daughters in school. Having been a vigorous lad in his youth, his memories of his own adventures haunted him when he thought of his daughters' suitors. He could see that young boys today lacked the propriety and integrity he had possessed, and you could have carried his in a thimble. He was known to say "The situation is worrisome, very worrisome," as he toddled about the village wringing his hands.

"What about the paper? What is it?" I insisted.

"I stopped by the print shop earlier today to pick up some flyers for the hardware store," Hugginbough began, "they were just proofs, really. I haven't decided if I'm going ahead with the promotion."

"I think you should. It sounds like a good idea." Stu encouraged Hugginbough.

"Are you sure, Stu?" Hugginbough expressed his apprehension. "I'm not convinced cotter pins hold the universal appeal necessary to bring in large numbers of customers."

I could have told him cotter pins wouldn't herd droves of buyers but I was more interested in the paper in his hand. Curiosity made me interrupt. "The paper in your hand, is it an ad for the hardware store? What does that have to do with the folks from the Philippines?" I was confused once more. It must have been a bad day for me. Conversation usually travels in a straight line for me from one topic to another. Yesterday's befuddling experience of skipping from unfamiliar topic to unrelated subject without so much as a hangnail of a common thread to relate them was wearing a hole in my patience. I pressed on reconsidering the idea of heading home and going back to bed, calling it a day.

"Why no, Harry, it's an ad for the new karate studio." Stu explained calmly and as if I should have known. He could see I had reached my limit and started trying to simplify life for me. He handed me the flyer. I took the gesture as a personal favor. Reading it calmed me.

"They have pretty good distribution throughout town. I got a flyer on my door." Clovis' father said. It seemed unlikely since he lived about three miles out in the country. Who would go door to door that far out for a flyer?

"One was tucked into the door of the tractor store this morning." Ward said, displaying his copy of the document. They all looked alike although some were different colors.

"Kick me." It said, a simple enough message but its meaning eluded me.

"I'm going to have a talk with them about the flyer. In the nub it's good, but it lacks sufficient elaboration for the average person to grasp the services they intend to offer." Hugginbough volunteered. His experience in matters of advertising was a valuable resource. They could learn from his wisdom.

"True. It might attract the naïve who would wander in to find out the details, but it doesn't seem like a good slogan for the karate-accomplished." Stu added. He was tight fisted and only rarely fooled by slick ads or flashy promotional campaigns.

"I would think 'You can't kick me!' would be a better slogan." I thought out loud. It was dangerous territory for me, given recent events. The desire to see immigrants to Blandtrap thrive in their new environment spurred me on.

"That's it!" Stu shouted and gave me a big clop on the back for my effort.

"Great idea! Creative and descriptive, everything you want in an ad campaign." Ward said, also patting me on the back. I felt quite honored.

Nothing makes a man feel better than recognition by his peers. It was just what I needed at the moment. After all the fuss and mayhem earlier, the day was beginning to show promise of better times ahead. Now I could go out and get things done.

"Before you go, Harry, I want to make sure I've got this down right. The slogan is 'You can't kick me,' right?" Hugginbough talked as he was writing on the back of another flyer.

I slipped on my jacket to the accolades showered by those in the diner and more pats on my back greeted me on my way out. It was a wholly satisfying experience.

"Having a bad morning are you, honey?" The waitress chatted as I paid my tab.

"I had a rough start," I said, "but things are looking up now." I assured her.

A sharp blow to my posterior distracted me from counting my change. It nearly lifted me from the floor. Clovis was standing there carrying a tractor part in his hand. He must have struck me with the object in his negligence. It was unthinking and not malicious. He apologized yet it seemed insincere and hollow with that big dopey grin on his face. I didn't have time to fool with him so I just nodded and departed for home, rubbing the insult to my person.

The walk home was delightful. It was a pleasant stroll and I was imagining the toast I would make when I arrived. Entering, I could hear Edith in the kitchen. Hanging my jacket in the closet, I joined her in the kitchen. "Did you hear about the family from the Philippines who moved here recently" I quizzed her as I passed by to take my chair after filling the toaster with a muffin pretending foreign origins.

"No, I hadn't heard a word." She said, not appearing to be interested in our new residents, "Why do you have 'Kick Me' signs taped to your back?"

"Oh, gosh!" I said. "They were all over town. Several of the guys at the diner had them. They have to do with that family from the Philippines I was talking about. They must have gotten stuck to my back somehow." I went on to explain about their new business and how they would fit right in with the townsfolk. Edith was amazed at the story but became suspicious near the end. It took hours to get her to stop giggling and questioning me. In one way I am glad I can bring humor into my wife's life, but I felt the incident came dangerously close to ridicule.

So, you can plainly see from the event of yesterday that Blandtrap has no time for the nonsense of April Fools Day. There are no practical jokes, no childish pranks, and no embarrassment of the unsuspecting occupying the valuable time of our esteemed residents. We are a more sincere people than you city dwellers and so I must leave you to your folly. I will tend to weightier matters!

Respectfully Submitted,

Harry Ellis

Harry Ellis

238 Persimmon Street

Blandtrap

To the Editor of the Tiskilwa Bureau Valley Chief

RE: Opening Day of Baseball Season

Dear Sir:

Your conjecture that we have no sports in Blandtrap is ridiculous. We observe all local sporting events most much larger communities enjoy. The baseball season opens soon and we are all looking forward to the games.

Opening day of the baseball season is a big event in the lives of most men, though it's not a big event in the way a wedding, a funeral, or your daughter's first date is a big event. In a man's mind, I suppose, it ranks in importance along side the opening day of hunting season. It wouldn't matter what hunting season you would choose. Women would rank holidays by an entirely different scale.

The topic comes up all the time. At the diner this morning, while the rest of us were pounding down hot cakes and planning the demise of rodents and insects, Stu Said, "Wednesday is opening day of the baseball season."

A simple statement delivered in a matter-of-fact fashion, yet it spurred lively conversation around the table like no other news could do. Starting about the same time each year, the day sneaks up on me in the way anniversaries do. Some say Memorial Day marks the beginning of summer. I say summer begins on the first day the game can be played in Chicago without wearing long underwear. It is an arbitrary measure to be sure, but I stand behind it.

Clovis' father piped in, "In a normal year, I'd have half my fields plowed by opening day. Don't suppose I've got more than a quarter plowed now." He was peering into his coffee cup as if a map of his farm were clearly visible in the cream he had yet to stir into the brew.

"We're pretty much in the same boat." Bill Whittacre added, looking out into space. Seldom socializing, Bill keeps to himself most of the time. Bob Hayes, his employer, asked him to meet at the diner that morning. Bill doesn't think much of himself, but is held in esteem by men in Blandtrap. It was a rare treat to see him in a relaxed setting and a pure pleasure to hear Bill speak. I wish he'd said more.

I commented that I was unaware if the president was able to throw out the first pitch this year. Business of State being what it is; free time must be scarce. I never held a job with duties that pressing. I wouldn't want one that did.

Clovis' father said he was pretty sure that the president, like any politician, might be able to skirt famine or circumnavigate natural disaster in order make it in time for the photo opportunity the first pitch of baseball season has become. Positive face time on the news is difficult to come by in this or any other political climate.

"I was driving my tractor from the barn to the hog confinement building when a rabbit ran across the road in front of me. It startled me and I jerked the steering wheel and jammed on the brakes when my muddy foot slipped off the middle bar and sharply depressed only the right wheel brake. This caused me to swerve into the ditch." Sigmund Allerman began with a glazed look in his eyes gazing at the tabletop. I'm not sure he was aware he was speaking out loud. What he told sounded more like a thought than a statement.

"My Ellen was standing in the yard witnessing the whole thing and she said it was sweet that I ditched the tractor rather than run over the bunny. She was right, too. When rabbit is road kill, the light cream sauce just doesn't cover that funny taste a puddle adds to the meat!

"Well," Sig continued, still looking down and lost in a fog, "I was stuck in the ditch at about a 45 degree angle and was lucky to climb off the tractor without it tipping. Just then, that Simon guy, you know, the hog-hauler with the gruff voice and the scruffy mustache that hangs over his upper lip, come by in his rig. I flagged him down and he offered to pull me out. At least I think he offered to pull me out. With that thick Swedish accent it's always hard to tell what he is saying but with the aid of loud pig Latin and wild gestures he caught the drift of my dilemma. My tractor in the muddy ditch was just the visual aid I needed to clarify my request. He must have understood because he started to position his truck for the task.

"I crawled under the tractor and secured the chain, bloodying my knuckles on the axel or something like it. Twisting my ankle as I scrambled up the slippery incline of the ditch, the ordeal left me bleeding and hopping while talking under my breath in language I don't use out loud except during national elections.

"We got the tractor back on the road, but I managed to get my shirt sleeve tangled in the chain and I had to sacrifice a piece of my forearm to save the rest of me. Wounded, I took the tractor back to the barn and called it a day, and then I went inside and didn't come out until noon the next day." Sigmund became aware of our stares and our wondering what had prompted this monologue.

He looked up sheepishly and shrugged his shoulders. "What in the world does that have to do with what we were talking about?" Clovis father demanded to know.

There was a long, uncomfortable silence, and then he said, "That was an opening day. Cubs and St. Louis, as I remember… Cubs lost a close one. I caught the ninth inning."

Sigmund started to stare off into space again and that was our cue for the rest of us to disperse. We grabbed our checks and lined up at the counter to pay. Once again I was stuck with Stu's tab. I've grown to accept it with only modest protest. Others wandered off to their chores and I headed for Hugginbough Hardware and Lumber.

Entering under the jingling bell over the door, I saw Mr. Walker arguing with the Hunter Boy who had been clerking at the establishment for some time now. Herman was always looking for a scandal and, in his mind, he was rarely unsuccessful in his search. It seems years ago you could get twenty-four seven penny nails to a pound but when he got home yesterday there were only twenty-three seven penny nails in his one pound bag. Scandal!

Herman Walker's standard for a scandal was low and it didn't have to be a clear-cut unscrupulous behavior to garner his ire. If a situation was vague or ambiguous, Herman erred on the side of scandal. Spending his time scouring the village looking for any kind of confusion or uncertainty to exploit as scandal, he was shunned by busy folks and given short shrift by shop owners. Clerks lacked the authority to throw him out so he worked them over whenever he found the owners off the premises.

In his mind, success was the hallmark of his reputation. He got to the bottom of the tenth of a cent discrepancy in the sale of gasoline. We know the penny is the smallest unit of currency and the gas station was only getting nine tenths of the penny. Where was the elusive last tenth going? He couldn't elicit a confession from the owner. The officer enjoying a cup of coffee on his break was no help. Still, Herman felt he had made headway and proved the gas station owner was jilting the customer.

Moving his attention to the consumer, he asked customer after customer what they were doing with the tenth of a cent they were saving on every gallon they purchased and he documented the answers: 18 said "This is the dumbest thing I've ever heard"; 15 said "Leave me alone I'm in a hurry"; and 3 said "Huh?"

Herman didn't get a chance to gather more information because the officer had finished his cup of coffee and said goodbye to the owner. The officer performed his duty, chasing Herman from the establishment.

He always hoped Calvin Farnsworth would give him a hand interpreting the data but there was never time in the busy schedule at the Institute for Idle Science. There were similarities between Herman and Calvin. Both relied on hard statistics to prove their points, but focus was completely different for each. Calvin's interests were to expand and advance the knowledge of science for the betterment of mankind.

Germaine to Herman's purpose was the need to expose consumer fraud and allow people to make the best decisions based upon true and accurate product and pricing information. Both were devoted to truth and the improvement of their community, but they diverged when their approaches were considered.

"It doesn't seem like much money per gallon, but when you consider the millions of gallons of gasoline sold, were talking about some serious money." He'd say. He was convinced that wherever the money was going, someone was getting rich with ill gotten gains. Even though he didn't know of many rich people around Blandtrap, he seemed to imagine them everywhere.

He also broke open the bowling scandal! You know: the unrolled ball in the 10th frame if you don't mark in the 10th. This was a remarkable discovery, really. Armed with only time on his hands, an abrasive personality, and the experience of never having rolled a single frame, he made himself sufficiently familiar with the game to detect the discrepancy. Herman postulated that bowlers who didn't mark in the 10th frame were 'owed' another ball and should be compensated, either in cash or with credits that could accumulate to a free game.

Marty Riccioni, owner of the Blandtrap Bowl, objected most vigorously to the insinuation that he was cheating his customers and was nothing more than a common thief. Marty stood his ground, conceding nothing to Herman. Eventually, Mr. Walker was banned from all parts of the bowling alley, except the coffee shop and lounge. Under a gag order negotiated by Marty, Herman was allowed to participate in a bowling league and held to the agreement responsibly until he was too old to be competitive.

Once Herman was finished with the Hardware Store lad, it was my turn. I was proud of the Hunter kid. He showed a lot of pluck because Herman's ranting and wild conjecture bounced off him like water off a duck's back. A good guess is he's had a lot of practice. My business actually had to do with the Hardware Store and the Hunter kid seemed relieved and gave me his undivided attention.

I asked if the decorative wall sconce mounts Edith had ordered were in yet. I had no reason to believe they had arrived. If they had, someone would have called. Years with Edith had taught me to check. Edith would certainly ask me if I had inquired about the mounts. Time had shown me it was better to check than to lie about it.

Sometimes Hugginbough would have Tommy deliver household items on his way home from work. Nothing is more damning than testifying to your wife that you have dutifully checked on the status of an item while your wife is standing with said item concealed behind her back awaiting your indiscretion. The lad indicated they had not yet come in. and so my tracks were covered.

I enjoy chatting with young people; it's a way of keeping current with the times. Tommy told me he would cut back his hours at the hardware store once baseball season started in earnest. The whole Hunter family was big on baseball. Even his older sister, Cheryl, was also good at softball…a short stop. She pitched some, too, as I remember.

All Tommy did was go to work and play sports. He had no time for women, liquor, or other nonsense that distract some of high school age. Women, mainly his mother, conspired against him on Valentine's Day and he had secretly confessed he enjoyed the evening, but it was back to work after that. His moral and financial interests were greater than his prurient pursuits. Good kid, that Tommy.

I commented that next week was the opening day of the baseball season. He too was surprised that the season had snuck up so quickly. He remembered that just a few years ago, the opening game for the freshman baseball team was played in the snow. I recalled the game well and had witnessed a few innings of the marathon event.

They were playing those snobs from Butte Crossing when flurries turned to a full-fledged snowstorm. This would have delayed or cancelled most ball games but the rivalry between Butte Crossing and Blandtrap eclipsed weather concerns and many other matters of reason. The game continued as scheduled. Neither coach would yield a quarter to the other, and the umpire was in financial circumstances which made collecting the full fee for a complete game a new rule for the book. The closeness of the score further complicated compromise. Both teams needed the win to retain their standing in the conference. The game could go either way and neither team was leaving until they knew the victor.

Visibility was diminished to the point that balls and strikes were, more or less, randomly determined. Pass balls didn't always advance runners because they couldn't see the plate or get a good look at the base coach for the run signal. The pitcher had to shout when he released the pitch to warn the catcher it was coming. Once on base, though, the runner had the advantage.

Pitcher's mound had begun to ice over, making balance more difficult. Runners were encouraged to take extraordinary lead-offs. When a pitcher tried their pick-off move, they lost their balance and slid off the mound before delivering an accurate throw.

Similarly, it was nearly impossible to know which infielder had the ball. The pitcher may start his windup and the runner lead-off, only to find the baseman with the ball hidden in his glove to make the tag and register the out, the old hidden ball trick. Fingers were pointed in every direction and the umpire ruled on every dispute. The official had a grin on his face no one had seen before, or since for that matter.

Snow around the bases tended to enhance the runner's ability to slide and the flying snow made seeing the tag difficult at best. With the exception of allowing the game to continue, the umpire strained to keep his integrity intact. He refused to call a runner out unless he saw the tag. This character attribute made the game a high scoring event.

Base runners were on their own after they left first base. The first base coach would encourage them to keep advancing because it was nearly impossible to get picked off and even more unlikely you would be called out if you were. After one of the many base-on-balls the game provided, a runner took the opportunity of the next pitch to steal second base. The following pitch sent him off towards third base when he encountered another waiting for the bag to free up for his use.

Knowing three on third was less lucky than three on a match, he tried to find his way back to second base but with his tracks covered by blowing snow, he wasn't completely sure where he came from. The three lads had been Boy Scouts, so they put their heads together to get them out of their jamb. Recalling how the ball field was laid out and the location of third base, they were able to plot a course using a compass one of the prepared boys brought with them. Knowing how they were supposed to tag up after every pitch, they believed they would be excused from that rule since it could not be determined when a pitch occurred.

The catcher's job was a nightmare, too. He didn't have a clue when the ball was to arrive at the plate. The pitcher would shout but it was hard to distinguish his voice from crowd noise. The game was delayed for about five minutes as the catcher and umpire waited for a pitch to arrive at the plate.

It became apparent they would have to talk to the pitcher to get him to speed things up. When they found him he told them he had thrown a bad pitch. Believing he had hit the batter, he went over to first base to apologize for his error and ensure no hard feelings. Returning to the mound, he was waiting for the ball to be thrown back by the catcher.

The umpire was in a spot. All the baseballs he brought with him had been lost and they had been playing with the last one. A thorough search around the backstop uncovered the missing ball so the game was still on. After groping around the batter's box to see if they had overlooked a player hit by a pitch, the umpire got things moving again.

The game went into extra innings and lasted for hours. In retrospect, some of us felt the umpire took advantage of the situation. Officiating over the longest game in Bureau County history, he also garnered the highest salary ever paid to a baseball official anyone could ever recall. Five times the normal fee!

Blandtrap prevailed on the last play of the game with a close, as far as we could tell, play at the plate- A thrilling end to an otherwise confusing game.

Checking the schedule I find the Blandtrap freshman baseball team opens their season next Monday with another contest with rival Butte Crossing. The game begins at 4:00 PM at the high school diamond. Varsity begins their schedule the following week playing against the same scoundrels.

Respectfully Submitted,

Harry Ellis

Harry Ellis

238 Persimmon Street

Blandtrap

To the Editor of the Tiskilwa Bureau Valley Chief

RE: Clovis Beagle and the Savvy Salesman

Dear Sir:

On the business page of your newspaper I found a story about some creative farmers who have made what you have headlined as 'A breakthrough in agriculture.' I want to share with you words of caution. In an ancient profession like the tending of crops, there remains little room for true creativity. 'Breakthrough' is what the plow does when it hits the sod. What may appear new is probably very old, so old that any calamity caused by the first time the innovation was tried has been forgotten and jokes about its application have also fallen from memory. You should choose to use better words to describe what you mean.

Because some jobs are, by their very nature, hot and sweaty work, it seems winter or early spring would be a better time to perform that kind of labor. Digging post holes is just such a job. Weather is a fickle friend, more often detracting from the accomplishment of work than facilitating it. In the business of digging post holes, because the ground is usually frozen in winter and too wet to keep its form in spring, the jobs are best planned during summer and early autumn, the hottest time of the year.

Clovis Beagle is large. Large people generally don't prefer to work in the heat. People who must work around the perspiring and who also enjoy being dry feel the same way. Hard labor encourages, even maximizes perspiration. I have visited Beagle Farms on hot days when Clovis was engaged in physical labor and it was not a pretty sight. In many ways he resembled bacon frying in a skillet. Clovis was sensitive about his appearance although he rarely did anything to change other's perception of him. Still, he would rather work alone where the opinions of others were of no consequence.

Last summer Clovis' father decided to try something different. Innovation is the fertilizer of business, but, as in gardening, you have to be careful where you spread your innovation or the smell may become overwhelming. Some innovations, changes, or improvements are the springboard launching humdrum, scratch-out-a-living businesses into a category of enviable profit. It is true of farming as well, but restrictions this industry places on its practitioners are more severe than for other occupations.

Regardless of the tack you take you will find it to be true. The farmer plants, tends, harvests, sells and prepares the soil for next year. It must be done in that order. A farmer could choose to harvest before the crop grows but it is universally understood that yield would suffer. The steps are set and cannot be altered. Creativity, then, lies only in how each step is accomplished.

Manufacturing is less strict in its process. In order to make a garment, a pattern must be made of the end product, pieces fitting the pattern cut from cloth, and pieces assembled. It is as straight forward as farming. Where manufacturing differs from farming is that cloth for the garment can be purchased precut or with two or more pieces already assembled which may reduce time or expense of garment production.

The farmer is without similar remedy. If he were to purchase pre-planted seed, he would soon learn his folly and become the laughing stock of his community. A wise and experienced farmer is aware of this situation and will not fall for ploys of this nature. Clovis, although experienced in all aspects of farming, is not so wise. Last summer the lack of this commodity cost Clovis his reputation and a neat pile of cash.

Aware of pitfalls with agricultural innovation, Clovis' father decided to participate in research on livestock. The nature of the scientific investigation required separating small groups, herds if you will, but usually the groups were no more than four cattle, into small pens. The small herds were then subjected to different chemicals, or diets, or environments and then medical condition monitored by the Beagles and by periodic visits by veterinarians.

I'm not sure I understand the research in all its detail, unfamiliar as I am with livestock other than those I encounter in government service. Calvin Farnsworth with the Institute for Idle Science explained it all to me but several conditions of the research got fuzzy early in the explanation. Seeking the advice of another may have shed more light on the subject. When educating you, Calvin insists you fully comprehend each of the small points, leaving precious little time to communicate larger ideas like the purpose of the study.

Some fencing had deteriorated over the years and needed to be replaced in addition to the new fencing to be installed for the project. Clovis' father briefly considered renting an auger to bore post holes recognizing how it would speed the process. That choice would waste Clovis' greatest contribution to the family business, immense strength and a strong work ethic. He would have Clovis dig post holes by hand.

The Friday night before Clovis was to begin fence repair, the Beagle family made their weekly Saturday night trek into Blandtrap a day early. It just works better sometimes to come a day earlier. Clovis had the grocery list to tackle first so he headed for the IGA.

Baking mix was at the top of the list so he went there first. When people make a shopping list they sit down and mentally go through the menus they have planned for the week and scan pantry shelves for items necessary to prepare the courses. There is no order to the items on the list, certainly they are not in an order lending itself to efficient shopping.

Clovis had been trained over the years to work instructions always from top to bottom. Skipping or rearranging steps frequently lead to disaster. He would get the first item then move to the second without looking ahead on the lists to see if several items on the list might be found in the same isle or next to one another on a shelf, as they often are. On any shopping trip Clovis may wander every isle as many as six times before completing his mission.

He tried to make up for inefficiency in organization with speed, racing down isles and through coolers without much regard for other patrons. It was hard to stop him when his talents were needed by the short or elderly shoppers to retrieve items they were unable to handle themselves. He knew if he kept his nose to the grindstone he would finish in the same amount of time as others. He would do much more work, but would finish the same. It was important to him that he didn't stand out.

Clovis was a thinking man. Most wouldn't believe it of him because of his behavior and the things he said, but they would be wrong. His problems came from over-thinking a situation more often than under-thinking. Baking mix, he thought as he searched for eggs in the dairy cooler, is a convenience. They have done much of the hard work of baking, pre-mixing the flour, sugar, baking soda, and salt, that are common ingredients to most baking. What a time and work saver it was.

Finishing the list, he saw the value in pre-packaged foods and wondered if he could take advantage of comparable convenience with some of his manual chores. Clovis thought it was worth investigation and he vowed to keep his eyes open for such an opportunity.

He finished shopping in time to dash to the bank to cash his paycheck before they closed. Although an heir to the Beagle Estate, Clovis was paid a salary for his work. 'No work, no pay.' was

Clovis' father's philosophy. The fact that most people carried cards, debit, credit or both, was not lost on Clovis. He entertained offers that came in the mail and had fancied the sophistication of card ownership, but he remained apprehensive. It seemed a bank card was a lot of responsibility. If it fell into the wrong hands, thieves could steal money he hadn't even earned yet. Clovis recognized he lacked the regular vigilance in his financial matters to make bank card ownership a pleasant experience. Many others would do well to honestly appraise their own behavior and reach the same conclusion.

Even though it wasn't for him, Clovis could see the convenience of having a bank card. Much of the hard work of finance had been done by the bank by offering the card to be a mediator between consumer and provider. The business of writing a check in a store could be tedious. You have to remember to bring the checkbook with you, carefully and legibly write the check while those behind you are dropping groceries because they didn't think they'd need a cart or are harrumphing because they are behind their time and you are delaying them.

The most annoying and least helpful aspect of check writing is the identification process. I have been stuck behind Clovis many times while he has written a check. I will acknowledge it is important to minimize fraud and proper identification of purveyors of financial instruments is the foundation of that effort. I also want to point out another truth. The line of people who want to become Clovis Beagle is a short one and they pose little or no threat to anyone other than themselves.

Clovis admired the bank for their ingenuity. He realized convenience was valuable and well worth the investment if it represented a significant savings of time and labor. Wondering if he might be able, some day, to take advantage of a similar convenience; he kept an eye open for that kind of opportunity. It was an eagle eye, at that.

Making the bank before they closed took the pressure off Clovis. He could wander about the village for a while and do his own bidding rather than that of others. With limited time to themselves, leisure is precious to farm folk. I'm not talking about the free time one has while plowing a field or harvesting a crop. The mind tends to wander hither and yon while performing routine tasks, but it sometimes comes at a heavy cost like the loss of life or limb. Those times are not truly free. You are a prisoner to the task.

Clovis had an hour and a half, maybe two hours at most, to do whatever he wanted. He moseyed by the theater to see what was playing. It was "My Fair Lady" again. He'd seen it several times and it didn't start for another hour. Time was wasting and he wouldn't have been able to see the entire musical if he had the inclination.

Passing the window of Plow Boy Diner, Clovis gazed inside. He wasn't hungry so he didn't go in. Noticing the daily specials written on the chalkboard, he was tempted. During holiday seasons a waitress would use colored chalk and draw interesting or funny pictures among the specials, tantalizing patrons like Clovis. Drawings were a big hit with him and with school children as well. At that very moment he saw why the diner offered specials. It was a convenience. A light bulb went off in Clovis' It saved the customer money and time by having certain foods ready to serve and prepared in quantity.

It was like when they turn all of the lights on in a stadium. He went from groping around in the dark to feeling his way through to a blinding light. They say mules that work their entire lives in dark mines lose their sight. If they are brought out of the mine in their old age they are incapable of sustaining themselves because they are completely blind. Perhaps Clovis' affliction is related to this phenomenon in some way. I think we will never know for sure.

Entertainment is in the eye of the beholder. He could find neither convenient distraction nor any gentle amusement to occupy his time or soothe his troubled mind. He's met a girl recently and if she were there, he would have enjoyed talking with her. She was not there, though, and his interest in her had not grown to the point of motivating him to seek her out. Love and courtship are complicated matters people are prone to rush into. Clovis was wise to wait until he had a sense of urgency before moving ahead.

Unseasonably warm weather was, at the time, pleasant and it was stimulating to be able to wear short sleeves so early in the year. Clovis window-shopped his way to Village Square taking a seat on the bandstand the way the villagers do on hot summer nights. Letting his mind drift back to the topic of conveniences, he engaged all his mental prowess to work on his idea.

Conveniences, he noticed, made hundreds, thousands, even millions of dollars for those who invented them and had the courage to offer them to the public in creative ways. Clovis wasn't interested in being rich. He had a couple of hundred dollars in his pocket right then and he couldn't think of a way he cared to spend it. The attraction to Clovis was the savings of time and work, mostly the work. Recognition for a brilliant invention meant more than money to him.

Irony was not lost on Clovis that as the first choice of someone to do any job, attributes of the worker would include manual labor or brute strength. No one would choose him to balance their checkbook or estimate their taxes.

If someone else was chosen for a job, out would come trucks, tractors, or augers. Great expense would be incurred to save the backs of others. If the work was to belong to Clovis he would be given a wheelbarrow, a rope or a bucket and sent off to work by himself. The thought of the injustice nagged at him.

On one level, he didn't mind working alone, especially if it was heavy work. Clovis had a good sense of his own abilities, how much he could lift and how far he could carry it. He was not as good a judge of others' abilities.

He assumed others were nearly as strong as he. Coworkers would strain muscles and injure backs doing work Clovis was convinced would be easy for them. He had to continually make allowances for the inadequacies of others. It was simpler for him to work alone rather than nurse someone else through a job he could do by himself.

On another level, he could see his father and the community at large had no respect for his opinions or ideas. It burned at him that they thought so little of him. On several occasions he tried to prove them wrong. Each of those attempts ended in miserable failure or utter disaster. If he were to change their view of him now, it would take something big and spectacular to do the job.

He sat on the steps of the bandstand thinking. Most great ideas occur to people while they're thinking of something else. Extraordinarily rare is the person who decides to think of something great and sits down to do it. Try as he might, the well was empty. He kept pulling up empty buckets.

Noise from a large truck competed with Clovis' thoughts for his attention. Few large trucks ventured into the village. Village Square holds tight confines for commercial trucks. They stay out on the county road where they can make better time. Hugginbough Hardware and the IGA accept deliveries during the day but it was way too late for that. This was something different and different was what captured Clovis' attention.

The driver parked along Village Square and shut off the engine. Climbing down from the cab of the tractor he stretched and yawned as he walked around in a small circle the way people do when their muscles are stiff and they try to loosen them. He scanned his surroundings to get his bearings and fetched a look at Clovis sitting on the steps of the bandstand and started toward him. "Not a bad place to start." The man said to himself.

Clovis liked meeting new people so he was excited by the stranger's presence. In a small village you don't get a chance to meet new folks very often. He took advantage of the opportunity every time it presented itself.

It was embarrassing when you went out of town with Clovis. He would stop to greet each new face he encountered. Once you broke him free of one person he would attach himself to the very next person he saw. It was like dragging a treble hook along the bottom of a pond: your pole bends a lot but you rarely catch anything.

In small villages and large cities most people are more comfortable with familiar friends. They know you and your quirks and often know why you have them. When you talk to old friends they hear what you say in context without having to explain how you got in a situation or why what happened affects you. They know because they were there or nearby when it all happened.

Clovis' preference for strangers was sincere, and for the same reasons most of us would rather spend time with old friends. Often the butt of jokes and rarely taken seriously among familiar friends, he had a fresh start with each new person me met. They didn't assume he hadn't thought an idea through when he began to speak. New acquaintances didn't hold the opinion he was stupid as so many in Blandtrap tended to believe. He could carry on normal conversations like he heard those around him enjoy, avoiding the overt condescension that clouded most chats with villagers. Clovis found regular communication thrilling.

Not being as aware as others brought its own set of problems. He tended to be just a little gullible, believing, without clear evidence to the contrary, everyone was telling the truth all the time. It was a trait that made him an easy mark for pranks. Clovis' nature was to be willing, sometimes eager to fall for the same scam over and over. This kept him busy when in the company of practical jokers.

Clovis was honest to a fault and was convinced that it was a universal trait of humanity. He was basically a happy man. He was relieved because truck drivers often stopped only to get directions. Either an honest mistake driving or a victim of poor directions, they find themselves in Blandtrap. Since all the roads into Blandtrap are filled with curves making it tough to maintain a sense of direction, logic doesn't help you when you choose a route under these circumstances. If you want to go south out of town you must choose the road leaving from the northwest edge of town. It bends around and heads south at Big Bureau Creek. You can understand how a truck driver, stuck in the mud of misdirection, might not be in the best mood.

Hair slicked back, a tight, skinny shirt a wee bit too small for his frame, and an attitude that came with a swagger was the man Clovis greeted. Sliding onto lower steps of the bandstand than Clovis occupied, the stranger spoke first once he got comfortable. "Hey there, big guy …looks like you have a pretty quiet town, here, haven't you?"

"It suits us just fine." Clovis said still leaning back on the steps, relaxing. "Haven't seen you around. Are you new to Blandtrap or just passing through?" He didn't really care what the man's business was or what he was up to but he'd heard his father address strangers so he applied what he had learned.

"I'm still trying to make up my mind. It's a struggle for a young businessman like me to find the right place to get started. If you are young or new, different in any way, it seems that people don't give you a chance. They assume you can't do much and never give you the chance to try or show what you've got. I'm looking for a place that will give me that chance. I can prove myself with the right opportunity." The young stranger was a shrewd judge of character and had Clovis pegged for a loner because he was sitting by himself. Persuasion is a powerful potion but it works best in a one on one situation. Convincing a group is a different matter entirely.

"I know what you mean." Clovis sighed in sympathy. I have a reputation of being a little slow. They're probably right. It takes me longer to figure things out than others. I still get there-it may take a bit- but I get there. My father and the others don't want to wait. They tell me what to do, down to the smallest detail, and I follow their instructions. It makes me feel stupid sometimes. I could figure it out myself if they would give me the time."

"I'm with you, big guy." The stranger said. He recognized Clovis was a step behind the rest of the parade, exactly the person he was seeking. It was the opportunity he was looking for when he rolled into town. The man had found the fish now he had to try the right bait. A smallish man, he found greater enjoyment in landing a bigger fish.

Sitting up and extending his hand to the stranger, he said, "Clovis Beagle is my name." The stranger accepted Clovis' hand and shook it. Trying to read Clovis' face, his mind was working as if he were taking inventory or performing surgery. I suppose it was a little of both.

As last the ship reached shore, he said, "Palmer Astoria at your service, sir."

Clovis liked being called "sir." He didn't fish for compliments or get puffed up at the gesture. He thought the term made him equal to other men in a way acquaintances seldom allowed him to feel. "Glad to meet you, Palmer." Clovis wondered if he was talking to a kindred spirit.

"You impress me as a man who works the land. Am I right?" The stranger was mining for better information. The obvious was the best place to start. From discussing the plainly visible, Palmer hoped to peer inside Clovis' brain to understand him.

"Are you a mind reader or something? My father and I work a good sized farm just outside town. How did you know?" Clovis was astonished this new friend of his could zoom in on something like that so fast. Oblivious to the thin flannel shirt, coveralls, and Pfeister Seeds cap he wore; he couldn't see his appearance screamed farmer. Anyone else would have caught it and would have been wary of the stranger.

"That's my business, farming I mean. Well, agriculture in general is more descriptive of my field. I don't actually farm, you see, but I have a line of products that save farmers time and money. I strive to make the agricultural experience simpler and less strenuous. It's surprising how resistant to change your particular business can be. It seems like they want to do each job the same backbreaking way they always have. They don't even consider an easier way."

The best way to find weakness in someone is to ask them about it. You can't do it straight out or they will balk, but if you give them a chance they will usually volunteer what kind of job they like and what kind of job they detest. He gave Clovis the opening and he delivered information the stranger needed for his plan. "I guess I'm babbling. Do you have any idea what I'm talking about?"

"Post holes, they've got me digging post holes tomorrow. It's a big job as I'll probably be digging for a week. They could have rented an auger but they think I might break it, so I have to dig them by hand." Clovis was ashamed to confess it to the stranger.

"My land, man," The stranger began. The phrase was not part of his regular vocabulary. He tried inserting it to be folksy. It wouldn't have worked on another villager but it skittered past Clovis unnoticed. "I'm in the post-hole business! The biggest problem with post holes is your have to dig them in the field. It could be miserably hot or bone-shaking cold, yet you have to go to the spot, the exact spot where you want it, to dig the hole."

"You're right!" That is the problem in a nut shell." Clovis was spellbound.

"What the people I work for have done is like what they've done with construction. Do you remember how they used to deliver a pile of lumber and you sawed it and nailed it all together to make a house?" the stranger continued. Clovis nodded; he didn't want to interrupt with words. "Now they deliver roof trusses already nailed together. Hundreds of sticks of lumber already out and properly assembled into a building component. All they have to do is slap it together when they get it to the site. Since they build it in a factory they can do it fast and cheap. It's the same quality work, just cheaper and easier." The stranger was on a roll and was pulling the big man behind him.

"That's what I need for the post-hole job!" Clovis exclaimed. "I need something to make the job easier."

"I think I've got what you're looking for. One of our facilities does something like what the truss building factory does. They dig post holes in the factory, one right after the other in sort of an assembly line. They dig hundreds of post holes a day and they store them in their warehouse. A few of us have a franchise to sell them. I had hoped to sell large shipments to the lumber yard, but I've run into resistance. I think it's because I'm different, but they say they don't have the space inside to store them. If you store them outside they could fill up with water and then they'd be useless." The stranger thought he might have gone too far in exaggerating the truth, an occupational hazard. Sometimes the stretched truth snaps like a rubber band and flies back to hurt you. He waited for Clovis to react before going further. The huckster could see his pigeon thinking. That was never a good sign to a flimflam artist. He readied himself to run.

"If you stored them upside down the water wouldn't run into them." Clovis suggested, hoping his idea made sense. Trying to be helpful, the young farmer had been working the kinks out of the stranger's problems rather than protecting his own hide. Clovis was most afraid of losing the respect of his new found friend.

"Why you're right. I'm going to put that in the brochure. I want to thank you, Mr. Beagle. This has been a most enlightening meeting. This is a highly specialized field and not many grasp the nuances of its implementation. You can't imagine the hours I've wasted emptying water logged post holes when all I had to do was store them upside down. Forgive me, sir, I'm not just stroking your ego when I say your idea is genius, pure genius."

Beaming from ear to ear, Clovis began to blush at the honor. This type of attention he didn't shun, but he was unaccustomed to enjoying it.

"You, sir, have been a fountain of wisdom for me. I really wish there was a way for me to repay you the kindness you have shown me. Time is ticking on, though and I have to get to the next hardware store by morning." The stranger pretended to leave, rising to his feet and looking around for his truck.

"You can help me." The big man tried to delay the stranger's departure. "You could sell me a load of those post-holes. It could help us both. I wouldn't have to dig all those holes and you could put a sign in front of our farm 'Palmer's Post-holes' or whatever you call your business. What do you say?" Clovis was thinking now. "Can we work something out?"

"I'd really like to give you a hand but I have to get paid when I deliver the post holes. They are inflexible on the practice. The factory expects me to wire them the money the next day after I make a sale. Besides, we like to sell them by the hundreds, not one at a time." The stranger kept dangling the bait in the water; making it dance seems to excite the fish's interest.

"I'm going to need about two hundred. It's not a small job I'm doing. I would pay you myself if they're not too expensive. How much would it be for two hundred?" Clovis readied to buy.

"Normally, they sell for at least four dollars a post-hole . I don't suppose you have eight hundred dollars on you."

"No. I don't." Clovis was crestfallen. It seemed like his plan was crumbling. His despair showed in him.

"That's the retail price, eight hundred dollars. I sell them wholesale for two dollars a post-hole. That would be four hundred dollars for the two hundred post-holes. Half price. How does that suit you?" Not as big a payday as he hoped for, but four hundred dollars would be a nice payday for late at night in a small village. Clovis was still in the dumps and the stranger knew why. "Still too much, big guy?"

Clovis nodded. It had been a good idea but he lacked the resources to take advantage of it. "Sorry. I guess this is out of my league."

"Not so fast, Mr. Beagle. Maybe we can still work something out. I make half of the wholesale price. If you would be willing to let me put several signs along the road to your farm, I'd be willing to forego my commission and consider the loss an advertising expense. Can you do that? Can we make a deal for two hundred dollars?" Not much money to the stranger, but better than nothing. It was certainly more money than he could make in an hour of legitimate work.

Producing the proceeds from his paycheck, Clovis started counting out the cash. Snatching the cash in his hand and plunking it in his pocket, the stranger said, "Bring your truck around to mine and I'll load you up." Clovis was off and back with his truck in the blink of and eye.

"What size posts are you putting in?" The stranger shouted back from the bed of the empty trailer. "I've got different sizes here."

"Just regular post-holes." Clovis said after a moment's pause. Clovis felt fortunate he had the stranger looking after his interests in the transactions. It would be endless ridicule if he were to come home with worthless post-holes. He wasn't sure he was right on the size and he hoped he wasn't fouling things up at the last instant.

"Good!" The salesman said. "They're loaded on the back of the trailer. I hate having to unload one size posthole to get to another. It's much easier this way." Clovis moved in to help load his truck. The salesman feared he would be discovered. "I wish you could help me, Mr. Beagle, but our company requires us to load your truck ourselves. That way any breakage is on us. There is a bit of a trick to moving these things without running into trouble." It was the first honest statement from the stranger.

"I'll sit down and let you do your job." Clovis relished the idea of relaxing while someone else did the heavy lifting. Boosting his ego was a rare treat for him. He wouldn't have gotten this kind of consideration from his father.

"All loaded. Listen, fella, don't try to unload these tonight. Leave them in the truck until morning and drive the truck to where you want the post-hole to go. There's no sense in carrying these things around the farm." He advised. "It doesn't look like rain, but to be on the safe side, I turned them upside down the way you suggested."

Clovis saw his point. He'd done his share of unnecessary work; enough to recognize opportunity when it passed by. A sudden fit of panic rushed through his mind and body, realizing his oversight he asked. "Wait a minute, how do I use these post-holes?"

It was a good question and one the stranger had anticipated. "It's as easy as one, two, three: One, identify exactly where you want the post-hole; Two, prepare the soil; and Three, insert the post-hole. I can write that down for you if you want but a bright guy like you won't have any trouble remembering it."

The last memory Clovis had of the stranger was when he scrambled up into the cab of the tractor and wheeled his trailer away with Clovis' money and partial load of post-holes.

The next morning it didn't go well with Clovis and his father. When Clovis pitched his innovation to his father he began to see the folly of his plan. Showing his father the truckload of postholes he saw the truck was empty. Repeated attempts to explain to his father what he had done sounded like gibberish even to Clovis.

"How was this supposed to work?" Clovis' father asked repeatedly. Clovis was glad he asked the question. It was the only aspect of the ordeal he could remember from the night before, except, of course, handing over his hard earned paycheck.

"It's as easy as one, two, three. The guy explained it so even I understood it." Clovis was proud of himself. "One, you pick the exact location where the post-holes go. You can see how I left them on the truck so I didn't have to drag them across the field. I can drive them to where I want them to go."

"I already picked where I want them to go. The little flags are planted in the middle of where the post-hole is supposed to go." Clovis' father reminded him. "So that's already done. What's number 2?"

"Prepare the soil for the hole." Clovis told his father. Clovis' father looked back at him and didn't say a word. He waited for it to occur to Clovis. Nothing happened right away, so Clovis' father prompted him. "What do you suppose you would have to do to the soil to prepare it for a hole?" he asked his son.

Clovis' brain works like those three-way light bulbs, the forty, one hundred, two hundred fifty Watt bulbs. One at a time the light brightens until what is there can be seen. He screwed up his face to think harder. His face beamed once he understood completely, then his head hung in shame as he saw the consequences of his actions. "You'd have to remove the soil to insert the post-hole wouldn't you?" Clovis guessed.

His father nodded and put his arm around Clovis' shoulder in support of him. A farmer only has a few moments to regret misdeeds before he must renew himself and begin working to correct his mistakes. Clovis' father handed him the post-hole digger and Clovis walked toward the field with flags marking where he would use the dreaded tool.

You can see why I have cautioned you against the hope of agricultural innovation. It's a brew that intoxicates us, a shadow that blocks the light of reason from illuminating what is clearly silly. We are all like Clovis in one way or another. Innovation is not necessarily bad. Sometimes it is simply new and not better. Often, we miss that point.

We strain our brains pondering new ways to accomplish old tasks. Landing on an idea, we rarely think it through to its ultimate conclusion. Logic is a foreigner in the nation that is our minds. I sometimes believe God listens in when we think great thoughts, and He chuckles.

Respectfully Submitted,

Harry Ellis

Harry Ellis

238 Persimmon Street

Blandtrap

To the Editor of the Tiskilwa Bureau Valley Chief

RE: The Enlightenment of Carla Dombrowski

Dear Sir:

You seem to be in the doldrums of news, lately. Only bad news graces your pages these days. This week's issue is a few pages short of the usual. It was the article about the stray dog that must have tipped me off to your dilemma. The prose was good enough but the content lacked anything remotely resembling news. A stray dog was found near your downtown. He didn't bite anyone nor did he even venture a bark as far as the story went. It was entirely unmentionable. The creature didn't save a drowning victim or wake a sleeping family to warn them of fire.

I would assume there were also cats, flies, and, presumably, several humans wandering about your city, all with somewhat interesting circumstances surrounding them, yet you gave the wandering dog the nod as the headline story. The dog takes a good picture, for a stray, and does appear to be a cute and cuddlesome animal. Still, I have to ask why you would select the dog story. Is it because he is the most interesting among your citizenry? I don't know and your story shines no light in this direction. I'm not a critic and I don't know you well, but I'm convinced you can do better.

Edith and the ladies have been taking on projects recently and I believe they have settled on Carla Dombrowski as their next victim, or project, depending on your point of view. She explained how the entire matter unfolded. Now, it is not my nature to intrude into the private and personal matters of others. Women, you know, don't always respect a curtain of privacy like men do. I have prided myself on my ability to mind my own business, leaving others alone. In this small matter, and only this once, I will deviate from my normal pattern.

Carla Dombrowski had a sheltered childhood as nearly every child would if parents had their way. She had an older sister and two older brothers. Her sister was bossy and spoke for her before she could open her mouth. She didn't speak regularly until kindergarten because her older sister was constantly hovering about ready to reply for her. There was simply no need to speak when her sibling was nearby.

Her older brothers were either protecting her fiercely from real or imagined dangers or they were teasing her mercilessly. It was often difficult to distinguish between protection and provocation where the two boys were concerned. Between brothers and sister, her life was not her own.

Carla was not one of the more popular girls in high school, shunning the kind of behavior that makes most girls popular. Neither was she a wallflower, having her share of dates with boys who managed to pass her brothers' approval. Their painful screening process narrowed the scope of her dating opportunities. It did net the benefit of never having to fight off a date's hands or endure the empty gas tank gambit played by so many young men. Her brothers checked the gauge before they left.

In college and nursing school Carla went a little crazy for a while, first time on her own and all. She wasn't very discriminating about who she dated and had her eyes opened regarding the depravity of men and was shocked to learn that so many women not only tolerated that kind of mistreatment, but encouraged it and sometimes sought it out.

After college and a few years of working, Carla realized that kind of life was not for her and she made up her mind to develop a set of standards for those she would date and vowed not to compromise those standards for the frivolity of emotion.

A few close friends were consulted to establish a set of iron clad standards for Carla to use in the evaluation of dating prospects. They bandied about criteria over several weeks and it became a popular topic with the girls of her age. Discussion of her proposed love life had reached the status of legitimate entertainment with many in her acquaintance, eschewing movies and parties for the opportunity to sit in on one of these discussions or hold one of their own chat groups without Carla in attendance. When a friend would conjure up a new, previously unconsidered requirement, an emergency meeting might be called for early the next morning at the diner.

Normally the diner is the exclusive haunt of old men during the early hours of the day. I remember a few occasions recently when these groups of young ladies entered the diner and sat at a table as far away from the 'regulars' table as they could get and not be dining al fresco. Privacy was a premium to them.

Their conversation was intense at times and animated with whooping and hollering at other times. They didn't display the dignity and reserved demeanor presented at our table. They are young and our kind of behavior is learned over time and with a variety of experience. It comes with the sacrifice a successful life demands.

Carla, eager to get on with the search, saw how the criteria committee had stalled in the process and decided to bring it to a close. She thought of ordering pizza or having tea. Both were inappropriate. Her hope was to avoid the sleepover atmosphere pizza sometimes suggests and the stiff formality of a tea would only serve to hinder conversation. Deciding on finger sandwiches with vegetables and dip, she freed her mind to tend to other items she would need for the evening.

It was necessary to trim the list of participants. If she were to invite all the acquaintances who had been offering advice, it would look more like a general session at the United Nations than a genuine meeting. Only her closest friends made the invitation list.

Lauretta Townsend used a flip chart when planning parades. Carla called Lauretta who graciously lent her flip chart for what seemed to Lauretta to be cryptic reasons. While widely known among her contemporaries, the search had not become common knowledge throughout the village. It was her greatest fear that word of her quest would leak out and her intentions be misconstrued by others rendering her the laughing stock of the community. The fear kept her up nights.

Driving back from Lauretta's home with the flip chart, Carla realized she was limiting the scope of her counsel. She had only sought opinion from her young friends regarding this matter. Two of her friends were successfully married, but not for very long. It occurred to her that ideas from ladies happily married for decades might also be valuable. She thought she might seek the advice of older ladies, ladies married for decades. She would give wisdom a fleeting chance before implementing a rash plan developed by her young friends.

A quick stop by the IGA was necessary to pick up some fresh ground coffee and replenish her stash of herbal teas. She had decided to serve tea despite the dangers associated with it. Tea can cause spurious conversation among women the way beer can cause wearisome brawls among men.

Remembering she was out of paper plates and plastic table service, she restocked those items as well as napkins, tea candles, and garbage bags. While fumbling for keys on her way to the car, she lost control of the rather large bag she was wrestling. Bag and contents went skidding along the sidewalk. Bill Whittacre was passing by and he came to her rescue, chasing down rolling cans and sticking them back into the torn bag. It was amazing he could salvage any use for the tattered paper remnant.

"I better carry these to your car. The bag is badly torn and I think I have a grip on most of this stuff." Bill got the goods into her car without dropping what he had. Most of the purchases spilled across the back seat and the bag was shreds when he placed it on the seat.

Bill vanished before she could thank him. Carla fussed with the items in the back seat so they wouldn't roll onto the floor on her way home. As she put the key in the ignition, Bill tapped on her window. "Here, I got you a new bag. It'll make it easier to get this stuff inside when you get home." He handed the bag through the window and was gone again before she could say a proper thank you. As Bill walked away he thought, "My, what an attractive young lady."

Immediately, he drove the thought from his head. Bill didn't allow himself the fantasy of love or feminine friendship. He didn't have anything to offer an intelligent and attractive lady. Bill Whittacre was a farm hand. That was what he was and it was all he would ever be. Before vanishing from her window, he said, "Ma'am." She couldn't see if he tipped his hat or not.

By the time the young ladies arrived at her home, Carla had made finger sandwiches and had appealingly arranged vegetables around them on a large platter she'd borrowed from her mother. Two kinds of dip were intriguingly displayed nearby. Dip containers didn't fit well on the platter so she put them alongside. They were the traditional ranch and spinach dip which is much better when served with fancy breads rather than vegetables. She knew it was unorthodox but cuisine wasn't the point of the evening. Still, two of her friends commented on the gaffe.

As the young ladies walked in, one or two at a time, they were surprised at the formality Carla had chosen for the meeting. The couch was central to seating and a folding chair, borrowed from the church reception hall, flanked either side. The flip chart was in front of the seating and the tray of the easel was filled with no less than six colors of markers! These would be handy for showing emphasis or if the plan got overly-complicated. Color coding seems to be the key to organization these days.

Cheryl Hunter was the first to arrive. Having wed last year, she was the veteran of the group with regard to marital bliss. She brought a cheesecake and some chocolate sauce to share. The baking had taken a toll on her energy and the disposition of her husband. The rigors of cheesecake preparation caused her to rise early and hubby's demeanor improved throughout the day as he saw the project near completion. His countenance crashed when he saw her stuff the delicacy into a cake carrier and head for the door.

It is a mistake common to young married men. They see something good going on in the kitchen and they think it will have something to do with them. In time, and after repeated disappointments he will learn to ask at the first opportunity whether it is to be given away or is for home consumption before he gets his hopes up. If he's lucky, a piece will be left over and Cheryl will bring it back for him.

Eliza Beeman was next to appear. Just married a couple of months, she was still ablush with the excitement of marriage and the thrill of knowing another intimately. It was too soon for her to be very concerned with his behavior. Before long, those cute idiosyncrasies that first attracted her to him would begin to grate on her nerves until they rose to the top of the list of things about him she would most like to change.

Eliza came straight from work with a layover at the IGA to purchase a pint each of mocha fudge and French vanilla ice cream. Some items in her refrigerator would have been suitable to bring but she thought better of it. Home had to be avoided if she was to be on time. Recently married, the groom still had regular expectations and she would, time permitting, have been willing to meet them, but the hour was late. It was better to delay the encounter than to create disappointment.

Arlene Libidowitz and Lucrecia Kwok came in the same car. On their way into the IGA, they passed Eliza on her way out. It gave them a minute to compare notes on purchases for the party. Better informed, Arlene found a very fudgy brownie she thought would liven up well in the microwave. Lucrecia uncovered some frozen strawberries that were nearly whole, with no added sugar. Mocha fudge would sit like a crown atop the warm brownies and the berries would be a perfect pedestal for French vanilla ice cream.

Carla put each item on her small kitchen table as they arrived. Once Arlene and Lucrecia completed the guest list, they started to fill their plates. I'm being kind, of course, because the truth is often ugly. Those ladies attacked that table with a vengeance too vicious for words. The carnage of slopped chocolate syrup, discarded and slightly irregular strawberries, and the confetti of bread crumbs from finger sandwiches rained onto the tablecloth while the floor resembled the streets of a ransacked village.

In the other room ladies sat with straight backs, observing the long established customs of affairs such as this. Each would eat a half a finger sandwich and at least three baby carrots or celery sticks before consuming a warm brownie, heaping bowl of strawberries and ice cream, and a slice of cheesecake (without chocolate sauce, because with would be piggish). It is important, after all, to exercise moderation in all matters. Only then were they ready for the meeting.

Carla began, "I think I have lost my focus. I'm no longer looking for an interesting conversationalist or a guy that likes to have fun. I am looking for a husband who will be both, but if a guy is both and is not husband material, I don't want to waste my time. I'm tired of the merry-go-round. I want a ride that's going somewhere and if I have to leave the amusement park to find it, I'm willing to do so.

"The men I have dated are not, for the most part, bad men. They just had plans that didn't include me. The doctor I dated was kind and attentive whenever he thought of me. The problem was that thoughts of me didn't cycle through his mind more that twice a week and those were often interrupted by emergency calls. I wasn't important enough to him to warrant his interest so it wasn't possible to capture his heart.

"The plumber was nice, too. He had a good job and was very good at it. He really liked to make money, which isn't a bad trait at all, but making money was more important to him than me. He would cancel dates if he got extra work. The last straw was when we were out to dinner on Valentines Day and his pager went off. He left me sitting there for a plumbing emergency.

I could tolerate the doctor's interruptions, I mean, how can you expect a doctor to deprive a critically ill person their very life and breath? But the plumber was different; certainly our romantic evening could take precedence over a clogged toilet!" Carla had worked herself into an emotional frenzy. It was time for friends to come to her assistance.

A collage of "You deserve better," "Men are bums," "It's their loss," and "You're better off without them," filled the air and surrounded Carla like a warm blanket. It bolstered her determination. She composed herself and got the meeting back on track, asking each of her confidants to list the qualities she should be looking for in a man.

Eliza, still high on chocolate said, "He should be dreamy, like my guy."

Cheryl Hunter and Lucrecia Kwok looked at each other as if in shock. Eliza's husband was a good man, a good provider, and would unquestionably be, one day, a good father, but there was no way a rational person could rate his appearance as 'dreamy.' If they were to rate his looks they would need to begin at a reference point nearer the middle of the scale, say, somewhere around 'not entirely repulsive.' It wasn't a bad rating at all, but still a good distance from 'dreamy,' which was the gold standard in picking a guy.

Realizing the infirmity a new marriage causes the bride, they decided not to bicker over her choice of words. The others agreed Carla should think the one she chose to be handsome. He didn't have to be strikingly handsome and it would be better if he were unaware of his beauty. Conceit and vanity can, in the initial stages of a relationship, be confused for confidence. As appealing as confidence might be, conceit and vanity are abrasive and wear through the fabric of a relationship in short order. Carla wrote "good looking" on the flip chart. They were on their way.

Cheryl spoke up next. "He should have a good job." The Hunters, to a person, were hard workers and admired that quality in others. They believed only hard workers get ahead in this world. In a perfect world that would be true.

With unanimous agreement Carla wrote "good job" under "good looking" on the flip chart.

"You should have lots of things in common." Arlene noted. Looking around she saw she was not well understood, so she added, "You know, he should like the same things she does. They should both like theater. They should both like the same kind of novels so they can cuddle together and read a good book to one another." This elicited deep sighs and a few "Aw"s from the ladies. Carla scribbled "things in common" on the list. That one seemed shaky to Carla but her friends' attitudes brought her around to their side.

Lucrecia was last to offer an opinion but it was accepted with the greatest acclaim. "He has to love you more than anything else."

Eliza and Cheryl leapt to their feet in exuberance and uttered a unison "Yes!" in loud voice. They felt strongly about this point and couldn't imagine why they had not thought of it.

Carla was satisfied with the evening's work. The young ladies needed to leave so they began the cleanup. By the time they were finished gathering the leftovers there were none remaining except a slice of cheesecake Cheryl had hidden behind the toaster. She wrapped it up for hubby. Everything that wasn't paper or plastic had been consumed. A quick wipe of the table and they were out the door.

Before turning in for the night, Carla transferred the list on the flip chart onto an index card, stuffing it into her purse for future reference. Should she meet a man of interest, the list would be nearby where she could refer to it if she believed she was straying from the plan. She carried the list for about two weeks, never really needing it, until she stopped by the church to return the folding chairs and to drop off some sheet music.

A quick fill-up at the gas station provided fuel for the trip to the church. Carla was struggling a bit with the contents of the car. When she borrowed the flip chart it was good weather and she drove with the chart hanging out a window. Now, with a gentle rain, it threatened to damage the entire pad of paper.

Bill Whittacre was also in the gas station and noticed Carla's situation. He approached her, "I don't know if you remember me, I'm Bill Whittacre."

"Sure, Bill, I remember. We graduated in the same class." Carla replied. In a moment of reminiscence she remembered he remained in the background, working on one thing or another, but never in the spotlight for even a moment. She couldn't recall ever having even the briefest conversation with him, except, of course, outside the IGA.

"If you keep driving like that you're going to ruin the flip chart pad. It will fit behind the seat of my truck. I could deliver it for you." Knowing his place was a comfort to him. Bill continued, "It wouldn't be any trouble." Bill suggested. He would have offered even if it was a monumental inconvenience and wouldn't have regretted it.

"It belongs to Lauretta Townsend." Carla answered trying to look Bill in the eyes, but he didn't offer them. Bill kept his eyes downcast, never presuming to be another's equal. "They live down by..."

Bill cut her off. "I know the Townsends. If no one is home, I'll put it in the breezeway. It'll be protected there. You can call to tell them where to find it."

"Thank you, Bill." Carla was impressed by his charity and initiative. A girl doesn't find that in a lot of guys. "That would help me tremendously." Still searching for some recognition of her in Bill's eyes, she was not rewarded in her effort.

Where most people would hang around to collect some emotional reward or accolade for their act of kindness, Bill quickly exited with his characteristic, "Ma'am." He didn't like to linger after helping someone. Not knowing how to do polite conversation, he knew he looked backward when he talked so he made it a habit to leave before he embarrassed himself.

Carla was a casual member of the church choir, making Wednesday night rehearsal and Sunday services as her schedule permitted. Since she worked in the city, she picked up sheet music the director ordered from the music store and brought it to the church.

In the basement of the church, several older ladies were convening for a meeting. It was one of those grand misunderstandings that so often occur in church organization. After an opening prayer the ladies had difficulty staying on topic. Indeed, the ladies had trouble finding any common ground for the session. It seems Lauretta Townsend had prepared for a meeting about the church grounds and had ideas regarding landscaping plans. Edith Ellis, my lovely wife, clearly remembered the meeting was to discuss selection of a new hymnal. Bob and Ruth Woods anchored the evangelism committee, so Ruth came to the table to explore preparations for a revival: "Tent, or no tent?" was her topic. Mrs. Wing had come to investigate whether repair or replacement of the church bell would be best. It no longer rang as loudly as it used to. The meeting, lacking a thread of commonality, began to get loud; not angry, just loud.

Carla heard the commotion and went downstairs to investigate. She found the four pillars deep in disagreement about nothing. This was the opportunity she was hoping to find, experienced ladies with time on their hands. Taking the index card from her purse, she intended to interrupt the group to seek their advice.

Ruth was the first to notice Carla approaching the group. "Hello, Carla," she greeted and waved her hand for Carla to come over. "How nice it is to see you. Can we help you?" The other ladies joined in with similar sentiments.

Carla was in full blush as she stammered out what she wanted to discuss with them. After swearing them to confidence, she said "This is the list of qualities we decided were important. I sort of rearranged them in what I thought was order of importance: One, he should love me more than anything else; Two, he should like the same things I like (this one had grown in favor as she thought about it, causing Carla to advance it up the list); Three, he should be hard working;, and Four, he should be good looking."

An uncomfortable silence fell over the group of ladies. Sharp tongued as they may be with each other, they had vowed only to be positive and encouraging when dealing with younger ladies in the congregation.

Mrs. Wing broke the silence. "Why, dear, that is a perfectly wonderful list. It is thoughtful and detailed. You should keep it with you always. If you ever decide you want to buy a dog that list will come in mighty handy." She said with her sweetest smile.

Edith was next. "Any man you choose should care for you deeply, dear, but the best two people can muster is human love, frail at best. It is very limited and not capable of much on its own. What is important is that both you and the man you choose love God more than each other. God's love can keep you together. Human love tends as much toward destructive jealousy as it does toward forever after forgiveness.

With God's love you will insult, offend, and disappoint each other a wee bit less and when these offenses occur, and they will occur, you will be hurt less by them. After having to humble yourself before God and ask forgiveness for your transgressions, it is much easier to grant the same to another."

Lauretta Townsend waded into the deep waters. "Hard work is admirable; there is no doubt about that. But men, as a group, tend to take the whole work thing too seriously. It can consume them and diminish you in their mind. More important is direction. It is easy for men to get caught up in the nitty gritty of work and lose sight of what is to be accomplished in life. They need direction from you and, more importantly, from above."

Ruth chimed in at the end. "You should feel an attraction to a man but appearance isn't all its cracked up to be. It changes over time, anyway, and the man you pick will not look like the same man after a couple of decades. Why, when I fell in love with Bob, I had no idea what he looked like. My brothers beat him so often his face was hidden behind a mask of scabs. I thought he looked pretty good after he healed up but I would have been happy with him however he looked. It was his determination that was his beauty, not his face."

"But shouldn't he love me? Shouldn't I love him?" Carla pleaded, beginning to become disillusioned.

"Yes, dear," Mrs. Wing took the lead. "But you are confusing love with affection. There should be affection for sure. Affection comes and goes over the years, mostly it stays around. Love is a different matter entirely. Love isn't a feeling. Love is action. Love is what he is willing to do for you without regard for himself. Love is what you are willing to do for him without regard for yourself. It always comes at a cost to the one who loves, and they gladly pay the fee."

"It's like what Christ did, only on a much smaller scale. He gave his life for us while we were still insulting Him. He could have raised His hands and said 'I love you, be well,' and avoided the suffering, but we would still be lost. He was willing to suffer for us and to take our burden upon Himself. You see, dear," Edith instructed with gentle words, "that is love."

Ruth summed it up. "And, that is why it is so important for the man you choose to love God more than you. He needs to see, understand, and do. Don't settle for anything less, Carla, it is what God wants for you. Don't cheat yourself."

The rest of the ladies agreed as Lauretta instructed Carla to turn over the index card and write: One, Loves God; Two, Has direction; Three, Is determined; and Four, Feels affection. "You need all four, but work the list from top down. Affection is a powerful distraction and can be the most difficult of the four to walk away from. Don't put your heart out there until you know he's a keeper."

"Where do you want to live, dear?" Mrs. Wing asked out of the blue.

"I guess I'm not sure what that has to do with what we're talking about, but I want to live in Blandtrap. I work in the city and I see what life there does to some people. It's okay for them, but I would prefer to live and raise a family here where my relatives are close and friends nearby."

"Good, good! You'll likely want to pick a local boy with ties to Blandtrap, then." Mrs. Wing made the whole thing sound so easy, like picking a ripe tomato.

"Won't that be limiting? Won't that eliminate most of the men on the face of the earth? Who will I be left with?" Carla was getting agitated at the business like manner in which the ladies were approaching her very sensitive life problems.

"Of course it will narrow the field. I thought that's what we were doing here. Why, my dear, you will be left with only the ones you might want to marry." Mrs. Wing calmed her. "Just add Five, Lives close to Blandtrap to your list.'

The ladies dismissed Carla, who wandered away in a fog from the encounter wondering what had happened, what she should expect, and what her friends would say about the meeting. Keeping it a secret from them would be a prudent option, at least in the short run.

I wish I could be of assistance to you in your search for meaningful news. A dearth of news is our lot here in Blandtrap, also. Since you have expressed an interest in animals, I will scour our village to find stories worthy of print.

In the mean time, let me suggest you scrutinize your front page stories. Try to apply a higher standard than you are now employing. If the story is not informative or interesting and you are not driven to remember the incident, it should not appear, in bold print and with pictures, beneath your banner.

Our neighbor has some entertaining cats. The Beagle farm has goats, but their antics are often unsuitable for mixed audiences. I'll keep my eye open for something worthy of news. Should I uncover an event out of the ordinary or if I encounter an otherwise noteworthy circumstance, I will contact you by the next post.

Respectfully Submitted,

Harry Ellis

Harry Ellis

238 Persimmon Street

Blandtrap

To the Editor of the Tiskilwa Bureau Valley Chief

RE: The High School Musical

Dear Sir:

Last week we were treated to an annual event that brings a smile to my heart, if not my face. I am speaking, of course, about the high school musical. The hubbub started more than a month ago. Casting calls are open to the public at Blandtrap High School primarily because they don't promptly lock the doors immediately after school. I got wind of the tryouts and stopped in for a few moments to see what was up.

Calvin Farnsworth, from the Institute for Idle Science watched the proceedings from stem to stern. He recorded each participant, what piece they prepared for the audition, and which selection they were asked to sight read. A table was set up for him when he arrived. The accommodation was the result of several phone calls to the director asking how auditions would be handled. Armed with his paperwork, Calvin was waiting long before student or director entered the auditorium.

It was Calvin's opinion that these records might prove invaluable to research some day, maybe providing the missing variable to some life-changing theory. His records are incomplete. After his fourth interruption to ask the correct spelling of a name, he was asked to remain quiet. His third interruption to ask the name of a musical number auditioned got him tossed from the event. He was asked to leave and escorted to the door by the custodian who locked it behind him. "It is a great loss for mankind." Calvin lamented as the door was slammed in his face.

Mrs. Twilly's Tiny Tumblers have no permanent address. She finds a location where the little ones can practice for a few years until a better offer comes along for the property owner. She finds herself out on her ear in a matter of weeks. When she came to town almost two decades ago she was fully endowed with ability and equipment. The gymnastic apparati were stored while she sought suitable accommodations.

Her decision to take apartments around Village Square above the bakery spoke to her unusual personality. Other accommodations were available to her yet she made her odd choice. Mrs. Twilly had the heart of an artist. She stayed up late, took coffee in the middle of the afternoon, and was seen sketching and painting in Village Square. She stood out from the other villagers. Standing out isn't a bad thing by itself, but it does bring one up as a topic of conversation more frequently than usual folk. People who are different intentionally don't, as a rule, mind that much.

Unable to negotiate a storefront large enough and affordable, she struck an agreement with the high school. She would donate her equipment to the institution but she would retain use of it during reasonable hours to be arranged with the custodian and when the gymnasium was not in use by the athletic department.

A couple of years later when she was more financially secure, a back room beneath her lodgings became available. Mrs. Twilly would use that location when gymnastic equipment was not required. She could teach tumbling and dance close to her apartment, avoiding the cold walk to the high school during winter months.

Small children were her only clientele when she first opened shop. Mrs. Twilly had a rapport with little ones. Her careful methods and eccentric behavior drew out the best in children and they tried very hard to please her. These classes became her bread and butter. She offered a full gamut of services. There was the popular tumbling for the younger children. Older students, after showing ability and determination, could take gymnastic instruction under her tutelage. She taught classes in social graces to young ladies and gentlemen. Teas were the backdrop for lessons on manners, dress, and proper speech for young ladies. Mother, aunt, or grandmother was required to attend with the student. Truth be known, more learning was done by the elder than the younger. This was all to the benefit of the village.

Training of the young gentlemen took a more basic tack than the young ladies' education. In the beginning she required attendance by a father, uncle, or grandfather but quickly relented on this condition. Scratching and spitting were two of the bigger hurdles the young men had to leap and they were receiving more instruction from the older men in techniques to enhance these skills than Mrs. Twilly could pound into their skulls about gentle behavior. The older men were out and the young men were the better for it.

Her teaching about social graces has not been without impact on the locals. At Plow Boy Diner, these days, more than half the spoons knocked to the floor will remain there or be exchanged for a clean one replacing the previous practice of blowing the spoon clean and returning it to use. It may seem like a small matter but it is a huge change in the thinking of patrons. One person, particularly a person like Mrs. Twilly, can make a difference.

No one formally responded to Mrs. Twilly's advertisements for ballroom dancing instruction. As far as anyone knew she had never had a student. Edith and I used to sneak in the back door and get a pointer or two when the mood struck us, but I'm sure we were the only ones availing themselves of her talent. I learned some interesting facts about Blandtrap as we were skulking about in secrecy.

Traffic patterns were not what you would expect them to be of an evening. Main Street, I always believed, carried the lion's share of vehicle traffic around Village Square day or night. It is designed for the purpose and does indeed handle many cars. In the evening, though, the alley behind Mrs. Twilly's shop was often clogged with cars. I wouldn't have thought the narrow alley would have competed so aggressively for the affection of drivers. In just one evening we passed Bob and Ruth Woods pulling out of the parking space when we arrived. The Hugginboughs were waiting to take our parking place when we pulled out after our lesson. Yet another car, I'm fairly certain it was the mayor's car but the passengers kept ducking down, was circling the block.

It is a shame the dance instruction part of her business never caught on. She still advertises, bless her heart. It is probably out of habit that she continues to do so. It doesn't seem to profit her in any way.

The primary difficulty a director encounters casting a high school musical is in recruiting enough boys to fill all the roles. Musicals have a reputation. Plays, in general, don't scare as many young men as musicals do. Singing and dancing doesn't appeal to young men. In the abstract, they see nothing wrong with the activities. Individually they aren't as threatening as the two together can be. The reality of standing on stage, spotlight shining on a dark stage, is another matter altogether. The idea of presenting yourself as a talented person in front of friends who know better instills a fear in the core of a young man that prevents him from forcing his feet to carry him to an audition. Rational fear depletes the ranks of eligible male actors to a point where a director has few to fill the roles of many. A good director, even in a community like ours where honesty and integrity are prized above all other virtues, must resort to dares, threats, and, eventually, blackmail.

A musical is a more complicated production than other theatrical performances. It requires coordination of three skills: acting prowess, vocal ability, and instrumental accomplishment. It is the rare director that is familiar with all three. Normally, three adults are needed to blend their artistry into one production. If the reader believes it is difficult to get children who are still young and moldable, not suffering from decades of habitual behavior to cooperate, he should try to get adults, who are more complacent and mostly self-motivated, to get on the same page with each other, literally as well as figuratively.

The pit band rehearsed on one schedule; vocal instruction was given on a second schedule; while stage direction was blocked on a third schedule. It appeared that progress was made in all three areas without incident. There were, of course, omens of impending disaster along the path to dress rehearsal, but it was easier to think pleasant thoughts rather than bad ones.

"Jimmy, this is where you stand when you sing 'The Asparagus Is in Bloom," the director told the aspiring actor.

"Mrs. Wellengood said I don't have the range to sing that song and it's going to be cut from the show." Jimmy whined, feeling a bit squeamish about telling the director how the musical would proceed. His reticence is understandable. One of Attila's deputies would also be concerned about telling the Hun about changes in an attack plan.

"We'll deal with it later." The director relented in disgust.

During a confrontation between the director and Mrs. Wellengood regarding Jimmy's limited vocal range, the band coach interjects that Jimmy is also having trouble with the trombone solo in 'The Asparagus Is In Bloom," and how can he sing the song and play the trombone at the same time? If he were a violin player it would be possible, awkward but possible. The director leaves it up to the vocal coach and the band coach to settle the matter, barking out the order: "Put Jimmy in the cast or in the band but do it today; and fill his vacancy today, too."

Later the director learned that the pit band, with the more accomplished Jimmy on the trombone, was having trouble with 'The Asparagus is in Bloom' song. The instrumental coach had more requests to cut scores from the script and announced the band was laboring with the overture. Bristling at this tinkering with her artistic perception of the musical, the director laid down the law with the coaches. "There can be only one director, so just teach the kids to sing the songs and how to play the music as we agreed. I don't want to hear of this again." Foot stomping and marching off in a huff are options but not always effective. They must be used sparingly or they lose the impact of surprise. A director knows this yet it is still hard to restrain the behavior.

Another snag of musical productions has to do with the physical limitations of the cast. It isn't long after characters in a musical break out in song until they start dancing around. Left to their own devices, young ladies and gentlemen dance like wounded elk. That kind of performance is unsuitable for audience consumption. That was when Mrs. Twilly's talents were solicited.

In a meeting with the coaches, the director discussed what, artistically, needed to be projected by the dancing. Mr. Orton, the instrumental coach, suggested clog dancing during certain numbers to drown out the pit band's inadequacies. The vocal coach said it would be a good idea for 'The Asparagus is in Bloom' as well. Mrs. Twilly explained clog dancing or, anticipating their next suggestion, loud tap dancing would be inappropriate and she volunteered to work with both coaches to see what could be done. Among these four, Mrs. Twilly is the only true professional performer and the only one who wouldn't rather be somewhere else. It showed in the quality of her work and the enthusiasm with which her duties were dispatched.

Trouble for the director began before they were aware of the impending doom. At the staff meeting when the director of the musical was announced, the principal, Mr. Paar, has tried each year to elicit an atmosphere of suspense over the selection. There was suspense, dread would be a better word to describe it, but suspense was part of it. A small stipend for the hopeless, thankless task was the source of envy for those who had never served in the position.

The compensation, if carefully calculated, worked out to be about twenty-three cents an hour if sleepless nights were excluded. It hadn't been an attractive salary since the great depression.

Following what Mr. Paar believed were subtle theatrics, he announced the winner and they responded to the honor with some comment like "What did I ever do to you?" and a director was born.

The director issue being decided, halls of the school came alive again. For weeks teachers had been avoiding the principal, checking the hall before leaving their room and sending students to the office to perform duties they should attend to themselves. No teacher wanted to be the last qualified person the principal saw before he made his decision. Unaffected teachers became friends of the principal once more and the mantle of pariah was passed from the principal to the newly crowned director. Life returned to normal for the relieved principal.

No longer bothered by the decision-making process, he was free to exercise his authority anew. The principal had been cheated of this luxury for a while because he couldn't find the hiding teachers, cowering behind corners or sitting in locked classrooms with the lights turned off in order to elude him. Now, only the director continued to avoid the principal. After he paid the stipend and released the paltry budget for the production, the director would no longer speak to him. "All the better," Mr. Paar thought.

The first order of business for a convicted offender doing time is to plot revenge against those they perceive played a role in their incarceration. So it was with the reluctant director. She stalked the halls like a roaring lion looking for prey. Her weapons were not teeth and claws but set construction duties and wardrobe responsibilities. These tasks would be distributed with a vindictive heart and a wicked smile on her face; the designee powerless to refuse, fearing a reputation of being uncooperative. It was much like a game of tag only with horrible, time-sucking, schedule-wrecking, life-changing consequences.

Leon, the history and civics teacher fell off the roof of his house and was hospitalized for the weekend. He came to school on Monday in a wheel chair, heavily medicated for the pain. They moved his classes to the first floor because he was unable to negotiate stairs. When he ran into the director at lunch he informed her, "I won't be able to do a very good job of set construction in this condition."

"Don't worry about it," she responded in a compassionate tone and with a sensitive hand on his only arm without a bandage, "I'll get you some help."

Help was hard to find. It wouldn't be prudent for her to give him a pass while he was still breathing. "You're going to have to do better than a simple fracture if you want to get out of this show," She was heard to say to others.

Sylvester Juan Ramirez and Raymond Johnson were the senior Romeos this year. The director was able to draft them to perform due to a marginal grade in English. It was indeed blackmail, plain and simple. She saw it as a win-win situation. If she could get those two to read the script, which they would have to do to retain a shred of dignity during the performance, she would have succeeded in forcing them to read at least one book during her class: One better than her current record.

Sylvester, known as 'The Sly One' and Raymond, calling himself 'The Ray,' were placed in the capable hands of Mrs. Twilly to teach them dance steps. They would prove a handful for her to manage; however, her experience with older men with similar inclinations served her well in this venture.

Young ladies who gravitate toward theater fall into one of two categories: the popular girls who are using the occasion of the musical to add to their popularity; and the good girls who have a conscience and a strong sense of right and wrong, and are unwilling to do what makes the popular girls popular. Girls from both categories find themselves in leading roles.

The Sly One and The Ray approached each rehearsal as if they came stag to a make-out party. Eying each girl who passes them, regardless of the number of times they pass. It becomes, with their limited ability to improvise, increasingly difficult for them to recall clever and suggestive innuendo to fill their remarks. Their small minds quickly overload and they repeat themselves, sometimes several times during the same rehearsal. Relying on their tiny vocabularies, they are disappointed when they reach into the pantry of their intellect for the correct word and find the shelves empty. Perhaps if they expanded their spectrum of reading to include literature without fold-out pages, they would be enriched and more fully prepared for intelligent conversation.

Mrs. Twilly utters the words that delight the young ladies but shoots pangs of panic through the ears of The Sly One and The Ray, "Let's dance!"

Pairing dancers by height was her first attempt at organizing the actors. It would do for then, but she knew there would be many changes before the final pairings were found. In the end, they would be grouped by ability. Since none yet possessed that characteristic, they were all in the same group.

The big production number, 'The Asparagus Is in Bloom,' was a rumba. Mrs. Twilly was aware they would have to learn to walk before she could teach them to dance, so she began by teaching them the waltz. It was a technique she had used several times before. The waltz is a simple step quickly mastered by those with any talent, while the untalented struggle. When she doesn't immediately discover profound talent and doesn't have time to grow a new crop, she uses this technique to separate the chaff from the doorknobs, so to speak. It would be unrealistic to hope for wheat.

"This is the position," she demonstrates expecting the students to mimic her. They just stood, looking down at the ground without movement of any kind, save the odd foot shuffle. Uneasiness was a cloud that enveloped the group. Young people, boys and girls, are generally uncomfortable touching in public unless it is in the back row at the movies or in front of old folks they hope to embarrass. Even the wolfish boys whom the good girls have to push away when they meet in the halls are timid in this setting.

She tackled the biggest problems first, "One!" she shouted, addressing Sylvester.

"That's 'The Sly One,'" He boasted, drawing on all the courage he had. Covering his growing fear he brought forward his brash attitude, thankful his voice didn't crack and his knees shake in the process.

"In the theater we tend to address actors by their last names, One, too many people have the same first name, fewer have the same last name. You are One." She said to Sylvester. Turning to Ray she moved into his personal space, nearly touching his nose, "Are you One, too?" The girls privately applauded Mrs. Twilly's handling of the boys.

"No, ma'am, I'm Ray," was his meek response. The Sly One chose to lay low along with The Ray. He knew this was not the time to stand and call attention to himself. They knew Mrs. Twilly would call a bluff in a second and just might continue to ridicule beyond their limits to contain themselves. She looked as if she were capable of that. She was, and willing to do it, too.

Returning her attention to the group brought sighs of relief from the boys. Mrs. Twilly ordered, "Assume the waltz position," without meeting resistance that time. The boys continued with uncharacteristic self-conscious behavior counterproductive to learning a new skill. "Come on boys!" she barked once again, "any other time you couldn't keep your hands off these ladies!"

The boys, under the barrage of Mrs. Twilly's verbal stimulation, quickly learned the step, more out of self-defense than a desire to learn. The ladies were gliding across the floor with movement resembling grace while the young men plodded along with them, with feet in the proper position but with a stiffness suggesting they were walking behind a plow horse rather than dancing. It was what she had grown to expect.

A stickler for detail, Mrs. Twilly was also a realist. This was musical theater, not ballet. No critic would evaluate the dance steps or dissect arm movement. The mere illusion of dancing was sufficient for the musical. This was good enough. From here she hoped they would not get worse before they got better. Inspiration struck her, though it would be a few days before she could develop her plan.

The director pulled Mrs. Twilly aside to discuss the big production number. She was concerned the dancers didn't look 'asparagusy' enough to convey the full meaning of the song. Mrs. Twilly listened to her and looked serious, nodding her head in agreement once in a while hearing all of the concerns. This was not the first director Mrs. Twilly had to placate. She made an insignificant change to the dance number and exaggerated the benefit to the director, profusely thanking her for pointing out the deficiency and saving her obvious embarrassment. Problem solved and disaster averted at the mere cost of momentary boot licking.

Rehearsals the last two weeks before a performance become more complete and time is spent on scenes that give the cast the most trouble. Mrs. Twilly has, at this point, finished teaching dance steps but she continues to frequent rehearsals to the relief of the director. When the dance coach found The Sly One had backed some polite young lady into a corner, she cuffed him and chased him away. It happened with surprising regularity and Sylvester often left rehearsal with a headache. Raymond, always striving for the upper hand, convinced The Sly One he was developing a bald spot from perpetual thwacking. He purchased a small mirror to monitor his hair line which he carried at all times.

At the diner I shared what I have gleaned from the few rehearsals I attended. Stu was looking forward to the musical. Being banned from the annual Christmas Pageant, he appreciated what he was allowed to attend much more that at any other time in his life. He was always on his best behavior during a show and would wait until he was home to critique the event. Stu seemed to think he had seen this particular musical before but when I described the 'Asparagus Is In Bloom' number he drew a blank.

At practices, the vocal coach and the instrumental coach persisted in sniping at each other. The vocal coach kept suggesting to the instrumental coach to lower the pitch of various songs because singers were having difficulty reaching notes. The instrumental coach would explain to the vocal coach what a monumental effort it would be to rescore the music and also how the pit band didn't so much learn the music as they memorized the notes to be played. If the music were rewritten now, several musicians would be starting from scratch.

The last week before opening night, the carping and bickering among the director and the coaches reached a crescendo, but still restricted to conversations behind closed doors. They presented a united front to the cast, pit band, and crew. After all, they had a common enemy in the audience.

Even The Sly One and The Ray are treated with kid gloves. The initial onslaught of ridicule and humiliation were replaced with compliments and encouragement. Young ladies are pulled aside and instructed in defensive maneuvers. When the boys act inappropriately they are to kick them in the shins, or that general neighborhood, rather than slap their faces. Makeup can only cover so much. It would be easier to explain a limp or hunched posture than a facial scar.

Genius is another term used so loosely it has nearly lost its meaning. Mrs. Twilly's insight into the dance dilemma caused her to solve the problem in a unique way. It was clear to her Sylvester and Raymond could not conquer the dance. If grace were a million dollars, these two would be in debtor's prison. She wrestled with the problem until a solution was devised. The idea struck her as she was reaching into the freezer at the IGA to grab a carton of ice cream to solace her concern.

Pulling the director aside Mrs. Twilly begged her indulgence one last time. It was the final rehearsal before dress rehearsal and the production was moving along well, building toward the production number. In front of the plodding teens pretending to be dancers wafted a bank of fog. Mrs. Twilly had borrowed a fog machine from nearby theatrical enthusiasts and pushed the special effect ahead of the actors with a small fan.

Fog concealed the performers from the waist down, obscuring the audience's view of missteps and trippery. The illusion of dance was preserved without all the talent necessary to pull it off in full view of spectators. The director leapt to her feet in applause and, with sincere gratitude and devotion, mentioned Mrs. Twilly several times as she stood on stage holding her flowers on closing night.

Dress rehearsal in Blandtrap is traditionally performed before the residents of the Nursing Home. Vans carry the more mobile elderly to the high school gymnasium. Those able to make the trip from Blandtrap's retirement village and surrounding facilities are also welcome to attend.

Director and coaches evaluate the performance by the actions of the performers. Making notes for last minute advice to cast and changes to the show itself. Pages are filled with scribbled comments and tiny diagrams that would take too many words to explain in writing. Some changes would be made after dress rehearsal and others just before opening curtain. Directors have a feel for that sort of thing.

Stu and I had a unique protocol for judging the likely success of a performance based upon the dress rehearsal. We count the number of old folks who nod off during the performance. If no more than twenty percent fall asleep before intermission and only a few more drift off during the second act, the show is a cinch to be a success. Greater than sixty percent noddage is doom for any production. We believe that process to be wholly accurate and it has never failed to accurately predict the outcome in the ten years since we perfected the method.

Dress rehearsal went well with hardly a sleeper in the crowd. The performance went well too, as Stu and I promised it would. Stu's wife and Edith agreed with us. The next day, everyone was talking about the 'asparagus song.'

At the diner the next morning, "The Asparagus Is in Bloom' production number replaced baseball as the featured topic. I was pleasantly surprised the 'asparagus song' would capture the imagination in an agricultural community where no farmers raise produce. Still, they were smitten with the song. Clovis' father vowed to investigate the feasibility of raising the crop; he was so moved by the musical. The fog effect was a big hit.

Asparagus is a vegetable that can be hard to prepare in a palatable way. Most people cook it into a green mush easily confused with overcooked pea soup or guacamole. It is a tender food which should be lightly peeled at the stalk, sprinkled with olive oil and salt, and nicely warmed in the oven. Overcooking is its death and the shame of many aspiring chefs.

I am aware of the professional performances your city attracts and I am sure the quality of performance is remarkable. In Blandtrap, though, we raise our own talent and, most years, enjoy the finest entertainment this village can muster produced by the best coerced direction we can find. You should be envious. We are proud.

Respectfully Submitted,

Harry Ellis

May

Plagiarized from the tablet of Calvin Farnsworth:

If you were to discover the brain of a brilliant scientist lost in the shaft of an old coal mine, wouldn't that be…

...an Einstein fine mind mine find?

Harry Ellis

238 Persimmon Street

Blandtrap

To the Editor of the Tiskilwa Bureau Valley Chief

RE: Fishing With Brimstone

Dear Sir:

The weather is beginning to warm and that means fish will begin to bite. I love to fish and have neglected the hobby for far too long. Letting the cares of the world weigh me down, I haven't been out with my rod and reel in a couple of years. It's high time I resumed the peaceful recreation and soothed my frayed nerves.

I gave it a good going over and after thumbing through your pages I saw no mention of fishing. There is no report regarding where the fish are biting or what kind of fish appear to be active right now. Nothing was found on your sports page. Not even a note was included in your community affairs column. The only reference to fish I could find had nothing to do with sport. It seems they are serving fish sticks and tater-tots at the elementary school on Friday. Informative, but not the tip I was hoping for.

Spending some time in the garage and basement last night, I discovered it has been far too long since I last fished. Accoutrements of the sport were scattered throughout the house from attic to cellar and from carport to guest bath. There was no rhyme or reason to what was found where. I believe this demonstrates a rare law of physics.

Calvin Farnsworth of the Institute for Idle Sciences joined me for coffee recently. It is his tendency to lecture rather than chat. As I recall his dissertation that morning was on the discipline of chemistry, or something like it. Somewhere between the time my mind first wandered to the idea of trading in my car, and the point where my eyes rolled back into my head, he talked about diffusion. It was his contention that things, he probably meant chemicals, moved from higher concentration to lower concentration all by themselves; that they were incapable of moving from lower to higher concentration without an outside force acting on them.

Stu, sitting in with us as he often does, expressed his skepticism, contending the law lost validity with practical application. Holidays, in his mind, were the greatest obstacle to proving the theory. On holidays, Stu's story went, in-laws moved in droves from their own houses, where they were thick as flies on possum road kill, to his house where he labored daily to keep it as in-law free as humanly possible. Certainly this phenomenon put a dent in the theory, because no visible outside force was acting upon the in-laws to draw them into his domain.

Clovis' father came to the defense of the scientist. "I can think of a very good outside force drawing in-laws to your home. You're forgetting about the dusty piles of cash you have stashed in your wallet, hidden under your mattress and probably buried in your back yard. Cash motivates everyone but it works best on in-laws."

Calvin butted into our discussion and tried to pour water on our fire. He said we were all wrong and had taken the idea in a direction it was never intended to go. Scientists are like that. It must be a disease of some kind. As soon as you uncover a useful application for one of their mind-numbingly, boring principals and start to have some fun with it, they drag you back to books and chalkboards, test tubes and fume hoods or beakers on Bunsen burners; killjoys all of them. Over his strongest objections and through his most detailed argument against it, I believe diffusion was responsible for scattering my fishing gear.

Let me explain the forces I see at work: When such things are stored, they disassemble themselves into their individual pieces before they find themselves hiding places. As an example, I found my rod in the garage, the reel in the basement, and line in my sock drawer. I had an idea where the line was located as I had come across it looking for a hammer not too long ago. I don't normally have to dig through my sock drawer on a regular basis because Edith keeps up with the laundry. I have a dozen pairs of socks but I only ever wear one of the top two pairs. Dirty socks get washed and returned to the drawer before I get deeper into the inventory. Until I observed this circle of life for socks I was amazed that all the socks in the drawer looked new, except, that is, for the top two raggedy pairs, the ones I wore regularly. These saw duty every other day while the others rested comfortably. Once a pair of socks worked its way into the 'top two' position, their fate was known. It's no small wonder they take the opportunity presented by the laundry to make their escape. I believe they help one another. If one of the pair finds freedom elsewhere, the remaining sock also finds retirement. Perhaps one creates a diversion while the other makes a run for it. This could be more fodder for one of Farnsworth's follies.

The rod had been jammed behind a sled and a post-hole digger on the back wall of the garage. The sled had provided me years of recreation in younger days but at my present age, its services were no longer required. While I hadn't fished in years, it had been decades since the sled saw action. Perhaps it was out of jealousy that it pressed against my fishing rod, creating what I feared was a permanent curve to its form. I hoped it didn't do its damage out of a sense of revenge. Gentle efforts to unbend the rod did not yield the desired results. Sudden and more severe measures ended its useful life as a fishing tool.

A fishing reel is a remarkable device, the penultimate achievement of engineering. Those elite who have mastered this discipline boast of providing sanitation to the problem of waste in cities, channeling clean water to the thirsty and desperate, and creating computers capable of thinking millions of times faster than the human brain. These are useful and clever applications of science, but a fishing reel is true genius.

The basement probably wasn't the best place to store a mechanical device with metal moving parts. Moisture and humidity tend to be higher in lower regions of the house much like Aunt Sadie who is only allowed to sit on vinyl kitchen chairs and is unwelcome on the sofa.

Oxidation had done its work on this reel causing the moving parts to seize up and refuse to perform their duty. Oil, WD-40, and a light hammer didn't free the parts designed to move and created new parts that probably shouldn't have moved. Its replacement would be necessary if I was to fish again.

Line found at the bottom of the sock drawer was very old. I could remember examining it the last time I was looking for fishing line and passing it over in favor of something its junior. By the look of the label and the quality of the product I imagine I had passed it over more than once. Frugality being the virtue it is, I gave the old line a chance testing to see if it could still do the job. Unwinding the line from the roll was easy enough. It hadn't melted together or bonded in some other way like it does if you store it in the back window of the car. When I released it, the line curled up into the position it was in on the roll. Perhaps all those years in the sock drawer had made it agoraphobic, causing it to return to the fetal position when it met the real world.

I began to think of new and unique applications for curly fish line. If I used a heavy sinker, the line would be straightened out as I cast. The power to recoil would be stored in the line. If the line had sufficient strength, recoil would reel in the line on its own. I wouldn't have to spin the reel at all. A rush of invention came over me and I began to see other advantages. After the lines were cast could the energy of the recoil be used to generate electricity? Imagine; an entire city powered by nothing but retired guys with time on their hands, once again performing useful services to society while remaining out of their wives' hair for hours every day. Excuse me, I don't want to get sidetracked, I'll move on.

Shopping is not an adventure enjoyed by many men and I am no exception to the rule. That's why men are such shrewd negotiators when buying a new car. Once we find a vehicle that will do the job we immediately enter into negotiations for its purchase. There may be better transportation at another dealer nearby or maybe even on that lot. It doesn't matter. In the time wasted wandering from newspaper ad to dealership we know we could make the buy and be home cleaning the glass and scraping the new car sticker off of the window.

Fishing gear is a more personal purchase than an auto. If I buy an ugly car people will point and snicker. They're likely to do that anyway. Tragedy comes when ineffective, unappealing fishing gear is bought. Fish won't bite and I would become the butt of jokes forever, eternally used as a poor example every time one was needed. I can hear it now. "He's got about as much chance of finishing a marathon as Harry has catching a trout "or," That candidate garnered as many votes as Harry's caught bluegill." Chuckles and guffaws would follow as all looked my way and elbowed one another. Such a risk couldn't be taken; I'm not that much of a gambler.

I headed for Hugginbough Hardware and Lumber to replace worn or injured components of my gear. Pleasant weather made the walk enjoyable. Passing Maybelle Oufsbacher en route I stopped her and quizzed her regarding the health of Clovis. If she was carrying a rumor that would kill off Clovis soon I wanted to put it to rest early so it wouldn't interfere with fishing. Exacting a promise from her that her report would be that Clovis was well and it would remain that way for the foreseeable future, I proceeded to my destination.

Most aisles in the hardware store are familiar to me. The section of shelves dedicated to sporting goods is not among them.

It was an eclectic mix of sport and hobby, depending on how you viewed the activity. The baseball area had three baseballs, a softball, a first base mitt but no fielder's gloves nor catcher's mitt, and two bats: one twenty-six inches in length and the other thirty-four. That was the long and short of it, I guess.

There was a set of horseshoes and one metal stake. I wondered when anyone would need only one horseshoe stake. Even if you were playing horseshoes solitaire or just practicing, a second stake, although not absolutely necessary, would be darned handy. I question whether the savings would be considered ample for the additional work required retrieving the shoes after each turn.

Like footwear, horseshoe stakes are sold in pairs. I was at a loss to provide another explanation for an odd number of horseshoes in Hugginbough's inventory. The idea that someone would shoplift one horseshoe stake was too remote for me to entertain. The most desperate thief wouldn't be that stupid.

Hugginbough still had two sets of Rolle Bolle balls. They've been there since shortly after Seth bought the place. He keeps them as a reminder of the importance of diplomacy in business. Many years ago a group of Lithuanians settled in a small area a few miles from Blandtrap, not in the direction of Butte Crossing but more on the way to Bradford. Lithuanians would frequent his establishment and, since they were building houses, garages, and barns, had become good patrons of his business.

After the International Rolle Bolle Tournament moved to the Big Bureau County Fair, interest in the sport blossomed. It was a pastime unfamiliar to locals and it looked funny to them. One day Seth and Clovis' father were joking about the lop-sided ball and how it hopped along during play when a prominent member of the Lithuanian community was shopping for drawer handles with his wife. Seth hadn't heard them come in or he would have been assisting them rather than telling jokes.

Overhearing his ridicule of a revered national pastime, they took offense to his comments and left abruptly. Seth saw them leaving and tried to smooth things over by waiting on them, but they left without a word. It took days before he learned it was his own comment that turned them against him. He vowed to make amends and win them back.

No amount of cajoling moved the offended immigrants. Efforts to discount prices fell on deaf ears. They would gladly pay more where they were respected and their traditions honored. Even free delivery failed to loosen their tongues, melt their hearts, or untie their purse strings. He had lost Lithuanian business forever. That wretched hardware and lumber dealer in Butte Crossing would benefit from their patronage.

One effort Hugginbough made to win back Lithuanian trust was to stock Rolle Bolle and Bocce Ball sets on his shelves and put them next to baseball equipment, giving them equal status, in his mind, with the American pastime. Lithuanians never came back so they didn't see the display. To some extent he still maintains it. While the Bocce Balls were sold, two dusty sets of Rolle Bolle Balls still grace hardware shelves.

Calvin Farnsworth bought the two Rolle Bolle sets for some experiment a few years ago. Not knowing they were lop-sided, he returned them as defective. The two sets of Rolle Bolle balls remind Seth to hold his tongue, and to respect traditions of others.

To my dismay they have changed the way they describe fishing line on the packaging. Discarding the familiar pictures and propaganda that suggested how the product could be used had been replaced with more technical terminology. I never had a grasp on the whole 'test line' designation mentioned on every package of fishing line. Technical definitions are the realm of Calvin Farnsworth and I have sought his advice before, but his explanations are so complete, they remove all mystery and intrigue from a topic leaving behind only science and the mathematics of a matter. I didn't want this to happen to fishing.

Experience and usage frequently provide definition from context. I had caught many one pound fish on ten-pound test line, as it was possible to catch fish smaller than the pound designation. That made sense to me. Never having caught large fish, I had to consult an expert in the matter. My brother-in-law is an accomplished fisherman, spending hours of time and tens of thousands of dollars on the sport. He also catches many large fish. I posed the question to him, "What's the largest fish you have caught on ten pound test line?" He leaned back in his chair, told a colorful story about a former mayor of Blandtrap, and answered, "About twenty-three pounds, I guess."

Fishermen are known to exaggerate, famous for the behavior, really. I believe it is a requirement to be welcomed into the brotherhood. Fishermen have described to me fish they have caught that are longer than the body of water they claimed to fish and significantly larger than the craft they fished from. An accomplished and well-lubricated fisherman can explain in minute detail how he caught a whale in a bathtub and provide witnesses to attest to the feat.

The most ardent in the brotherhood hold to high standards not recognized by rank and file members. Twenty-three pounds was a raw number, which needed to be interpreted; it has no relationship with reality until it is manipulated by reason. 'The better the fisherman, the less the exaggeration' is a general rule. Good fishermen don't need to stretch the truth as much as one that never gets a nibble. His lies are more like window dressing than deceit.

Poor fishermen are forced to lie if they are to be credited with catching any fish at all. The brotherhood of fishermen includes both good and bad anglers; and they observe few rules. While they are informal in nature, these rules are strictly enforced. If you can't catch fish you can't call yourself a fisherman.

Depending on your method of fishing they would bestow other titles upon you. If you fished from the beach, you could be a sunbather; if you fished while wading, you could be a swimmer; or if you fished from a boat, you could be a sailor. You could pretend to be an astronaut for all they care but you couldn't be called a fisherman if you couldn't catch fish.

All I could find at Hugginbough's store was a rod. Seth agreed his selection of fishing gear was limited and said he used to sell more, especially to kids during the summer. "They don't buy fishing gear like they used to," he lamented. I noticed that he didn't bother selling bait anymore either. The only suggestion he had was to try the foreigner who had that little shop behind Tilly's shack by the boat launch.

To describe a man in Blandtrap as a foreigner was faint detail. We were awash in foreigners. He might as well have told me to see the man with a nose. I took my rod and wandered toward Tilly's shack with brief stopovers at the post office and the bakery. I took coffee and a donut with me. They are the universally accepted symbols of greeting and welcome. I hoped it would break the ice with the foreign fellow.

Behind Tilly's shack was a small building, a one car garage is what it was and it didn't appear it was a business. No signage of any kind graced the structure. I knocked on the door unaware of what would happen from there, bracing myself for any and all possibilities.

Some of what Seth had told me was true, but not in the way he intended it. The proprietor of the establishment showed me his inventory and I was interested. One thing was clear to me; if we were to negotiate or communicate in any meaningful way, I would have to find an interpreter. The man knew a little English but not enough for us to connect.

Jose Wong was familiar with many African languages and Mrs. Tilly could navigate many European tongues but neither was available just then. I thought I had heard the dialect before so I went in search of an expert in the field. Returning in an hour with Maybelle Oufsbacher and Mrs. Wing in tow, the women were of great help to me, particularly Mrs. Wing; I began to communicate with the man. After listening to the proprietor for a few minutes,

Mrs. Wing ran to the phone and called her sister-in-law from southern Tennessee. She was sure the accent was from a county in the northern end of the Volunteer State. You can rely on the experience of old ladies. Mrs. Wing was right on the mark. When her sister-in-law made it to the little shop, we struck a deal in no time and I acquired not only a reel but also line I believed to be adequate for any task I may ask of it.

Essential equipment was in place, freeing my mind to consider the finer points of fishing. Opening my tackle box I began my inspection of its contents. On top were rubber worms that were once all the rage. They came in a variety of colors and could be found without hooks or with up to three hooks already in place. I had at least one of each. A couple of spinners filled compartments in the top tray with an assortment of hooks nearby. I would think that something intended to be in and out of water would resist rust. Years of neglect in a damp basement had ravaged the tackle.

Raising the top tray revealed a lower tray and the bottom of the tackle box. The second tray was a little deeper than the top tray and held bobbers, weights, swivels, things like that. It also held a few plugs I had been talked into buying. They were supposed to look like bait, you know, small fish or frogs and such. Manufacturers must believe fish are either blind or stupid because these plugs don't resemble God's creatures in any way. I cast the lure thinking I am enticing fish to bite, but in reality I fear the fish giggle as I repeatedly send these silly things their way. Never having caught a fish using them is evidence of their futility.

The bottom compartment housed heavy hardware. The needle-nosed pliers would be used to remove hooks from the inside of fish's mouths were I to actually catch one. A brand new fifteen-year-old stringer was also on the bottom, still wrapped in its original twist-tie. Other incidental items were found down there, like a scale to weigh my catches, a scaler and a filet knife, and a retractable tape measure to ensure the fish I don't catch are big enough to keep. After all, I wouldn't want to run afoul of fishing regulations.

Everyone has to be a critic, including my friends. I recall fishing with Stu many years back. We were in a new boat on Big Bureau Creek. I was providing entertainment for Stu as I made my many attempts to maneuver the craft into a small inlet when the game warden appeared on shore and asked us to produce our fishing licenses. Stu had his in his pocket and produced it immediately. It wasn't that easy for me. I was wearing a pair of jeans with four pockets, a two-pocket shirt and a light jacket with four pockets. Clothing serves as a filing cabinet for me: the left front pocket is for banking receipts; the right front pocket is for keys and change; the right rear pocket is for shopping lists and coupons; and the left rear pocket is for my wallet.

While I sorted though the papers in my shirt pockets Stu questioned the warden and said I shouldn't have to purchase a fishing license since I had never caught a fish in my life. He contended I sat with the fish more as a companion or custodian than a predator. The warden acknowledged the merit of his argument and told Stu if I couldn't produce a fishing license he would be willing to accept a valid day care license and would consider the fish my charges.

Shirt paperwork didn't reveal a license. The pockets of my jacket, which I wear only rarely, held nothing current. The search was more like an archeological dig than anything else. I had no idea the jacket was so old. It was trendy by my standards. I put some items aside for Edith to put in a scrapbook and others I thought would interest the Smithsonian I returned to the filing pocket.

Stu and the game warden were chuckling pretty well by this time. Despite the fact I had not been listening, I knew I was the butt of the jokes. My search for the fishing license was annoying. I remember buying the license at the hardware store, and I was sure I had it with me. It was unlike me to overlook a detail like that. The warden said he had to be on his way and could he please see my license. When I apologized and said I couldn't find it he told me to look in my tackle box. Lifting the lid I saw the fishing license grinning back at me as if it had chosen the perfect spot in a game of hide and seek and thus had won. It was another in a long list of bad maneuvers.

I formulated a plan in my mind. Fishing alone was never for me. Consistent failure to land fish made it boring to do solo. Having honestly earned my reputation for a lack of fishing prowess, organizing an adventure with me as the lead would yield few participants.

The trip up the creek would be easier than in the old days. Rowing is a labor-intensive mode of transportation, slow and painful under ideal conditions. When in water that is fast moving it requires experience to maneuver a small craft where you want it to go. Boat motors are more readily available and reasonably priced now than ever before. A small motor on the boat could make the difference between agony and comfort.

My hope was to horn my way into some group with a fishing trip already planned. I kept my ears peeled for more than a week waiting to hear mere mention of fishing. Unfortunately, like the pages of your newspaper, the topic never arose.

As usual, luck was not my companion. No one in the village was currently a fishing enthusiast. I would have to generate interest on my own, unable to piggyback on the adventure of others. I would have to convince others that they should organize a fishing trip that included me. Plowboy Diner would be the best place in Blandtrap to search for fishermen. The next morning I set about my scheme.

Attendance around the large table at the diner was below average. Only Clovis' father preceded me. Unsolicited advice comes by the truckload but legitimate help for an ongoing problem must be dug out like diamonds from a remote mountain. Neither have much value until they are mined, cut, and polished.

I asked Clovis' father for advice regarding whom I should invite to accompany me. It peaked his interest. He said he hadn't been fishing in years and, now that he thought about it, he missed the relaxation the sport provided him. If I was planning a fishing venture, he wanted to be included. How could I turn him down? I had a partner in crime.

We put our heads together and pooled our resources discovering we had gained nothing in the brain department by pairing up. Each of us had our own gear or was going to acquire it soon. Neither of us had a boat or a motor. Unless we were willing to wade or sit on the shore, our recruitment efforts should be focused on those with the missing mode of transportation.

Our memories aren't what we remembered they were. The names of living boat owners didn't immediately spring to mind. We only entertained the idea of asking for widow's boats for a moment, fearing we would be snared into unwanted conversation, trapped in painful reminiscence of the deceased or subjected to a high-pressure sales presentation to purchase the no longer useful watercraft.

Both of us fell into the "softy" category, unable to resist plausible requests from widows. We made a solemn vow to each other not to solicit widows directly nor send word that the other might be interested in their boat. Agreeing to meet the next morning with a list of gullible boat owners to exploit for our recreational pleasure, we returned to our homes. I felt it unwise at this juncture to seek advice from Edith. Exploiting weaknesses in friends and family wasn't her strong suit.

Breakfast reunited Clovis' father and I. My list had two names on it, his had three. I was reticent to call mine, both of them relatives. Borrowing from relatives never ends well. Whatever is borrowed will suffer real or perceived damage, or will fail in some way that will ruin the experience resulting in accusations of blame flying in all directions. I avoid the practice at all costs.

Stu was at the table when Clovis' father and I sat down. He had been talking to Simian Swagg. Ed's Polka Band and Hip-Hop Review was adding a few songs to their charts and Simian was seeking Stu's advice. I can't imagine what value Stu's opinion of hip-hop would be since he listens exclusively to big band music.

I was able to speak openly with Clovis' father without being overheard until Seth arrived. He was excited about my recent interest in fishing equipment at his store. He'd had two inquiries for fishing equipment in two days. He was thinking of expanding his display if demand increased. Clovis' father and I recognized that we were the two inquiries Seth mentioned. We felt that Seth was misled by our recent interest in tackle.

Putting our heads together again and combining our lists gave us the greatest opportunity for success. Separately our minds kept wandering. Clovis' father brought a map, and he indicated the best fishing holes with a red marker. The map also noted what kind of fish was caught where. His information came from fishermen he knew. He had been up way past ten o'clock badgering these fellows to give up their favorite fishing sites. It was clear he had worked hard on the map but I questioned its validity. Few fishermen would give up their information without a struggle. Sleep deprivation alone wouldn't be enough to loosen their tongues. It was more likely they lied.

Consumed with our plotting and planning we didn't notice what was happening around us. The number of men at the table had swelled to about eight, in total, before a sudden exodus. We looked up from our precious documents to see we were alone. Men were pulling on jackets as they speed-walked to the door. We didn't have time to ask each other what caused everyone to leave when large hands were placed on our shoulders and a voice boomed from the specter behind us, "Are you boys planning a fishing trip?"

It was Reverend Brimstone, the scourge of Plow Boy Diner. He only showed up when he was stuck for a sermon topic. Not afraid to name names during a sermon, his presence caused any crowd of decent size to scatter when they saw him coming. The owners of Plow Boy Diner talked with him on several occasions begging him not to come in during peak times because they couldn't afford the loss of business. Brimstone didn't listen to them, claiming he was doing the Lord's work. They were members of the Lutheran church, anyway.

Not getting a response from his first inquiry and accustomed to having to talk to himself in similar situations, he pressed on. "Looks like you boys are planning to fish a little," said Brimstone with that large voice that loosened ceiling tile. "I haven't been fishing since I was a boy. It's a noble pastime, scriptural, you know. Peter was a fisherman." He sat down with us. "I must have delivered a thousand sermons about or concerning fishing yet I haven't gone recently. I believe it high time I remedied the problem. When are we going?"

I thought it was rude of him to butt his way into our trip without benefit of invitation. Clovis' father kept clammed up. He and Clovis had been the topic of far too many sermons to speak freely when Brimstone was around. I, as all the men in the congregation, had also endured the same unsavory fate. Here he was, though, and we would have to deal with him.

"We haven't picked a day yet. We're working out some of the details right now, but I'm not sure you would want to fish with the likes of us. We don't have a reputation as good fishermen." I tried to distract him, make him think he would be better off fishing with others.

"Nonsense!" Brimstone boomed to background music of the plate glass window rattling. "You boys will do fine. You may not have a reputation now, but with luck, you will when you return. What have you got for a boat?"

"We don't have one," Clovis' father decided to contribute to the conversation. He hoped our lack of preparation would dampen Brimstone's interest in our expedition. "We were trying to figure out where we could get one but we're running out of ideas."

"That's a simple matter. We'll find someone with a boat and I'll tell them the Lord needs it." He said it in a very matter-of-fact way. I was taken aback by the comment. It seemed to be stretching the truth more than a little bit in my opinion and it didn't seem to bother his conscience in any way.

"Wouldn't that be misleading the victim, I mean donor, of the boat?" Under normal circumstances I wouldn't dare challenge Brimstone on a matter of integrity but it seemed he was out on a moral ledge here. I hoped to talk him down before he jumped.

"Poppycock!" was his answer. I couldn't remember when I had last heard someone use that word. Sure, you hear it in old movies but it doesn't come up in the normal course of conversation much anymore. "The Bible is full of examples where stretching the truth or even outright deception is praised: Jacob got Isaac's blessing over Esau by deceit; Joseph lied to his brothers about his identity; and Rahab lied to the citizens of Jericho which lead to its complete destruction. It's done all the time in the service of God.

I remained skeptical and was beginning to question whether this 'service to God' business was truly all it was cracked up to be. It seemed mighty convenient to say everyone else ought to tell the truth all the time, but lies are OK if he can get what he wants. I thought I should pursue this line of reasoning with Brimstone. He was wrong and I knew it. Letting something like that slide wasn't part of my nature, but two obstacles prevented me from convincing him he was wrong. First, I didn't have my reference Bible with me to help me find scripture key to my argument, and second, his tactics, wrong as they were, had an excellent probability of getting us the boat we needed. I let it go.

Bob Townsend walked through the door of the diner. He was among a handful of parishioners who didn't run when they saw Brimstone on a week day. Having been the object lesson for innumerable sermons, he was unafraid of pastoral embarrassment. Lauretta, Bob's wife, wasn't moved by the opinions of others either. Immune to Brimstone's tirades, he slept through the few sermons he managed to attend.

"Bob Townsend, my fine fellow," Brimstone addressed him. "Come join us and let me buy you a cup of coffee. How long has it been since we sat and chatted?" I swear he would have hugged Satan himself if he thought he could wangle a boat in the process. I felt uncomfortable in company that behaved this way and was weary of standing too close to the man should God decide to smite him where he stood.

"Probably the last time Lauretta and I had some serious trouble or the church needed some fast cash. Don't you remember? You told me I should spend more time at home and cut out the drinking; same as always." To our amazement Bob sat down with us, genuinely engaged in conversation with Brimstone. I had always been surprised when reading the Bible how casual the conversation appeared between Jesus and Lucifer during the temptation. Perhaps Brimstone and Townsend were having a moment like that. It didn't seem natural to me.

"I seem to remember you have a boat. As I recall, the boat belonged to Lauretta's brother." Brimstone got down to business. Bob wasn't a man you danced with, it was better to get your cards on the table right away.

"I have to write a check every month to store the (word deleted for decorum) thing." Townsend was truly touchy about it. It amazed me that Bob felt comfortable swearing in front of the preacher.

Several questions remained unanswered regarding periods of Brimstone's past and one of them was why foul language didn't offend him unless women or children were present. He didn't talk that way himself, but it didn't rattle his cage if other men did in his presence. "We'd like to borrow the boat to do some fishing. Is it available?" Finally getting to the point, Brimstone popped the question. "We'll be gentle with it as we can be."

"You can borrow it or you can have it. It's parked in a storage shed at the edge of the village, behind door 6A. It's not locked. I keep hoping someone will steal it. The hull hasn't seen water for about a decade but it was in good shape then. The motor doesn't work so you will have to get another one. All I ask is if something happens to the boat, you don't tell me about it. I'll notice the stall is empty and stop renting it soon enough." Townsend covered all his bases.

"Done," Brimstone struck the deal. "And we all thank you. With that Townsend finished his cup of coffee and set about his day.

After Bob had left, Brimstone took stock. "All we need is a motor and we're all set."

I had to excuse myself. Watching Brimstone work was like watching sausage being made. I had to stop looking if I was ever to enjoy fishing or church again. By the time I got home, Brimstone had left a message with Edith that he found a motor and we should meet at the diner at 4:30 AM, gear in hand. I questioned whether he relied on coercion or took a more honest approach and used a handgun to get the motor.

As the sun rose the next morning, so did my anxiety. Brimstone might have been a man of God but he was no prophet or he would have seen the handwriting on the wall. Three old men who hadn't been fishing in recent memory were going out in a boat that hadn't floated in a decade with a motor of questionable origin. I had no idea how this would turn out but I thought there was an even chance the story would end up on the front page of your paper, provided they could locate our bodies before you went to press.

Carrying my gear, bait, and lunch; I walked to the Plow Boy Diner beating Clovis' father by a few minutes. First to arrive, I started the coffee pot and waited for employees to show up. After the elder Beagle made his appearance, we both had a cup down the hatch by the time Brimstone arrived. Our provisions were piled outside the diner door. As Brimstone pulled up in front of the diner we piled into the parish's station wagon and headed for the storage shed. After hitching the trailer to the wagon and attaching the light cable we headed for the highway.

The trailer provided more resistance than Brimstone thought was right. He pulled over and a quick inspection revealed a flat tire on the driver's side of the boat trailer. There was no jack for the trailer but after unloading the station wagon we were able to modify the car jack to lift the trailer. The spare went on slick as a whistle and we repacked the wagon. Pulling ahead, Brimstone told us that although the symptom had improved he believed we still had the disease. Indeed the passenger side tire on the trailer was also flat. It was just our luck, there had been only one spare.

Disconnecting the trailer, drove back to the Plow Boy Diner, and coerced Seth into opening the hardware store early and selling us a similar although not identical tire. This was where Clovis' father shined. He was always modifying new parts to fit old tractors on the farm. A handful of odd-sized washers and nuts guaranteed success.

The sun had been up for awhile before we got the boat and trailer on the road. Clovis' father and I watched as Brimstone turned in the direction of Blandtrap rather than big Bureau Creek. The two of us were past the point where we questioned what he was doing, we were simply holding on for the ride. Eventually, he looked over to see our bewildered faces and solved one mystery for us. "The motor," was all he said.

I was chagrined to see him turn down Paw Paw Street, or Dead Ed End as many referred to it. He came to a stop in front of Maybelle Oufsbacher's house of all places. He hopped out of the car and headed toward the door. "I'll just be a minute," he said back to us. We knew better. Even if he were measuring time in dog years he would not be correct. Maybelle's reputation as a chatterbox had been hard-earned and was well deserved.

Clovis' father and I chatted for awhile, ate our lunches, and then napped. Brimstone woke us and we grabbed the motor from the garage. The ancient motor was of odd vintage and didn't easily secure to the boat. Clovis' father stepped in once more and went to work solving our dilemma. Four shims, two furniture C-clamps, a wire hanger, and duct tape made a pretty job of it with only one trip to the hardware store.

Brimstone tried to get the trailer turned around on the cul-de-sac but it had been quite some time since he backed a trailer. Clovis' father had to take the wheel to get us out of there. Brimstone resumed driving duties to discover he was low on fuel. We had to drive out to the county road to get gas. Once more Brimstone's inexperience with towing a trailer got us into a jamb. His corrections made things worse. We had to disconnect the trailer from the wagon to untangle the mess. For a man who can look at a collection plate and estimate contributions to within ten dollars, he was surprisingly weak in math skills. I, after torturous long division out loud with hand gestures to "borrow" from one column or another, volunteered to pay the whole bill rather than split the tab.

We hadn't gotten up to road speed yet when flashing lights reflected from our rearview mirror. The officer motioned for us to pull over and we met him at the boat trailer. The trailer wasn't displaying a license plate. The three of us rummaged the boat and found one in storage under the seat. We presented it to the officer and he was impressed with our exhibit. He said except for antique vehicles, he hadn't seen a license plate this old, but even those vehicles needed valid registration. I suggested to the officer that perhaps the trailer predated vehicle registration laws and was grandfathered into the system exempting it from current legislation. He said no but took the time to write down what I said so he could share it with his peers. He suggested I might be in line for an award or some other recognition for my creative evasiveness. I fondly await the ruling of the judges.

Brimstone went on the offensive. He explained to the policeman how he was a preacher and we were parishioners; how the boat and motor were borrowed; how much trouble we had and expense had been incurred in our pursuit of much-needed recreation. Without drawing a breath, he launched into scripture to justify our situation. Halfway through Genesis the officer cut him off by handing him a citation saying, "It doesn't sound like this ticket will amount to much compared to your other expenses today! Have a nice day!" He headed back to his cruiser with that all-knowing smirk you only get form the police after you've done something stupid.

Brimstone shouted after the officer. "How much is this ticket worth?"

Turning around the officer told him. "It's not worth anything, sir. I think you'll find it's going to cost you about seventy-five dollars, though." He still wore that grin.

"How are we gonna get around with this trailer, now?" Brimstone pleaded.

Putting his foot inside the police car we heard him say, "If you get stopped again today just show them your ticket and tell them you're returning the trailer. It won't work tomorrow but it should do for today. Good day, gentlemen." Tipping his hat, he returned to his hiding spot behind the billboard where he lurked to catch speeders.

Not to be denied his angling pleasure, Brimstone forged ahead. Well past noon, we caught our first glimpse of water. Clovis' father exercised the authority that comes with being senior member of our expedition and backed the boat down the ramp to launch the craft. All aboard ship, Brimstone tried to start the motor. It refused to turn over.

"Is the battery dead?" Clovis' father inquired of Brimstone.

It's just like a preacher to answer a question with a question. "It needs a battery?" he asked.

We had drifted a few feet from the dock while we had been toying with the motor. Not wanting to get wet, we searched the craft for a paddle or a rope. All we found was an anchor. Brimstone thought he could toss the anchor and snag the dock to pull us back in close. I was impressed with Brimstone's toss. It was higher than I would have chosen, but the direction was dead on. In flight, the anchor managed to free itself from the rope and was completely separate when it crashed through the deck of the dock. I pressed myself into service by climbing into the water and pulling the boat back to the dock.

Brimstone made me ride in the back of his station wagon so I wouldn't get the seats wet. I got some funny looks as we passed Village Square on our way to buy a battery at Hugginbough Hardware. A brief chat with Seth sent Brimstone and Clovis' father back to see what electrical demands the motor had. I stayed at the hardware store to dry out. The strategy worked well enough that they let me ride in the seat back to the dock.

Our ordeal began to chip away at Brimstone's stance on temperance. When I said I wished I had a bottle of champagne to christen the voyage, he confessed he probably wouldn't waste the bottle breaking it against the hull of the boat. He thought it might have a higher calling, so to speak.

The motor barked right off and we headed up creek as the sun was beginning to set. "Let's hurry. We don't have much time left. Open the throttle and get this thing moving," Brimstone demanded. The old motor was wound-out to its limit, but we were making scant progress against the current. Our destination wasn't more than four miles upstream but it was going to take more than an hour to get there at that speed. We would have to get more out of the motor.

"All stop!" was the command we heard from a megaphone. It was game wardens. They quickly navigated their nimble craft alongside our cumbersome boat. We peered with envy at the powerful and quiet motor powering the officials' boat. Ours was so loud we could hardly hear one another.

"We've all got fishing licenses," Brimstone anticipated the officers' questions. "Hold up your licenses so they can see them." He was ordering us around but we didn't mind. Both of us complied with his command.

"I'm more interested in registration on the boat. Do you have the papers?" the official was direct and to the point. His request initiated another boat-wide search. We looked in every storage bin and crevice, under every feature that had an under, and between and among seat cushions. The official occupied the half hour we wasted searching in vain for registration papers by writing in his little book. In the end, we gave up and confessed we had none.

"I knew you wouldn't find them," he seemed to be pleased with himself as if this provided him some kind of entertainment, "because we don't number boats the same way as we did when this boat was last registered." Handing Brimstone the ticket, he added, "You'll have to follow me back to the dock."

"The traffic ticket I got earlier allowed me to drive the rest of the day. Does that ticket work here or does this ticket work in the same way as the other?" Brimstone was determined to continue regardless of trouble he was having keeping track of the crimes he had committed that day.

"Normally I would agree to that, but it's almost dark now and the lights on your boat don't work so you'll have to follow me to the dock. Let's get to it, gentlemen." It wasn't a request. He wanted us to go and go now.

The motor began to sputter as we turned around to follow the warden. It shook the craft for a while before it seized up entirely, and, I fear, forever. We were dead in the water as the sun set. Brimstone walked to the front of the boat to hail the officer. He was met with a line tossed in his face. "Tie it on." was the command.

I had to get back in the water to push the boat onto the trailer until the winch could pull it into place. We retraced our steps from earlier in the day. Returning the motor to Maybelle Oufsbacher was as painful as the pickup and as time consuming as well. We parked the trailer back in the storage shed and made our way back into town where they dropped me off at home. Clovis' father had his truck parked on Village Square. My home and shower were a welcome sight after a day in soggy clothes and squishy boots.

Before I retire for the evening I want to apologize for my lack of assistance in this matter. My efforts to garner information regarding fishing conditions in Big Bureau Creek were extensive and intricate. I labored from well before sunup until nearly midnight, never getting a fishing line wet or wounding a worm. It is not my nature to give up on a task because it is too hard, yet I must be honest with myself here. This fishing business is beyond my ability to gather meaningful information. You should look elsewhere for someone more capable to perform this task.

Respectfully Submitted,

Harry Ellis

Harry Ellis

238 Persimmon Street

Blandtrap

To the Editor of the Tiskilwa Bureau Valley Chief

RE: Mother's Day

Dear Sir:

I read advertisements in the present issue of your paper for flowers, chocolates, cards, and garden plants and supplies. Since Valentine's Day has past, it can only mean Mother's Day is near. Valentine's Day sells product because of hope. Hope for sparking an interest, hope for fanning a spark into flame, or hope for keeping the flames burning. Hope is a powerful motivator for men.

The motivation for Mother's Day is gratitude. Thankful for all the sacrifices mothers have made for their children wells up on this day and overflows into displays of love and recognition for their loving devotion to duty. To a person, mothers deny it is duty or could even be called work at all. They profess it is undying and unconditional love.

Although the motive may be gratitude, the driving force often is guilt. Mothers wield the sword of guilt with the same skill and with the same hand as they apply the salve of nurture. Capable of both at the same time, it creates a situation where it is easier to go peacefully than to struggle against a force you, in the end, are unwilling to resist.

227

A gift is mandatory. The value of the gift will not be weighed in dollars and cents nor will it be measured by liberal social or historic standards. Nothing remotely similar to this will occur. It will be examined for the amount of thought the gift required. Extra credit may be earned for originality, spontaneity, and cleverness but the underlying thought required to conceive of the gift and to bring it to fruition will be the primary measuring stick. Pain or sacrifice required to obtain the gift also counts in the giver's favor.

A good mother's absence is an emptiness felt so deep in the breast it is difficult to express with words. The wedding of our daughter was such an occasion. I needed desperately for a year before the event to speak to my mother, seek her guidance, and include her desires in the ceremony. Instead of the comfort of her voice and wisdom, I was, and still am left with memories and longing. There is nothing suitable to fill the empty pit, not pride in my daughter or the full satisfaction in her choice for a husband. I still love the lady dearly and miss her so.

My sister, in many respects, is a reflection of my mother. In some ways her life was more difficult than my mother's. It was certainly challenging in different ways. Her husband left her while her daughter was still very young and he moved to the city where he lived an unorthodox life style and openly engaged in what some would call questionable activities. He provided very little support, moral or financial, to my sister and niece.

Mother and father helped as much as they could but the kind of help a young mother raising a child needs most cannot be provided by even the most loving and well-meaning parents. It is beyond the scope of parenthood. Mother and child are often left alone to manage as best they can.

Their life resembles the high wire performer in the circus. Although a net may catch them if they fall, it does not erase the failure. It is better not to fall to certain death. A greater truth is that when death is avoided, more frequent failure often lies ahead.

When mother couldn't help, she could encourage. Her faith and her persistence in it gave her a perspective of promise for the future. If by no other way she could uplift with music. The entire family is musically inclined. I hesitate to say musically talented because opinions on the topic vary, yet I believe that is the case. All of us could read music and sing.

If the day was dark enough and tragedy seemed all around and closing in, she would bring out the big gun. Mother would yank out the piano bench and loosen her fingers. Having memorized many notes in the first twenty-one measures of "Moonlight Bay," she would butcher her way through the song until, some testified, the composer could be heard crying in his grave. When the task bettered her, she would frequently start back at the beginning of the piece thinking momentum might push her past memory lapses. The tactic was not successful but provided comedic relief from the tension. Tears of sorrow and frustration would turn to tears of laughter. Mother was something of a genius in this respect. She uplifted and encouraged and was loved for it.

About the same time trouble was haunting my sister, a young lady my mother worked with suffered catastrophe. Both of Tina's parents were killed in a traffic accident. Mother stepped in as a friend to her. It probably would have been easier for her to try to be a mother, but Tina needed a friend; she had lost her mother.

Tina's parents instilled good values during her upbringing which still serve her well today. Mother could, at an opportune moment, remind Tina of what she already knew, and reassure her that what her parents and God had taught her would, though painful now, serve her well throughout the rest of her life. It was a close relationship to which I was not privy.

Tina was a good friend to my mother as well. She provided youthful vitality to Mother when she learned of my father's cancer. News like that drags people down to depths they didn't know existed. When we are diagnosed with a disease that means death will greet us soon or sooner, we can become paralyzed.

Encouragement mother gave Tina was returned to her in the form of companionship and compassion. I was grateful to Tina then, and few days pass without thinking of her and her friendship to Mother. She was a better friend to her than I ever was a son. I must take the time to thank her some day. She is among the greatest people I have met and it has been a privilege to have known her. It will be a privilege to tell her.

I have so many memories of Mother it is difficult to express them without feeling a rush of nostalgia. It overcomes me. If I babble this week, please chalk it up to unbridled emotion. It is hard to keep my mind focused on one occurrence at a time.

Mother had a streak of larceny in her. Her birthday was June 14th which is the national holiday known as Flag Day. In our youth, the day was well recognized and most people in our neighborhood flew a flag from the porch of their residence. One year when she was young, my sister asked Mother why everyone was flying flags and she told my sister it was because it was her birthday. It was indeed my mother's birthday, so there was no reason to doubt her answer. My sister accepted it as fact.

The piece of trivia stuck in my sister's mind and lay there many years like a pimple just under the skin waiting for the most opportune moment to erupt. In a high school civics class they were discussing minor holidays throughout the year and the teacher brought up June 14th. The teacher asked "Does anyone know why they fly flags on this day?" My brave sister's hand shot into the air and she was selected to respond to the question because she seemed so confident. Allowing dramatic pause before she answered, "They fly flags today because it is my mother's birthday. They do it every year!" was her unfortunate response. Peals of laughter and a little ripple of applause told her she must be in error. Such were the lengths my mother was willing to travel to practice her own brand of chicanery.

Service to community was one of Mother's finest qualities. The junior high (I believe they are called middle schools today) presented a musical review each spring. It was the ambition of Amanda Wellengood's work with this age group that the eighth grade put together an evening of what was advertised as entertainment, and sometimes was.

Mrs. Wellengood was a good educator, challenging her students to reach out beyond their current abilities to become something more. She would select musical numbers just beyond a performer's skill and experience. Some years the group responded to the challenge and the audience would leap to their feet in applause at the sparkling performance. Other years the audience would leap to their feet looking for an exit to end their suffering.

Audiences at these affairs must always rise from their chairs and erupt with applause. It is expected and should not be used as a gauge of performance. I have, through the course of time, tried to resist the practice but jabs from Edith's elbow always convince me to comply with the trend. It has sullied the good name of a standing ovation. Having seen an audience rise in response to a quartet where only two uttered words, I am not impressed when I hear of another performer receiving similar recognition.

The annual Christmas Pageant was an extravaganza demanded by parents and public. A poor choice of seasons to require extra rehearsals and additional practice at home, the show must be presented each year. It was a strain on Amanda as well as the families of students. Mrs. Wellengood took yuletide solace in the medication spiked eggnog can provide. Once she was pretty well dried out from the Christmas Pageant, it was time to get started on the Spring Extravaganza.

As important as the performance is to the audience, the costume is every bit as essential to the performer. "Summertime" cannot be properly presented to an informed audience in a flannel shirt and ski pants. It tends to send a message of shoveling snow rather than steamy afternoons by the stream. This number must be performed wearing a simple sundress.

I don't know this to be true from personal experience; I learned it from weeping teenage divas as I accompanied Mother while she helped prepare costumes for the Spring Extravaganza. An army of ladies accomplished in the art of sewing costumes were assembled each year to meet the unreasonable demands of the cast and director. Each had better things to do than to listen to the whining of spoiled teenage girls and their mothers. It was a task requiring the skill that negotiating world peace would demand. No mere human could be asked to accomplish this task. They looked to Mother to do the job.

I remember sitting with mother while she listened to a pretty young girl explain in minute detail the fabric, the style, the type of stitch, and adornments necessary for her to be heard and recognized for the talent she was. Next Mrs. Wellengood would present her need that the costume should fill the desires of the prima donna, but also flow with the rest of the production.

Mother would nod her head as she listened and pretended to take notes when their volume increased or gestures became grand. I'm not sure she was listening to them. How could she? They weren't making any sense. They were not talking in words, only mental images and feelings which one had to sew together into something wearable. She could have been making a mental shopping list or figuring out how to juggle the budget to make ends meet. It wasn't necessary to listen because what they were asking was impossible.

After getting the commission, Mother would return to the room full of sewing machines brought by the volunteer seamstresses and they would go to work. They would decide on the style of the dress based upon the skill of the seamstress and the time remaining for the task.

A second order of business was to select an appropriate fabric for the costume. Underfinanced as it was the costume budget for the production was exhausted with the purchase of a box of straight pins so the ladies were left to resources they brought with them, like unused fabric from home. They weren't scraps, just unwanted fabric. You know the fabric that looked so good in the store you had to purchase, but when you got home and got a good look at it, you couldn't imagine being seen in public wearing it.

Usually their type of cloth is colorful. It attracted you by tugging at an old memory, more of a feeling than a memory. Once you got it out to sew with it, you remember where you'd seen it before. It was part of an ensemble. The other parts were orange hair, a red nose, and giant shoes. It was not what you had in mind for an evening out. Still, it might be salvaged. You could always wear it if tacky clothing wouldn't stand out, say, at the in-law's house.

Seeing a snotty little pretentious performer strutting across the stage thinking they were something special sporting clothes the seamstresses wouldn't be caught dead wearing was all the payment they desired for their services.

Not much attention was given to boy's costumes. There is only so much that can be done with teenage boys. No matter how you dress them up and present them as respectable; in your mind you know they are smelly, rude, and going to scratch a lot in places that will be hard to politely explain in the script. Backstage magic can only do so much.

The sweat shop would go into full production, each lady tackling a costume that in no way resembled what was ordered but would do the job nicely. Understanding your client is the key to success in business and my mother was keenly aware of who she was working for. If the director and the diva could not be made happy, no effort was made to humor them. Whatever they received would have to be good enough. No end product would go long without lengthy critical review.

The secret to fulfillment lay in the timing of delivery. Regardless of the status of the garment, it would not be ready until dress rehearsal. If it were to be brought out too soon, there would be adornments and other improvements that would need to be made at the expense of another costume. Mother knew that if she expressed doubt as to whether it would be ready for show time, when the garment was presented at dress rehearsal it would be greeted with joy, thanksgiving, and relief and no further work would be expected. She was wise in matters such as these.

The love Mother had for Father served as an example to me. Likewise, the love Father showed for Mother was also an encouragement to me. They consciously tried to out-work each other around the house. There was a general understanding that house work was mother's domain and income production was Father's. This arrangement served them well until mother began to work the year I entered first grade.

After that, it became competition. Mother would work hard on household duties after she got home from work. Father worked second shift at a factory and got up early to work on a farm. The factory was employment while the farm was the love of his life. It was the very blood that pulsed through his veins. He would arrive home from the farm with just enough time to bathe and get ready for the factory job. He often sacrificed some of that precious time to do a small job around the house to ease mother's load. Father would have already run the vacuum or washed the dishes by the time she came home. I never caught him doing the ironing, though. It's understandable. All men have their limits.

Saturday was laundry day. We had a wringer type washing machine which was just one step up from beating clothes on a rock by the stream. Still, the convenience of no longer having to carry the laundry to the stream was a work saver. Father would fill the washer and the rinse tubs with water while mother fixed breakfast and got the family started.

During the summer, when it wasn't raining, we would hang the wet clothes outside. If it was raining or cold we would hang clothes in the basement. Father had about two miles of clothes line strung through two basement rooms, steering clear of the furnace and the coal bin where ash and dust would counteract our efforts.

They worked hard together to finish this laborious task because once the laundry was done, all that remained to do was to mow the lawn, iron the clothes, do the shopping, repair the car, mend the fence, patch tears in clothing, do the dusting, run the vacuum, and cook dinner. It was practically a day of vacation.

When all the wet clothes had been hung on the line, it was time for my brother and me to get started. We had to carry dirty water from the washer and rinse tubs in the basement and dump them in the alley. Wash water and spent motor oil kept grass from growing in the alley and kept the dust down during dry summer days. My brother was older so he could carry two buckets, but I had trouble with just one. Always looking up to him, he looked back at me with little more than contempt. I held nothing for him other than envy and appreciation.

One day my brother and I were outside waiting to be called to empty wash water. Mother was nearly finished with the laundry, winding down her labors in the basement. My sister was washing dishes in the kitchen directly above mother. As mother faced the rinse tubs, a window was directly behind her. It was convenient for calling us when she needed help.

My sister said some smart-alecky remark to my brother who responded in kind. This was the first time I learned a teenage girl is nothing to trifle with unless you expect to get burned badly. You would think a young man would remember something this painful and never go near it again. That's not the way with teenage boys. They continue on the same path until they incur third degree burns of the heart.

Not normally given to that kind of behavior, my brother kept taunting my sister through the window over the sink. It was not worth the punishment to stop in the middle of a job, even for something as important as pounding your little brother. His position under the window gave my sister an idea. She pulled the spray nozzle from its resting place in the sink and proceeded to give my brother a good soaking through the window screen. The surprise attack worked and my brother was sopping wet before he could escape the powerful spray.

That morning was the perfect morning for laundry. The warm, dry west wind dried clothes faster than any automatic dryer of today could manage. The stiff breeze redirected the kitchen spray bringing water into the basement through the window onto Mother who was still slaving over laundry tubs.

Panic overcame her. Laundry was the most labor intensive, time consuming chore of the week and it had to be done each week if her offspring were to escape ragamuffin status. Clothes left hanging in the rain would not dry and may need to be rewashed before they could be worn. She reacted with the urgency the situation demanded.

My brother was still taunting my sister through the screen and she hadn't given up on trying to give him one more good dousing with the sprayer. "It's raining," Mother screamed as she exploded through the back door with a laundry basket in each hand. Throwing one to my brother, she shouted, "Get the clothes before they are ruined." Her gait slowed as she neared the clothesline in bright sunshine. Mother squinted from the brilliant light as she assessed the situation. We were frozen in our positions. I was in the swing enjoying the show. Not having participated in the frivolity that caused mother's panic did not guarantee I would escape her wrath.

Under the kitchen window, my brother stood holding the laundry basket while my sister's finger was stuck on the sprayer trigger unable to release it. She had seen and heard Mother coming from the bowels of the house but was powerless to react to the information. We all were frozen as if posing for a tableau.

It was one of those moments of truth you experience from time to time that could have gone either way. It was still early on Saturday and the biggest job was nearly done. Mother was feeling a sense of relief and that helped her to laugh at the situation rather than draw her sword of retribution and cut a swath of retaliation that would have ensured she wouldn't have to suffer the same fate again. Even though we got away with it, we knew we were on thin ice. No unnecessary chances were taken for the remainder of the day. We were on our best behavior for about a week.

One of my favorite memories of youth was the most painful at the time. During the summer, Father would work two jobs full time, the factory job and farm work. If we hadn't seen Dad for a while, Mother would insist we wait at the dinner table for him to come home. Dad always finished a job before he would leave so it made estimating his time of arrival home pure guesswork.

As my young mind measured time, we often waited an entire day for him to get home. Mother would get up as necessary to keep dinner warm and edible, but our rears were glued to chairs until he arrived. Any excuse to get up and sneak off to play was met with severe resistance. My sister and mother could pass the time talking about current fashion or hair disasters. My brother always had a book to amuse him. Asking what he was reading annoyed him. Neither scholarly nor interested in my appearance, I was left to my own devices for entertainment. Never mastering the art of sitting quietly and not bothering those around me, discipline focused its harsh attention on me. I was powerless to deflect it away from me to another target.

While waiting at the table was painful, the real test of patience came when Dad got home. Dirty from farm work, he had to bathe before coming to the dinner table. Being mere inches from food and just a few feet from the freedom of outdoors, I could feel the energy burning inside me. It was a fierce force for folly in the heart of that boy. Mother was busy getting the remnants of her preparation to the table leaving me the luxury of torturing brother and sister unencumbered by parental oversight. Bruises were the reward for my effort.

Finally ready to feast, we would pray and dive into the meal. It was a treat to have Dad at the table with us. The irresistible urge to play with toys or run outside was gone. Financial times what they were; we had precious few evenings like this. Mother was vigilant and provided us with as many of these moments she could.

Mother's Day is celebrated in Blandtrap much differently than in your city. Your day is consumed with the purchase of flowers and chocolates and greeting cards with clever rhymes. We express ourselves differently and more often. Sharing our hearts and our time with our mothers as long as we have them is our tradition. Once they are gone their memory is with us and their teaching still guides our actions.

Spend some time with your mother, sir, or with her memory. She will be honored and you will be the beneficiary of the experience. From our village we wish you well and pray you will enjoy the holiday the way it was intended to be celebrated.

Respectfully Submitted,

Harry Ellis

Harry Ellis

238 Persimmon Street

Blandtrap

To the Editor of the Tiskilwa Bureau Valley Chief

RE: The Selection of Carla Dombrowski's Prospects

Dear Sir:

Your criticism of 'small towns without even a stop light to their name' seemed to be aimed conspicuously at Blandtrap. Standards by which you measure the value of a village are as faulty as the logic you use to apply them. The tenet that if there is no stop light then there is no traffic, suggesting there is insufficient population to generate what would legitimately be called traffic, let alone traffic to the extent it would need to be controlled, is superfluous. You should reexamine your literary yard stick and make any necessary adjustments.

By your reasoning we would not have weather until the place was demolished by a tornado. It would not have snowed until we could measure movement of the glacier. One would not be hungry until looked upon with envy by Gandhi! Everything must be exaggerated in the city. It is much different here in our village. The pace is slower and the demeanor kinder. Still, we manage to accomplish as much as you.

Bill Whittacre is an example of a man who quietly works hard and achieves results. Bill is one of those fellows who fly under the radar. Work and church is all he knows. Everyone in Blandtrap is familiar with Bill personally, yet few know more than that he is a hard-working, church-going young man. His name rarely comes up in general conversation, unless the topic of hard work wiggles its way into the discussion: "That conveyor could move as much hay as Bill Whittacre." might be an example of what would be said about him. The other person would respond, "yeah, but it can't stack it as neatly." Both would be amused at the comments without knowing why. If you ever worked along side Bill, you understood the analogy of comparing him to a machine. The mechanical device always paled in comparison to Bill.

On a hot July evening, Edith and I would often take a walk ending on a bench in Village Square. Young men, high school lads and the like, still gather around the bandstand to relax, particularly on summer evenings when they are too tired from farm chores to chase girls. Muscles would ache from baling hay in the hot sun, manual labor that didn't end until the job was done. It was how boys learned to be men.

Being too tired to chase girls didn't mean they weren't interested in them. They knew they would be better off to rest at home, but the chance of meeting girls was substantially greater at Village Square. The usual competition among boys would ensue. "What were you doing while I was picking up bales from the ground and tossing them on the wagon? Were you sitting in a chair sipping iced tea?" is the way it would begin.

"I was stacking bales while you were going for a walk alongside the wagon." would be his response.

"I was heaving bales and you were just pushing them around a bit. What you did was like ants moving grains of sand." Another would venture.

Banter was endless and unimaginative. It was boring until someone would mention stacking hay in the barn with Bill Whittacre. Every boy who found part-time employment putting up hay tried to out-work Bill. Without any success whatever, I might add. It would end the same way every time. Three boys would lay bales of hay end to end on the conveyor, sending them up to Bill in the loft. He would grab the bales, one in each hand, and toss them halfway across the barn with such accuracy they were not only stacked, but stacked tightly.

Each load brought to the barn started a new contest. After the last bale was placed on the conveyor, one boy or another would ride the conveyor to try to catch Bill with a pile of unstacked bales or, perhaps, a broken bale. All the boy would see when he arrived at the top was two bales sailing through the air to the place Bill had assigned them before the toss.

Hay and straw scratch the skin unmercifully so all the boys wore long sleeved shirts to avoid the abrasion. Bill had command over the bales. They couldn't get close enough to his body to inflict a minor rash, so he would work in a t-shirt or without a shirt when the mood suited him.

That was when the boys got a lesson in what hard work could do for them. Bill's body was something they had only seen in the back of comic books, in the ads for body building. He was the perfect specimen, the 'after' picture they all longed to be.

That kind of information was closely held by the witnesses. Few young men are comfortable talking admiringly about the body of another man for fear of what others might think of them. Also, you would not expect Hunts to advertise for Heinz with regard to ketchup. The boys remained mum on the subject and since Bill didn't toot his own horn, few had intimate knowledge of his physique. Those who did weren't talking.

I found myself on my own for lunch today. Edith and some other church ladies were going to give it another shot this afternoon to accomplish what they had failed to complete a few weeks earlier. Edith had received a note from Lauretta Townsend who had gotten a phone call from Ruth Woods who was informed in church by Mrs. Wing to whom Edith had mailed a letter regarding a meeting. Church organization has it own circle of life.

The first order of business would be to establish the topic of the meeting. This would be a battle of the wills. I wish I could have observed. The four ladies comprised four committees. Each was chairman of one committee and a member of the others. The work of each committee was important and the chairman would not find peace until her business was done. Trying to accomplish more than one topic at a meeting had, in the past, consistently resulted in no progress being made on any topic. The ladies were fully vested in the meeting, though, and were prepared to cast lots, if it came to that, to determine an order of topics and accomplish some kind of church business since they were all in the same room at the same time.

Carla Dombrowski dropped by the church often to pick up or deliver choir music. Since she worked in the city, she was asked to play courier for the choir at the music store. It was rare when she would find anyone in the building other than Asher, the church custodian, or, of course, Reverend Brimstone.

That day she was again delivering some music she had picked up for the choir. The sound of clanking china and the tinkling of silver spoons wasn't altogether familiar to her and it attracted her attention. Carla investigated and found the ladies deep in discussion over tea; argument, really, but it hadn't gotten loud yet. They didn't relish confrontation; neither did they shrink from it. Still, they would rather be doing something else. The ladies were thrilled to see Carla again and begged her to sit and join them to provide distraction from their argument.

Reluctantly, she sat, intending to do so only for a moment, just be polite. She inquired of their health and welfare. It was a dangerous venture with Mrs. Wing present. The widows tended to give more detail than was necessary and started farther back in time than most people would choose to begin. If you asked her how her cold was progressing she might begin with an explanation of the separation pain she felt when she lost her first tooth. The other ladies were expert in navigating the deep waters of Mrs. Wing and were prepared to intervene at the right moment.

Before Mrs. Wing could get wound up about her latest malady, Lauretta hurriedly asked "Have you given any thought to what kind of man you would pick, dear?"

Carla answered frankly, "I'm a little old fashioned about that. I don't call men or ask them out. I know that kind of thing is done all the time now, but I am not comfortable with the situation. I want the man to pursue me. If he's not interested, why start at all?"

"How charming and admirable," Mrs. Wing said, "but men, if left to their own resources, will wander off after the next shiny object they see. That complicates a search for the right man if you're going to wait for him to come to you. Men aren't often the first to know they are interested in a lady. Some men have to be told. They have other matters on their mind which make them so thick and dull they will never see it themselves. Indeed, men can be so self-absorbed at times; they can miss what is right in front of them. Other men must be led to the conclusion by a carefully laid trail of intuitive bread crumbs until they reach the conclusion of love."

"What you want has a lot to do with who you pick." Lauretta Townsend launched into what seemed to be a new direction. "I know we asked you before, we want to know if the answer is the same. Where do you want to live?"

"I've thought about it more and the answer remains the same: I want to live here. I don't like the city and the hectic life there. Other small towns would be alright, I guess. Blandtrap would be best." Carla concluded her comments looking at the ladies. In previous discussions with the ladies most of her responses had been made with her head down because she was embarrassed. At that point her head was up and she was looking them in the eye as she spoke. By tackling her personal problem head on the old ladies had instilled a confidence in Carla she didn't know she had.

"Do you want a church-goer? Do you want to raise kids going to Sunday school, church picnics and pot luck suppers?" Edith weighed in.

"Sure. That's the way I was raised and I want that for my children, too." Carla thought out loud.

"Do you want a big house, big yard, several cars, or will a modest house and having to walk downtown during the day suit you?" Ruth Woods wanted to know.

"Money isn't that big of an issue. I make good money as a nurse. I'm able to save most of it because my needs are simple." Carla hadn't really considered some of these things, at least not in rapid succession like the ladies were now firing questions her way.

"Will you work or will you stay home with the children?" Edith inquired of her.

"I am deeply dedicated to my profession. I will always be a nurse. Seeing the children of families where both parents work full-time, though, I see the longing for companionship, for mothering and nurturing in the eyes of the children and in the expressions of the mothers. While children are of school age I want to be at home. I will have to keep my license current but that will only take a few days now and then." "Carla didn't, until this moment, realize she felt so strongly on the topic.

Nursing was a good job. She didn't recognize it as a profession or understand what the word meant until that moment. This exercise was enlightening for her. The process was oversimplified, she thought. This is too easy. It was like going to a drive-through window at one of those hamburger joints in the city. You drive up to the clown's head to look at the menu and order, and then you drive to the window and pick it up. She wondered if the order gets mixed up when selecting a man as often as it does at the pick-up window.

"You are a professional lady. We can see that's important to you. Does the gentleman have to be a professional, too?" Mrs. Wing asked.

"What do you mean?" Carla didn't see the relevance of the question.

"Do you need the prestige associated with, say, a doctor or lawyer or will a hard working regular Joe suit you?" Lauretta explained to Carla.

"Oh, I'm pretty secure that way," she said "a regular guy would be fine."

"That's a very good point of view, dear. Most young ladies aren't mature enough to see that a plumber or carpenter is much handier to have around the house than a doctor or lawyer." Mrs. Wing stated with an experienced perspective. "CPR or open heart surgery won't fix a leaky toilet."

"What about character? Women's tastes vary on this quality. Is honesty and integrity important, or can you tolerate a bit of a scallywag?" Lauretta asked painfully.

"Such a question!" Carla was taken aback. "I want a man I can trust. When I'm home knee-deep in diapers I don't want to be wondering what my husband is doing or who he's doing it with. I'm not flexible on this point."

"Good, good." Lauretta pressed on. "What about passion?"

"Passion?!" Carla blushed so fast it surprised her. As a nurse she had to discuss topics of this nature with patients and it was difficult then, when she had time to prepare for the discussion. It was an entirely different matter when she was the subject of the discussion and it wasn't required by medical emergency. This was a subject she never expected to discuss with church ladies. She was squirming in her seat and checking where the exits were in case she should decide to run.

"Passion." Lauretta was determined to explore these waters. "Do you want to have to drag it out of him at your pleasure or do you want to have to slap his hands in public? There's quite a range of behavior, here, so you just need to figure out what you want."

"You don't want to bite off more than you can chew!" Mrs. Wing observed. The other ladies tittered and Carla's face deepened in redness to a shade of maroon. She wondered if there was enough blood left in the rest of her body to sustain life. Her blush stayed that way a full hour after she left the ladies.

"You know what I mean." said Mrs. Wing. Turning to her contemporaries she bristled, "Ladies! Really!"

After several moments to compose herself in the company of old ladies winking at one another, Carla revealed, "Well, I don't want to be embarrassed all the time, but if I had to slap his hands in public every once in a while it wouldn't be so bad."

Edith leaned over and whispered into Carla's ear. "Honey, this is one of those topics you need to consider but you can keep the answer to yourself. It's not the kind of thing one discusses in polite company." Carla blushed even more. Apparently, rules of etiquette were different for her than for the ladies of the church.

"I think we have all the information we need, ladies. I believe we can compile a list of eligible candidates." Mrs. Wing thought she had heard enough and decided to push the meeting forward. "Any suggestions?"

"Clovis comes to mind." Ruth Woods tossed out the first name. "There's always Clovis."

"Hiram Swanson." Lauretta offered the name to the group. "He's an oldie but a goodie. We didn't discuss age. If that's a problem, dear, just strike him from the list."

"Bill Whittacre." Ruth Woods added another to the list. "I see Bill in church every Sunday and he is the most helpful fellow when you find yourself in a bind."

"I know Bill casually and I don't think there's any interest there…" Carla began to explain.

"Honey, listen, here's how it works. We make a complete list of all who are eligible, even the borderline cases. We will give the list to you and you can do with it whatever you wish. Now is not the time for your opinion on these men. You see, while you are considering why you should eliminate a candidate, we may overlook an excellent prospect. So, you just sit quietly unless you have a name for the list." Mrs. Wing disciplined Carla kindly.

"Tommy Hunter, that kid at the hardware store." Edith offered the first person to pop into her head.

"Isn't he still in high school?" Lauretta questioned. "I'm sure he is. I think I saw him in the cast of the high school musical."

Mrs. Wing patted Carla's arm, "If he's still in high school you strike him from the list." Looking her square in the eyes she said, "You're a little long in the tooth to wait for him to grow up."

Carla winced at Mrs. Wing's words. She had learned that it was better to remain silent when the ladies were wound up like this, offended or not. Opening her mouth hadn't yielded the results she anticipated.

"Alvin Solomon." Lauretta was digging deep. The mention of the name met with silence. No one had heard anything about Alvin Solomon or the Sebastian girl, Margarite, since the day they both fell of the face of the earth. The whole matter was very mysterious. When the parents of either were asked about what happened, they would only reply that they were doing well and immediately change the subject or leave. Eventually both families moved away and no one learned anything more about it.

"Randy Bean." Carla said, surprised the name occurred to her and even more surprised she would bring it up in present company. "I don't think he's married and he lives as close as Butte Crossing. We dated for a while near the end of high school and got along fine. Put him on the list."

"But he lives in Butte Crossing." Lauretta pointed out, trying not to let her snobbery show.

"Randy's on the list." Carla said with confidence. "Put his name down."

"Calvin Farnsworth is the last of the eligible males, I think." Mrs. Wing began to close the discussion. "If we think of more, we can let Carla know." The meeting broke up rather abruptly. Edith gave hand written notes of the meeting to Carla. Since the matter was personal, she wouldn't type and file the notes for posterity.

As Carla drove away from the Church, her mind wandered back to high school and memories of Randy Bean. She never really felt 'ga-ga' about the guy, yet she remembered how comfortable the relationship had been. There was no hand slapping, though, and only a couple of kisses, neither of which stood out as remarkable. Her mind was made up; she would hunt him down and see if anything was still there and let the chips fall where they may.

Days later, milk curdled in her breakfast coffee and her pantry was nearly bare. A stop by the IGA was needed to remedy the situation. Pulling up to the curb on Village Square, Carla saw Bill Whittacre entering the IGA. Through the window she could see Maybelle Oufsbacher. "With luck, he'll steer free of her before she gets started." She felt pity for any man caught in Maybelle's verbal trap. It was a common sentiment when folks saw an innocent bystander with Maybelle glued to their ear.

Nodding to the oldest Beeman girl as she passed, Carla exchanged pleasantries with the lady, noting that she was due in about two weeks. Carla expressed good wishes to her and asked about Eliza. She didn't work the maternity ward any more. It was too painful for her after the Williams baby was lost.

Carla heard Bill's voice. Soft yet firm in tone, she was surprised she recognized it with the limited communication they shared. "Mrs. Oufsbacher, you shouldn't be carrying those heavy bags. Let me get them for you."

Mrs. Oufsbacher spoke so softly Carla couldn't hear what she was saying, but she could hear Bill ask which car was hers as the door to the store closed. A favorite trick of Maybelle's was to speak more softly, forcing the listener to pay closer attention to hear her words. It was a tactic that had served her well over her many years of manipulating the innocent. Bill had to lean in close to her to hear what she was saying.

Carla set about her business of tossing items into her cart while mentally planning meals she would never feel like cooking.

Grocery shopping can be dizzying if you're not in the right frame of mind.

When Bill returned, Mr. Fezzizzi asked Bill to move some cases of canned goods out of the way of customers and put them in front of the shelves where the product would be stocked. Bill didn't say a word. He jumped right on the job at hand.

Bill and Carla met in the cereal aisle. Bill was bringing a case of inventory up the aisle while Carla was struggling to get a box of 'Crunchy Sweets' off the top shelf. She was embarrassed her poor choice of breakfast food was outed in such a public manner but she managed to greet him, "Hello, Bill." Carla said.

"Ma'am" Bill responded in his usual manner while looking down at the ground.

"Bill" Carla interrupted his thoughts and it caused him to look up at her face. Carla got her first chance to look into Bill's eyes. Women think they can look into a man's eyes and see his intentions and even into his soul. Most men hope to God they can't. "We went to high school together, Bill. We were classmates, you can call me Carla."

"As you wish, Carla.", Bill wondered if he would remember when he saw her next. Uncomfortable with small talk, he had been noticing, recently, his social skills were lagging behind those of his peers. In fact, they may be lacking altogether.

Bill ventured a stab at conversation. Noticing the deep color in Carla's face, he asked, "Have you been getting a lot of sun lately?"

Carla realized she was still blushing from the ladies probing inquiries. She dared a response, "Not as much as you would think." An awkward few seconds of dead silence passed. The ball was in Bill's court and he was all played out of small talk.

"I'm sorry to trouble you, but could you get me a box of 'Crunchy Sweets' from the top shelf" Carla decided to keep the conversation going to move past awkward. Bill reached for the box and handed it to her.

"Here you go." Bill offered.

"How long have you been working here?" Carla asked.

Bill seemed surprised at the question. "Oh, I don't work here. I came in to pick up a few things. Some ladies needed help with their bags and Mr. Fezzizzi's back has been bothering him so I pitched in to ease his load, just trying to be helpful. I still work on the dairy farm. Here's your cereal."

"I'm sorry for the confusion…" Carla began with apologies.

"I'm not offended. There's nothing wrong with working in a grocery. It's honest work. You will have to excuse me. I'm behind schedule and have to get back to work." Bill left with a tip of his cap. He felt foolish since he wasn't wearing a cap but the whole conversation with Carla had been exhausting and exhilarating at the same time. He could work all day and all night without a break. Conversation, though, could wear him out in a few minutes. Talking to Carla didn't wear on him the same as talking to the older ladies, but he figured it was just a matter of time until it did.

Carla mulled things over on her way home from the IGA. She only put her foot in her mouth three or four times in the space of a few minutes. It wasn't her personal record but a good effort for a week night. Letting the embarrassment abate, Carla allowed her mind to return to thoughts of Randy Bean. She decided to make a few phone calls and investigate whether any possibilities remained.

Relaxing with a cup of coffee at home, her kitchen being recently restocked with coffee condiments, Carla pulled the list of eligible men from her purse. Thoughts of Randy would have to simmer overnight and she would seek the counsel of her friends in the morning. She left messages for Cheryl Hunter, Arlene Libidowitz, and Lucrecia Kwok. They agreed to meet her at Plow Boy Diner for breakfast. Eliza Beeman would get the word from Lucrecia.

The ladies drifted into the diner over a span of about a half an hour. Cheryl and Eliza were late due to family responsibilities. They agreed with their husbands that they would die of hunger if meals were not prepared for them. Cheryl had a map of the kitchen showing where cereal, milk, bowl, and spoon could be found. She was saving it for an argument requiring her highest level of sarcasm.

Arlene had been up late reading and had trouble getting started in the morning. Lucrecia told them, "I was out late kissing frogs last night. I think I need help. I'm sure one of them was a toad in frog's clothing." Unable to decipher the metaphor, or parable, or whatever it was, Carla moved ahead.

"I've got a list of all the eligible bachelors in town." Carla passed a copy of the list around the table. "Don't worry; I've already scratched Clovis from the list."

"Hiram Swanson!" Eliza questioned those present, "Are you sure he's still alive?"

"I'm pretty sure he is," Arlene witnessed, "I saw the emergency squad over at his house last night and they didn't take him with them. He must still be kicking."

"Scratch him." Carla ordered.

"Bill Whittacre is a nice guy. Wasn't he in high school with us?

"Hey! What's my little brother doing on your list of guys to date?!" Cheryl Hunter shouted.

"Already scratched." Carla noted.

"Friend or no friend, stay away from my little brother!" Cheryl bristled

"Alvin Solomon is a ghost. No one knows where he went or why." Arlene thought, unaware she was heard.

"Calvin Farnsworth isn't a bad choice. He's not too old. He's odd, though, and he's already married to that Institute for Idle Science and to recording every meaningless event of the village." Cheryl commented.

"Scratch him too." Carla said with a sigh, "The names are falling fast from a short list."

"Last but not least, Randy Bean." Lucrecia read the name. "You two had a thing senior year, didn't you? He doesn't live in Blandtrap. Wasn't that a rule, they had to live in the village."

"Butte Crossing," Carla answered, "I heard this morning he lives in Butte Crossing."

"It's not his full-time job, but he tends bar at some watering hole there. I didn't see him myself. Hubby said he was working when they stopped for a drink after golf last week. I guess he stays on the list." Eliza had been a fountain of information.

"Was it Skinny's Tap?" Carla asked.

"No, it was the other bar." Eliza said she was sure. She couldn't remember the name of the bar but it couldn't be too hard to find in a town as small as Butte Crossing.

Work seemed to drag the next day. As soon as it was over, Carla headed for the watering hole in Butte Crossing. Out of her element being alone in a bar, Carla took a seat at the rail. It was the only time she could remember sitting at a bar except waiting for a table with a date or friends.

She noticed the bar help approaching from the far end of the bar. What a piece of work he was. With an indoor tan, shirt opened to his socks, and three gold chains around his neck he looked like the poster boy for men Carla detested.

"Dombrowski" she heard this joke of a man say, "Carla Dombrowski, it's me, Randy Bean."

Carla's heart sank; try as she might to hide it, she was sure the disappointment showed on her face. Randy was oblivious to signals women send, thus his demeanor and attire. He proceeded to hit on her before she could say hello.

"That's certainly an interesting offer, Randy, but I just came in to get some change for the phone." Was all she said.

He continued to work her. "I live upstairs. I could take you up there and you could use my phone." Randy persisted.

Carla was all too familiar with the kind of man Randy had become. She ran into them in the city all the time. "Just the change, Randy; I've got to go…and make it snappy." She added to emphasize the point that she hadn't come to play. Randy had turned into one of those men that make women feel like they need to bathe after speaking with them.

"Bill Whittacre was it." Carla pondered on the drive home. The old ladies sure knew how to handle matters of the heart. They were brusk, matter-of-fact, and they got to the nub of it in a hurry. Good ladies." Carla thought. She would take their advice and give Bill Whittacre a fair chance if she could get more than two words out of him. The first thing she would do was to break him of calling her 'ma'am.' It caused her to feel old.

Although there is no traffic in our streets, much is still happening in Blandtrap. We get more done before your light turns green than most city folks do all day. We enjoy freedom from the frustration traffic escorts into our lives. The time we save honking our horns and swearing at other drivers, we spend helping each other.

Respectfully Submitted,

Harry Ellis

Harry Ellis

238 Persimmon Street

Blandtrap

To the Editor of the Tiskilwa Bureau Valley Chief

RE: Memorial Day

Dear Sir:

Amost important day is upon us. Many use it as a simple marker indicating the beginning of summer. To those who think about liberty or ponder the sacrifices other men have made for our freedom, this day represents an opportunity to express gratitude for men and women who gave their lives in that struggle. Your paper stated the ceremony in your town would begin at ten o'clock. No other information was provided.

In Blandtrap, our tradition differs from yours. It must seem strange to you in the city, with your rushing about to make appointments and meet deadlines, that people would surrender an entire day to honor others, most of whom are dead and can't reciprocate. It is our custom, here to recognize the sacrifice of others; particularly, we make special recognition of those who gave life or limb to let us live free.

The day will start with a formal military service at the edge of the cemetery where the old Lutheran Church used to stand. The American Legion and the Veterans of Foreign Wars put their heads together each year to hold a solemn event lasting about an hour. They work hard to make each year different in some way without losing the sincerity of the moment. Creativity isn't their goal. Fear that the day will become a mechanical ritual devoid of sincere meaning drives their preparation.

The last bugler in the American Legion died a few years ago. Some high school kids play the bugle for the service. A couple of kids practiced echoing taps which is moving for military and civilians alike. One of the lads will stand among the larger monuments in the graveyard and the other will position himself in the back of the small woods adjacent to the burial ground. When the boys finish the musical interlude I will find more than one tear on my cheek, and as I look around, I will see more tears on other faces and many will be weeping openly and unashamed; so great is the gratitude of this village for those who gave so much for us.

From a distance we will hear the bagpipe playing a marching tune as if he were leading a platoon of soldiers into battle. The music will be loud at first as if a platoon was stationed nearby. Acoustics of the cemetery with sound bouncing off grave stones and statuary make it impossible to determine the direction of the music. As folks find their way to their cars the music will fade away as the piper symbolically leads the souls of fallen soldiers to their new homes in glory. It has become as meaningful to me as any remembrance.

The afternoon will offer a program in the American Legion hall where one or two veterans will share their war-time experiences with the audience. An opportunity for those of us who didn't serve to learn what it took to survive their strife.

It is usually painful for the speaker. Not many veterans care to talk publicly about their time in the service. The Legion tries each year to get new people to share at the program or at least to share experiences they haven't presented before.

Wars are fought by young people. The young are attracted to military service because it is an opportunity to prove themselves before peers and elders. It will teach them discipline and they will learn that success relies upon doing your own job and trusting the other guy will do his. Wondering or worrying about what the person next to you is going to do is not useful in conflict.

College and work experience teach something like this but military service, particularly in time of conflict, teach these fundamentals of life and death in a way available no where else. It is the master's degree in maturity. There exists no doctorate.

Young men who serve in conflict are young men no more. Each responds to combat in his own way but none are unaffected. They grow up fast when they spend any time at all at the end of a barrel of a gun. A person gets the answer to questions they can only guess at in most other settings. "Will I stand and fight or will I run?"

Folks outside the military aren't, as a rule, faced with that challenge. Police and firefighters get the answer to the question too often, but the rest of us never know. In our world as it exists today, there is little opportunity to demonstrate bravery of any kind except in the face of dire circumstances.

The law requires a man, if the option is available, to abandon his family and run from even an armed intruder, leaving his family to the fate of the perverse intruder. If he stays and forcefully defends the ones he loves it is certain he will go to prison. Lawyers will twist what happened until the defender is made out to be the aggressor. It is injustice.

In today's society, we are not allowed to be brave in the traditional sense, but the truly brave exhibit their character without societal permission. They adopt children removed from horrible home conditions, children completely neglected except when they were abused. These children are quite likely permanently changed and not for the better. Any shred of honesty and trust has been long since beaten from them. With all this baggage they are still adopted and loved.

These parents face obstacles I cannot imagine. They love and care for children who are incapable of loving them back, at least in a way we can understand. The children will be a continual source of heartbreak and trouble to the parents. Knowing the ultimate reward of their efforts will be pain and suffering, they take on the task in spite of their pain because every child deserves to be loved and cared for by parents who want the little comfort they can offer, and these few families are willing to show it. They are remarkable among people.

My own father, Maurice, served in time of war. It wasn't a topic of conversation often and when his personal service was brought up he quickly changed the subject. He wasn't ashamed of what he did but living it once was enough. Reliving it for the amusement of people who wouldn't understand what he was talking about was repugnant to him. My sister and brother don't really recall him sharing stories of his service to country. As the youngest, I was around later in my father's life when he was beginning to mellow a little. It was a time when the fears of life melt into an acceptance of finality.

Military service trains rigidity into a person. There's no other way for an army to organize and prepare its soldiers. A person's natural response to a threat will vary. A commander needs to know that each soldier will react with the desired response. It must be drilled into a recruit's head until he no longer needs to think about it. It is natural to him. In time of war the same is true. A sense of urgency, immediacy is foremost, intensifying training and making the exercises real. Recruits don't know how long it will be until they find themselves in a real situation against an enemy with the intent to kill. They know they must be prepared in every way if they are to survive.

Father was always aware of his surroundings. Knowing what he had and where it was, he could rise in the middle of the night and dress himself in the dark without having to grope about or guess what he was wearing. The exact location of every piece of clothing he had was etched in his brain and he could reach out and grasp whatever article of clothing he sought. I never possessed this skill.

Brassy as a child, I didn't develop my kind, patient, benevolent nature until later in life before acquiring the vast wisdom I now command. I remember when I challenged Father to a contest. The winner was the one who could change clothes the fastest. Usually these contests took place after church when I couldn't wait to get out of my tie and jacket. Neither of us felt comfortable in a suit. I laid down a challenge: I could change clothes faster than him. Standing in my bedroom next to the chest-of-drawers that held the every day clothes I was going to wear, victory was assured. Father accepted my dare and exited the room.

The mind of a child can be set on accomplishing a task, even single-minded at times. No matter the intent or goal, it is also true the mind of a child is easily distracted. Toys lying on the bed needed a moment's attention. Soldiers had to march to the storage box where they should have been billeted. It took some time because a jeep broke down along the way and they fell victim to an ambush. When I noticed Father was standing and watching, clothes changed, I was humiliated. All I had managed to do was to remove my shirt.

He waited a few minutes while I completed my change of clothes, instructing me about the importance of remembering what I was doing and knowing where my things were at all times. These were problems he didn't have to struggle with when he was a child. Grandfather died while Father was young. In those days, much as it is today, that meant poverty. Life was consumed with the urgent need to sustain them so there was no time to play. If fun was to be had it would have to come from labor. He didn't have many toys to keep track of and even less time to play with them. An axe for chopping wood became a friend and a hoe for gardening was a good buddy.

At the time of Grandfather's death they were among the wealthiest in the county. His death coupled with the Great Depression and the greed of relatives signaled a crash into poverty. Relatives snatched the property for a song, permitting them to stay in the house and work a small plot for vegetables thus earning their subsistence. It was a common story at that time. Pride is a powerful elixir that sours in the mouth long after the bottle is passed to another. Shame takes its place ruining pleasure and destroying peace of mind.

He attended a three year high school in a tiny town nearby home. It was filled with children in similar circumstances to his. There is some comfort in mutual misery, in shared shame. The school had a basketball team but no gymnasium. They practiced outside and played all their games at opponents who were blessed with an indoor facility. The team played in work boots and t-shirts for uniforms. Success was not alien to them, winning nearly every game Father's third year of high school. They won their first game of the state tournament and it looked as if they would go far.

A minor rule infraction, playing too many games in the regular season, reversed their victory and they were excluded from the tournament. The eventual winner of the tournament was a team they had defeated twice that year. Disappointment was added to shame.

For the fourth year of high school he had to travel to the county seat each day. A small town by today's standards, the county seat was nearly a metropolis in its day. It hosted every kind of business imaginable and every kind of trouble you could hope to find. Father managed to avoid trouble in the city.

As I have tried to point out to you, cities have different customs, ways of dressing, and patterns of speech than in the country or small villages. Appearance is more important in the city. Time has always seemed to be the most valuable commodity in the city making real friendship difficult under the best conditions. Since no one has time to explore the charracter of another, appearance is substituted for substance. Acquaintance is confused with friendship yielding a false familiarity based upon how things appear. I suppose that is why friendships are so weak in the city.

Father's pride and poverty were the building blocks of the shame he felt. Other students carried tins for their lunches and enjoyed sandwiches or fried chicken for lunch. All Father had for lunch was some cornbread soaked with sorghum. His humiliation drove him to hide in the custodian's room in the basement of the school to eat his meager lunch. Father's shame was great but I always wondered how his actions made the custodian feel. His office was a hiding place for Father, a place where no respectable person would see him.

Because of the many jobs he worked, I didn't get to spend much time with Father when I was young. I was jealous of my older sister. She would work side-by-side with Father when he did jobs around the house. Lacking age, size, or any ability to concentrate for more than two minutes meant I was no help to him; a burden, if anything.

When Father gave instructions, they were thorough and complete. He thought every job through to the minutest detail before he began working. When he made a request it reflected the same level of detail. He couldn't make himself simply ask for a screwdriver and send you on your way. The request might go something like this: "I need you to go down to the basement and get me a tool. You'll need to walk to the basement door and turn the knob. The door opens in so you'll need to step out of the way as you open it. Close the door behind you. Walk down the stairs and through the room to my workbench. On the workbench you will find the toolbox. In order to open the toolbox you must lift up on the latch and remove the hook securing the lid to the box. If you don't release both latches you won't be able to open the toolbox. Once it's open remove the top tray. The tool I want is not in the top tray, put it to the side. In the bottom of the toolbox there are many tools. I want a screwdriver. I don't want a Phillip's head screwdriver, that's the one that looks like a plus sign. I want a flat head screwdriver, that's the one that looks like a minus sign or the number one depending upon how you hold it. Put the flathead screwdriver aside, return the top tray to the toolbox, and secure the lid with the latches. Carrying the flathead screwdriver, walk back through the room and up the stairs. The door to the kitchen will open away from you this time so just turn the knob and walk through it. Close the door behind you. Bring the screwdriver to me so we can finish the job."

Nothing was ever lacking in his directions. Their length is what created a problem. It took so long to get to the task at hand; the mind of a child had wandered off into a mental playground long before all direction was received. I disappointed him too often to remember them all clearly.

Chairs were set in rows at Legion Hall and a lectern placed in front of them. Two men played with the amplification system without discernable improvement in performance. Their diagnostics didn't determine the exact cause of the failure but narrowed it down to one of two possibilities: a low hum or a high pitched squeal. Surely the problem rested in the microphone, the cable, or the amplifier. That was the extent of the equipment. Believing they were close to a workable cure, they were disappointed when the chapter president came in and made the decision to go forward without amplification.

A couple of guys had been sitting at the bar all morning. It had been one beer after another since they came in, some they paid for and others were charity. "The free ones taste better." one of them would say every time a passerby donated to their cause. They weren't intoxicated, neither were they sober. Existing in a state somewhere between both states, they strove to be distracted by inane conversation rather than wallow in memories. A hard childhood, a brutal war, and the stress of life beyond youth make a vivid mind a vile curse. To remember is hell, to forget is paradise.

This time of year they relive the same skirmishes. They are weary from the struggle to recall specific details, yet bored by the repetition. Running faster than the mind can think is exhausting, making them to flee from logical thought. The two will break into song at unpredictable intervals. One song will be a lullaby sung as a dirge while another will be a song of lost love sung as a sea shanty. The bartender knows the proper time to cut off the beer, only temporarily, and bring them some new distraction like a deck of cards or dice. The game will consume them for a few hours, quelling the boiling spirit invading their souls.

An empty auditorium has a hollow sound like when you thump a dry gourd. The event would not draw a large audience. If half the seats were occupied it would be an overwhelming success. What the speeches accomplished was unclear to me. In some way they held untold value. The rest of the day's activities were divided between honoring those who gave their lives for their country and those who survived the encounter. Speeches gave the appearance of therapy for survivors. What ever they need to get through the day is owed them.

Encounters of war are personal and different for each person. In some small way they are like stories of college. College stories lack meaning if you haven't attended the institution at the crux of the tale. Similarly, if you have never experienced combat or the terror of war, you can never fully appreciate the sentiments of veterans.

The program won't begin until the chairs have more than a few veterans holding them down. Media will be present. That insipid radio station in your town will have a reporter sitting on an aisle and your paper has sent reporters in the past. I suppose it is good they are here yet they are not the intended audience.

They will listen, take notes on their pads, and return to their chambers or cubicles to write what they think they heard. Observers can only fashion their thoughts through the words they hear. What they know is second hand. Veterans saw what happened, felt the pain and can empathize with the visions of horror the speaker experienced. What is presented is more of the soul than of the spoken word. God knows; and they know God knows.

Articles will be written and editorials will be voiced with glowing language and flowing phrases that tug at readers' heart strings. Polite folks will be moved for a moment. The most stoned-hearted man may shed a tear. Only veterans in the audience will leave with a shadow of understanding. If the speaker is a good communicator, listeners will see a small part of his experience. They will sympathize but can only guess the horror speakers are relaying.

Al Fornoff rose from his chair and headed for the lectern, shuffling his feet to keep his balance. It was hard to remember this frail old man and more like him were once all that stood between freedom and surrender. A faint and failing voice is all that is left to tell the stories of Pearl Harbor. Some of his stories aren't about himself, as far as he can remember, but he tells them as if they were.

When we tell stories of our accomplishments, we focus on those that make us more attractive to the listener. Tales of how we were generous, valiant, or wise are tucked into our quiver of half truths. If we were honest with ourselves and our audience, we would confess that some moments of generosity were really times when we miscounted, our valiant deeds were often foolishness in disguise, and our wisdom appeared by pure chance rather than a relentless pursuit of knowledge. Most heroes reach that status by circumstance. They don't set out to perform heroic deeds. Effort is not an ingredient to become a hero. Selfless action is what is required. Most don't possess it.

Mr. Fornoff stands to tell stories of moments of truth. His sagas are not pretty or polished stories and Al's remembrances don't always end well or flatter characters in the story. They're just true as he remembers them. Someone else can decide right and wrong, heroism or cowardice.

Having become part of him and forming the person he has been since, they provide insight into his understanding of life. It is remarkable that most of us never get around to grappling with the meaning of life until we are reasonably sure it's nearly over.

Soldiers in and near conflict have faced that moment many times and are disheartened they do not have a better grip on the answer. All they can tell you is it has something to do with God, family, and mankind; and how we relate to one another.

A brief and unnecessary introduction is made by the ranking officer. Rank is a necessity. Some must lead and give orders, others must pass orders along, and still others must carry them out. One isn't more important than the other. What is of life-saving urgency is that each carries out their assigned duties without delay. It is no wonder that extreme excesses occur with those in positions of power. As long as the powerful are not abusive or slow to act, it doesn't matter much how they do their job.

Careful scrutiny by those unsympathetic and uninvolved with an incident will, with all the time in the world to second-guess the split-second decisions of soldiers who have not even one to make crucial decisions that can save their life and the lives of fellow soldiers. Those self-righteous analysts belittle the brave.

The deck is stacked against the soldier or police officer or fireman. To make it completely fair and grant a level playing field to all involved, analysts should have to arrive at their conclusions in a period of no more than ten seconds. I would suggest they would reach far different conclusions than they often do.

Al worked his way to the microphone and cleared his voice several times before he spoke. Chairs with their backs to the speaker had been placed on both sides of the lectern allowing the unsteady to brace themselves as they delivered their message. Al took advantage of the chairs and nodded to the two healthy young men who flanked him, seated close enough to come to his aid if needed. More than one relied on their help that day.

"Maurice and I were looking down from Diamond Head at our Pacific Fleet aflame in Pearl Harbor. I didn't lose family in the war but Maurice's brother Doane was assigned to one of those ships. It would be weeks before Maurice learned his brother escaped serious injury to his person.

As it was with so many survivors, permanent and fatal injury had been inflicted on his mind. Symptoms would appear at least annually but it took decades for the injury to take its final toll. Civilians don't understand it. Soldiers do. They hate it but they understand it." Al's mind had wandered away from his speech and present day concerns but he caught it before it was completely lost.

"At Hickham Field, we had our own problems to deal with and were not able to come to the rescue of ships in the harbor. No one knew what was going to happen next. After the attack, we got our weapons and assembled for deployment, awaiting orders that didn't arrive. Expecting enemy troops to be landing at any moment to take the island, contingency defense plans were yanked from drawers once they were found and dust was blown off the papers. These were the only plans we had. They were unsuited for the situation we were facing.

"Our duties had been training recruits in anti-aircraft artillery. We drilled hayseeds and hillbillies in essential geometry to fire mighty weapons that could knock airplanes out of the sky. Regulations were strict and we followed them to the letter. Dummy rounds were fired during practice drills. Live ammunition was rationed for only experienced training classes and then just a few rounds were made available.

Since we simulated firing at enemy aircraft we were surprised how unprepared we were for actual combat. It was a glimpse of what our trainees had experienced after graduating from our instruction. Classes took on a more personal meaning after the attack.

"While enemy planes attacked Hickham Field, we took cover immediately. By the time we made our way to our guns, the threat had passed. The attack was over. It would have made no difference if we had gotten to them sooner. All we had were dummy rounds. It would have taken weeks to requisition live ammunition. We might as well have been throwing rocks at them.

"Until that time, military service hadn't been that bad. It was like a vacation in every way it wasn't like a nightmare. Sure, we were away from home and missing family and loved ones. Of course, we were two boys from rural counties billeted on an island paradise. We wrote letters home describing the profound beauty of the place. My guess is they didn't comprehend what we were telling them. In fact, we lacked the vocabulary to explain it fully. It doesn't exist. You can say beautiful only so many times before you are no longer believed, unless you are talking to a woman."

Al grinned for a moment. More comfortable with humor than with serious subjects, he wished he could recall more funny stories about the war. Then, like so many thoughts he had these days, they left his memory as quickly as they arrived. On closer inspection he would agree they weren't that funny anyway. He returned to what he knew.

"After the attack our unit drilled for infantry duty as well as anti-aircraft. Even constant, monotonous hours of training were accentuated with fear that filled our days and nights. We continued to train on our own when it wasn't ordered. The men didn't mind additional drills. It was better than endless nights with only your own frightening thoughts as a companion. We took our pistols apart and put them back together. We reached the point where it wasn't a challenge unless we were blindfolded.

"One day I was repacking my footlocker, for lack of anything better to do. A man on one of the top bunks (for the life of me I can't remember his name, I can see his face though) was handling a grenade. He had removed the pin and was replacing it when his arm slipped and he released the trigger, dropping the grenade. Scrambling to the floor he pulled it from under the bottom bunk and ran toward the door to throw it out of the barrack.

"Before he could release the weapon it went off in his hand removing a large part off his arm. As I looked out the door I saw Maurice approaching the door. He had no idea what was going on yet he witnessed what happened. Maurice ran to help the man injured man who turned, reentered the barrack with life blood ebbing from his severed limb begging his fellow soldiers and God to save him from a certain fate. He died on the floor in front of his comrades. Nothing could be done for him. He had signed his own sentence.

"Maurice was shaken more than the rest of us. He was hurting for his fellow soldier but he knew if the man had been successful in launching the grenade it would have been his demise rather than the other fellow. Maybe the guy didn't throw the grenade in time because he saw it would kill Maurice if he released it. He would never know for sure. Army life was full of episodes like this. We chew on its meaning until it softens. It's the hardtack of life.

"I never thought of myself as a lonely man. Never a good idea to set out on your own in a foreign port, I stayed close to friends when I left the base. Some entertainment was better left to those with more experience in worldly endeavors. Playing cards wasn't a good strategy for me if I wanted to keep company with my cash. Maurice and I had been overseas for many years and it came time for us to get extended leave to visit home. Both of us couldn't go at the same time because the one remaining had to take over teaching duties for the absent one. Our commander flipped a coin and Maurice won. I don't think I've ever been as jealous of another man as I was of him at that moment.

"He returned home and got married; Elizabeth was her name. Being home was wonderful for him and he regretted having to come back. He did, fighting every shred of logic in his brain, and it was my turn to go home, a glorious moment. It had been so long since I had been home I wondered how comfortable I was going to be with family and old friends. Would I still know them? Was I the same man who left? I was also terrified about returning to Hawaii. Paradise it may be; home it wasn't.

"During my leave they dropped the bombs on Japan. It wasn't long after that the enemy surrendered. I was discharged during my leave and didn't have to return to Hawaii. So, as the loser of the coin toss I became winner of the prize. Maurice won the coin toss but it was another six months before he found his way home."

Al began to tear up. He couldn't continue so he walked away from the lectern and took a seat. I don't know what was bothering Al. It was probably a flood of emotion he couldn't sort through. Applause is out of place at a moment like that. Everyone in the audience stopped by his seat to thank him for sharing the experience. He just nodded. Sometimes he smiled. He was spent emotionally and so were those who heard him. It was a privilege to be in attendance and I told him so on my way out.

I don't remember the purpose of my letter and am unmotivated to glance back to discover it. The business I am about these days seems unimportant compared to the efforts of these brave men. I am humbled and I am going to end this communication. You will not hear from me again until I become aware of more important matters. Good day and God bless.

Respectfully Submitted,

Harry Ellis

June

Borrowed from the notebook of Calvin Farnsworth:

If a troubled palmist were to warn you of a future rough patch regarding your spouse's objections to your inadequacies polishing cutlery, wouldn't that be…

A life line strife time knife shine wife whine?

Harry Ellis

238 Persimmon Street

Blandtrap

To the Editor of the Tiskilwa Bureau Valley Chief

RE: A June Bride, With Sponsors

Dear Sir:

Your paper is crowded with accounts of the social events of your city. Benefits, galas, even teas are recorded in your paper. I am sure this information is convenient for you readership.

When they want a cup of tea and have heated the water, but can find no one qualified to pour, they can rifle through your pages to find an expert in the field.

We have social events in Blandtrap too, and they are as good as, or better than yours. The month of June means weddings in Blandtrap, just as it does elsewhere. A few months ago I was sitting in the Plowboy Diner and I had an inkling that it was going to be an extraordinary day. Few customers were gracing the tables. On a normal day, the door of the diner hardly closes for folks coming and going. Let a day come when you're busting at the seams to tell some good news or so down in the dumps where only a friend can pull you out and no one is around. Since I was on an even keel, someone else was bound to have some scintillating news and I was staying in the game until I heard it.

Clovis' father came in, but he was just talking about crops. Mr. Doubet, who was always good for a joke, told one of his older, more tiresome stories. It was unusual his jokes missed the mark. Everyone has an off day, I suppose.

Stu arrived in a pretty chipper mood and, for a while, I was convinced he was going to provide the day's excitement. As it turned out, he was grinning because he was distracted yesterday and forgot to buy a new set of channel locks. On his way into the diner he noticed the channel locks on sale today in the window of the Hardware Store. Stu is so cheap, that kind of price reduction could keep him happy for days and his good fortune would be mentioned in casual conversation for months.

Craig Beeman wandered in and, although it wasn't his custom, he headed straight for our table and plunked himself down after grabbing a cup of coffee. He looked like he was about to burst unless he could unburden himself, but he wanted to be asked. Our table had dealt with this situation before. Clovis' father, Mr. Doubet, and Seth looked toward me as if I should decide who would stick a pin in Craig's balloon.

It was no time for levity, so I passed on Mr. Doubet. I nodded to Clovis' father. I would have gone to Seth if I had more time on my hands. It would take a while, but Seth could find out the most minute details about a matter without committing himself to a specific topic. Brevity being at premium, I opted for the direct approach.

"What's new?" Clovis' father started.

"My youngest daughter, Eliza, is getting married in June!" He was excited. The Beemans were blessed with four daughters. This was the last to wed, a moment Craig dreaded as well as desired.

Craig and Lucinda Beeman were hard working, regular folks raising a family like the rest of us. They hoped for more for their children than they had when they were young. A good aspiration in concept, but, like so many good intentions, often hits a target other than the intended in application. The more they provided for their daughters, the more they demanded.

Craig began, jokingly, referring to them as the princesses. Sadly, it turned out not to be a joke at all. Trendy clothing and fashionable makeup kept Craig in the poor house. Lucinda tried to rein them in on occasion, but in her heart she felt her daughters were entitled to all they could provide.

"Last one, eh Craig?" Clovis' father continued.

"Yeah, boy!" Craig responded with a grin, and then it faded into a serious worry.

"Big affair again this time?" Clovis father was digging for details now, although it was sort of a rhetorical question. Three daughters and three weddings so far, each one had been far superior to the previous. And the first was as posh an affair as Blandtrap had seen before.

"I suppose so." Craig resigned himself to his fate. "I've been up all night trying to find a way to pay for this thing. I haven't really slept in about a week. You know those other weddings have ruined me financially. My only asset is my ability to repay debt. I went over our budget again and again. If we live frugally, repay debt aggressively, forego any vacation or recreation of any kind, and I live to be 105, I can die broke."

"I'm sure it seems bleak now, Craig, but its not as bad as all that." I tried to cheer him.

"Oh no, Harry," He said, "It may be worse. I think, though, I may have found a way out if I can sell the idea to the ladies."

"What's that?" Clovis father inquired.

"Sponsors!" Craig said proudly but searching our faces for reaction.

"Sponsors?" We all asked in unison. Clovis, who had been wandering Village Square trying to remember what he was supposed to be doing, came in, sat down, and remained uncharacteristically quiet. He could tell we were in the middle of something, so he just nodded hellos and sat quietly. Our poker faces overrode the incredulity in our minds, so Craig explained more.

"Everyone is doing it these days. Sports arenas have been renamed for sponsors willing to pay a handsome fee for the privilege. Why, college bowl games are named for snack chips and cell phones, all for a pretty penny. If I play my cards right, I might just come out of this thing well heeled." Craig was showing the signs of strain. No one challenged what he was using for logic.

Sleep deprivation and financial crisis are an ugly combination. He had been thinking so hard, I was convinced the hamster had finally fallen off the wheel. Craig seemed suddenly inspired as he nearly jumped from his seat to leave abruptly. He made no further comment. He was on a mission.

As he ran by, Grace, the cashier, could not believe he dashed out without paying for his coffee. It wasn't all that rare. A couple of times a week one of the old guys would get up and wander off, forgetting to pay. Someone or other always steps up to take care of the bill. I still considered Craig one of the younger guys, but he was aging rapidly. I motioned to Grace to give me the check.

No one gave the matter much thought after that day. Craig was absent from the diner most of the time and he didn't mention the matter to any of us again. It simply slipped our minds.

The wedding was earlier today and it was an affair such as I had never dreamed. The invitation should have been an omen, yet I never guessed Craig would follow through on his idea. The invitation read:

Craig and Lucinda Beeman, owners of the Mudwaddle SUV available at Blandtrap Motors, proudly announce the marriage of their daughter, Eliza Beeman, a student at Bureau Valley Business College, to Frederick Aragon, insured by Butte Crossing Mutual, the son of Georgio and Annamae Aragon, whose home was built by the progressive builders, Armenian Homes, at 2:00 PM, as timed by the featured watch in the window of Walker's Jewelers, at the Blandtrap Community Church, home of the local food bank (Donations Welcome), on June 15th, the day Plowboy Diner, Blandtrap's only downtown eatery, was founded. The reception, catered by Jose Wong's Ye Olde Fashioned Chuckwagon Smorgasbord Luau Buffet, will begin immediately following the vows in the church reception hall.

The invitations were the talk of the town for weeks after they were received. We learned later that Lucinda had insisted upon a tasteful font of clearly visible size. This condition required the invitations be printed on legal sized paper, both sides.

At the wedding, decorum demanded a minimum of discussion during the ceremony. Craig had his eye out to see if criticism would be harsh, so little was said at the time. I'd like to call someone now and compare notes, but Edith and the ladies of the town are going to have the phone lines lit up all night.

The wedding itself was a most anticipated event, after the intriguing nature of the invitations. An invitation list normally contains many names of those who will not attend, but to whom an invitation should be extended. Vacations were delayed or cancelled and surgeries rescheduled in order to make the ceremony. Everyone invited attended this one, and even several who were not, I'm sure, invited at all.

We rose for the entry of the bride and as she passed, I could swear there were words written on the train of the gown. Fuzzy, almost indiscernible words were incorporated in the filmy fabric. It seemed to suggest 'Jose Wong,' but I couldn't be sure nor make out the rest. By the time I figured out what I was seeing, the bride had made her way to the altar and my vision was blocked by the scratching ring bearer and a fidgety flower girl.

"Did you see anything?" I whispered to Edith.

"I don't know." She was flustered and words were not readily at her command, "Luau Buffet?" she softly guessed.

"I did see it then!" I announced proudly but quietly. "Subliminal advertising! The parts of this event that are not pure brass are genius.

The preacher rose to throw out the first pitch. I was surprised to see it was not Brimstone on the mound, but some other fellow I'd never seen before. The preacher got right to it with 'Dearly beloved' and kept pitching from the stretch. Everything was quite traditional.

The unusual amount of conversation and occasional tittering led me to believe we were not alone in observing the train message. The mother of the bride was unnerved by the crowd's inattention and appeared not to understand the source of the distraction.

When it came time for 'Speak now or forever hold your peace,' Craig Beeman rose to his feet. Gasps from the audience, daggers of stares from the bride, and seam-popping tugs from the mother of the bride did not discourage him.

He began with clarity and sincerity, "I have no objection to this marriage, but want to take this moment to express my unconditional approval of the groom. Eliza could not have chosen a better man. I can recall dreams of this moment and it has been all I dreamed it would be, and more."

Chuckles from the audience were agreement. The event had been more than they hoped for, too.

Lucinda and I have dreamed of growing old, sitting on our backyard deck, watching Eliza's children, our future grandchildren, playing on the deck. Then I realized, we don't have a backyard deck. What will I do? Am I doomed to a tedious and boring retirement?"

Seth Hugginbough, owner of the Hardware Store and Lumberyard, also rose and said, "No, Craig. I can build that deck for you for four thousand dollars. You can enjoy your autumn years."

"Done." Craig responded, and they both sat.

The preacher must have been informed of the matter because he started again without a warm-up pitch. The rest of us were left on the bench. It was a hard grounder, but I think I fielded it cleanly. Craig and Seth had conducted just enough business to allow Craig to deduct the wedding from his income taxes. And, Seth got a plug for his new deck building service. The preacher took it all the way home this time, without further noticeable incident.

Reverend Brimstone was hanging around the periphery of the reception and I got a chance to ask him why he didn't preside over the ceremony. He said the first time Craig pitched his idea to him he had balked, so Craig benched him and brought in a reliever who would throw the pitches he wanted. After witnessing the day, Brimstone was at peace with his exclusion.

After the ceremony, the wedding party boarded cars for the traditional drive through town with horns honking, dragging cans and boots behind the car which was decorated with the traditional 'hot springs tonight' and the rarer 'you can own this car for $89.99 a month from Blandtrap Motors.'

After the wedding party's return, the reception line was next and it seemed normal, although the receiving line was directly under a banner for Walker's Jewelers. You don't, as a regular course of affairs, see that sort of thing in a church reception hall.

Jose Wong delivered on his promise of culinary diversity with suckling pig, potato pancakes, asparagus crepes, and black-eyed peas. Such diversity is novel but I am uncomfortable with many new trends. I don't keep up with international affairs, but I am convinced that more than one item on my plate may well have been at war with some others.

The cutting of the cake held promise for entertainment. The crowd had taken to moving 'en mass' like passengers on a cruise ship, moving from port to starboard to view featured sights.

Like the rest of the day's events, cake cutting was almost traditional. The cake was four tiered with white icing, a tiny bride and groom on the top tier. With camera flashes forming a nearly continuous blinding light, they cut the cake. The groom carefully put a piece in the mouth of the bride. She followed suit after pretending to smear the face of the groom.

The cake was a masterful piece of engineering. The decorations on the cake, the sugar flowers and icing brocade, were intricate, yet regardless of the angle a photographer attempted, the words 'Betty's Bakery and Beanery' in green icing could not be positioned out of the frame without also losing the bride and groom and most of the cake.

Some of the ladies, mostly the older ones with failing memories, began slipping away to take notes on the little pads in their purses in order to document these events, thinking they may need evidence in order to be believed. Others were bolder, directly soliciting the photographer for pictures, with a premium being placed on the video. The photographer was smiling big; he knew he had something special here. He was overheard laughingly muttering that he would make more from the guests than the family.

Stu and I cornered Seth Hugginbough trying to pry out of him how much he knew in advance of the ceremony, while Edith hustled over to witness the throwing of the garter and the bouquet. Hugginbough stuck to his story, no matter how Stu and I tried to crack it. Apparently, he knew nothing before the rehearsal last night.

Edith returned before our conversation could develop fully into recanting golf stories and baseball scores. Edith said it was anticlimactic. The bride and groom tossed the appropriate object and there was a only a modest amount of increased pushing and shoving than you would expect. It must have leaked out among the unmarried young men and women that a coupon for a free candle from the notion store and a coupon for a free oil and lube from the gas station were attached to the bouquet and garter. The coupons were 'buy one, get one free,' which was disappointing to the victors. Unlike the hype suggested, they had to spend to save.

Against our better judgment, Edith and I chose to leave a bit early. The neck craning and scurrying about to get a good view had tired us considerably. As we were gathering our things to leave, they were announcing the dollar dance.

Of course, Craig had raised the stakes a smidge. It was a five dollar dance now, but it wasn't just a price increase, the increase came with additional value as well. For five dollars you not only got a dance with the bride, but you got to choose the song. It was a good attempt to steal home, but the slide finished short of the plate.

The band for the reception was Ed's Polka Band and Hip Hop Review. Their music tended toward either extreme and it took a considerable amount of time to find common ground, musically, so the dancing could proceed.

As we exited, I saw Craig looking at his watch. As the reception dragged on he was sure the rental cost for the hall was going to exceed his budget..

This, I suppose, constitutes the main social event of the season. Although unconventional, I challenge you to show me an event in your city that can rival this day.

Respectfully Submitted,

Harry Ellis

Harry Ellis

238 Persimmon Street

Blandtrap

To the Editor of the Tiskilwa Bureau Valley Chief

RE: The Institute for Idle Science – The Precise Speed of Smell

Dear Sir:

Your editorial of last week presented an argument for urgency in scientific research. You contended we should focus on medical research to lengthen life, advance food safety to minimize illness, and geological investigations to understand our world more fully. All are noble pursuits. I don't argue against any of them. In Blandtrap we are working toward similar goals. Calvin Farnsworth of the Institute for Idle Science is beginning his fall term of experiments soon. Nearly free from his self-imposed summer obligations documenting community events, Calvin's calendar showed free dates in the near future. Research could resume.

The next topic of research had not been decided. Calvin had been toying with a few ideas but nothing had gelled yet. He always wanted to do something with 'The sun never sets on the English Empire' because of its wide-ranging implications as well as sounding like it would involve considerable travel. Calvin was a good historian but he fell short on current events. He was unaware the English Empire was not the world power it once was. When I informed him of the news, he discarded the project. Calvin had learned long ago, and on more than one occasion, that in order for the research to be valid, the premise must be true.

Truth alone isn't sufficient to qualify for research either. The research must carefully weigh the risk of injury during against the value of the knowledge learned. The 'Monkey See, Monkey Do / A Watched Pot Never Boils' fiasco was proof of that. A newfound respect for safety led Calvin to discard the very promising 'Never Run with Scissors / The Bridge Freezes before the Roadway' experiment in light of the more obvious dangers. He was also concerned the latter premise, wise as it was, was not an adage at all but simply a road sign.

Not long ago, Calvin had been reviewing constants. You know; those numbers that keep recurring but are always the same value, like pi. He would recalculate constants every few years to confirm they were truly constant.

If constants were to vary with time, it would suggest we know little about the interaction of our four dimensions with other, less familiar dimensions. The consequences could be far-reaching. "What if another dimension changed the relationship between Celsius and Fahrenheit units of measuring temperature?" he would postulate. No one else he knew was doing this ground-breaking work. Others were just continuing to use constants without concern for the possibility of change. That was far too narrow-minded for Mr. Farnsworth.

It was during a period of recalculation that Calvin noticed a vacancy among the known constants. He reviewed the speed of sound first because he could calculate that himself. The experiment was relatively easy and he could do it by himself. He preferred to conduct research alone, removing the variable of participant error, but he enjoyed the company when assistance was necessary to the experiment.

Recalculating the speed of light was more difficult. He had to review existing research because he lacked resources to do it himself. No one, let alone a scientist, likes to have their procedures and calculations questioned. They must submit to the scrutiny of peers, and it is marginally tolerated from the other scientists.

When letters arrived from The Institute for Idle Science, they wondered what the Institute had to do with them; and why it claimed dominion over their work.

He did, through persistence and regular correspondence, receive the information he requested. Calvin was able to recalculate the speed of light from the work of these renowned experts. He returned a letter of congratulations to all who contributed to his endeavor.

When the letters were received I am sure more than one eyebrow was raised and, when phone calls were exchanged among this august body of minds, I am also sure that inquiries were made regarding The Institute for Idle Science and the scope of its discipline.

Calvin's calculations showed, except for refinements in the procedure that allowed more precise measurement, both the speed of sound and the speed of light had remained constant and did not appear to change with time. However, he had only been performing these exercises for about ten years. "Ten years" Calvin thought, "was but a speck when considering the span of time. An imperceptibly small change, one too small to measure given current methods could still be present."

That kind of logic was the reason Calvin founded The Institute for Idle Science. He hoped others of his caliber would be attracted to the Institute and it would carry on his vision beyond his brief life. Don't we all hope something similar?

There was one calculation that remained elusive. No one in the scientific community was currently working on the task. Calvin journeyed from one major university to another, scouring records for previous work in this area. None was unearthed. No one in all antiquity had ever tackled this task before. He could be famous. His name would be included in textbooks: Calvin Farnsworth, the man who first measured the precise speed of smell. Maybe he would name the constant the 'Farnsworth Factor.'

"Hey you kids! You need to stay at least 20 'Farnsworths' from that dead skunk!" He imagined people using the term in normal daily events. "We should locate the new dump three 'Farnsworth Years' away from town." It might even be part of the zoning code one day.

The excitement of discovery gripped Calvin and wouldn't let him loose. He had trouble getting down to the work of science because his mind wandered to the probability of fame and recognition in the scientific community. It was a heady brew for a man like Farnsworth.

The first step in any scientific venture, I have been told, is to carefully define all terms. When it comes time to define physical phenomenon, it is often found that words don't really mean what we have traditionally thought them to mean. Smell, odor, scent, stink, and stench are often used interchangeably. Some of these terms, Calvin observed, operate in a small arena of reference given normal usage.

Odor, for instance, is a generic term for anything that can be smelled. Calvin eventually defined the term 'odor' but, to avoid a circular definition, he defined other terms first. The term 'odor' is more often used in polite company to refer to objectionable sensations when offense is to be avoided at all costs.

Scent is a term, he decided, reserved for animals. Dogs find their way around largely by scent. They mark their territory, as do many other animals, by leaving a scent behind. Canines and pigs are trained to search out particular odors, such as drug-sniffing dogs or truffle-seeking pigs.

Scent is used to refer to people also. Perfumes are referred to as scents. I had to use Edith's expertise here, but the amount of scent actually determines the quality of the product. Parfum has the most scent, eau de cologne has less, and eau de toilette has the least. The difference in quality is reflected in the price of the product. Not that I don't trust Edith, but I went to the drug store to confirm this information. There is a substantial difference in cost across the spectrum of scents confirming what I was told.

Aroma seems to be reserved for reference to food and drink. Biblically, of course, it refers to sacrifice. Unfamiliar with the original language, Calvin did not know if it was a literal translation or whether it was an idiomatic phrase. Aside from scripture, he was convinced his definition would hold up to scrutiny.

Stink and stench, he contended, were used to describe only objectionable odors. Stink was a detectable odor found objectionable by most, while stench applied to a strong stink found nearly universally offensive. These definitions formed the foundation of Calvin's study. His work was to determine that fine line between stink and stench.

I want it made clear to the editor: I had no foreknowledge of the experiment and, although I was present during the exercise, had no opportunity to warn the innocent who were about to be nasally assaulted. Stink, Calvin documented, involved a mild physical response usually including audible utterance which showed unmistakable dislike of the odor along with an attempt by the subject to separate himself from the odor. It often included a warning to subsequent subjects of the pending smell.

This varied significantly to observations Calvin had made regarding taste. When a subject encountered an objectionable flavor, it was often followed by an invitation to share the experience. It is true, I have encountered this phenomenon myself and it often occurs at the refrigerator. "This tastes awful, try this!" is the normal scenario.

While stink involved the nose, stench, Calvin discovered, involved the entire body. He noticed that in addition to covering their nose, the eyes started to tear and the attempt by the subject to remove themselves from the stench resembled flight, as if from a bomb or a natural disaster. The response was immediate, severe, and was instinctive, requiring no thought on the part of the subject.

Again Calvin compared the observation to what he had seen in experiments with taste, noting a similar response with that sense. When an unwitting subject was given a substance unrighteously sour, a response involving the entire body is also observed. For the experiment with taste, Calvin had used an under ripe persimmon. The experience was enlightening and memorable. It has become a point of reference ever since.

After carefully defining both stink and stench, Calvin set about the task of defining smell. This would prove the more difficult job. Smell, it seemed to Calvin, was the act of sensing or detecting an odor. He couldn't help wrestling with the familiar dilemma: "If a tree falls in the forest and no one is there to hear it, does it make a sound?" I tried to convince Calvin of my opinion on the issue. I explained that if a carcass rots in the woods, it has a stench whether anyone was there to appreciate it or not.

Calvin needed hard proof and my opinion did not constitute such a commodity. We spent two days picking up road kill and placing it in plastic garbage bags. The job easily could have been completed in a few hours if it were not for Calvin's careful documentation of each unfortunate creature we acquired. He photographed the carcass, measured the distance from some convenient point of reference, and filled out a chain-of-custody form for each bloated animal we put into inventory.

Next on the docket was to place these carcasses in the forest. We had been delayed a couple of days due to problems Calvin encountered getting owner permission to use wooded areas for the experiment. Objections to dumping rotting road kill on private land ranged from "won't these attract scavengers?" to "are you crazy?" By word of mouth we heard about Clovis' uncle, Sam Willey, who had not only lost the sense of smell, but his hearing was pretty well shot as well. When Calvin pitched the idea to Sam, he left the car engine running. This was enough background noise to stifle Sam's hearing altogether. Vanity prevented him from admitting his infirmity and he wouldn't let on he had no clue what was being said. He judged by the expression on Calvin's face that what he wanted to do was good, so he nodded his head in agreement. He would never discover his mistake and the experiment would not be an inconvenience to him. A stench wouldn't bother Sam in the least.

At our designated dumping sites we found that three days in a plastic bag didn't help these creatures any. We dropped the first carcass then I had to stand around while Calvin photographed, notated, and otherwise fussed about until he was satisfied the conditions were well-documented. I informed him the procedure had to change if I was to continue to assist him. In the future, he could measure and scribble to his heart's content but only while the critter was still in the plastic bag. All I was willing to do after we freed the road kill was to run as far and as fast as I could. I refused to stand in stench any longer.

We left the animals over the weekend, returning on Monday to monitor what had transpired. We left a total of four carcasses in different areas of the woods trying to keep them about a half a mile apart, more or less. The first two carcasses were missing. Not a bone or tuft of fur was left behind. Calvin was conflicted as to how to categorize the results. At first he put them in the 'yes' category because there was an odor present when no living creature was around, a living creature happened by and followed the odor to the carcass to drag it away. It was attracted by the odor.

"What if the animal didn't smell the carcass? What if it just stumbled across it by chance, you know, dumb luck?" I asked. Calvin had to chew on that one for a while but in the end he scratched it from the 'yes' column and put it in the 'uncertain' category. We continued searching for the other two carcasses.

The third carcass had been moved and about half of it remained uneaten. Something had been snacking on the carrion. There were tufts of long red fur and much shorter blonde fur lying around the site. The ground had been scratched up pretty good and twigs on small bushes had been snapped and were left hanging. It looked as if it could be the scene of a struggle. Two animals were fighting over the same prize, no doubt. This situation, too, didn't seem to fit well into one category or the other resulting in another entry into the 'uncertain' column.

The fourth carcass proved very difficult to find. We searched for about an hour before Calvin consulted the photographs he had taken when we dropped off the animal. Locating the carcass was not a challenge due to profound odor even if we couldn't see it. By olfactory chromatography, we discovered a tree had fallen over the carcass.

Neither Calvin nor I recalled the tree. It was absent from photographs or outside the frame of the picture. Its falling had changed the appearance of the small clearing rendering the position of the dead animal impossible to discern. Once we moved the log, we found the carcass. Now there might be some question if the odor is there when people are not, but I can testify that as soon at the log was moved, the stench arrived simultaneously.

The ride back was mind-numbingly boring. Since we used pry bars made of tree branches to remove the tree trunk from the carcass, I was subjected to the complete lecture regarding the physics of levers. The dissertation seemed endless. I kept interjecting every few moments what the ultimate consequence was, "We need to move the log." I like to get to the end result quickly. Calvin starts way too far back to make a story interesting. If you ask him how to change a tire, he'll begin by explaining how to grow a rubber tree. He includes entirely too much detail in his explanations.

It took Calvin several days to reconsider the experiment. Clearly his tactics were flawed. Consultation with other scientists led him to the conclusion that settling the smell in the woods question would be of no help to him in calculating the precise speed of smell. He hoped to design an experiment that could be performed in a laboratory because most prestigious research is performed in a laboratory. Calvin resolved there would be no wandering the countryside until the experiment was finished.

A question or two remained. They were confusing to Calvin. "Did pleasant odors travel at a different rate of speed than objectionable odors?" His experience suggested they did. Recalling his college days, he remembered being in a bar reeking of spilled beer and cigar smoke when a young lady entered and the smell of her perfume traveled across the room through the air, shoving flat beer and stale cigarette smells aside. The fragrance seemed to arrive at the nose of each man balancing on barstools uncontested. It wasn't entirely clear whether they had smelled her perfume, heard her voice, or seen her beauty first. It was the scent of her perfume he remembered most so it seemed first.

Perhaps pleasant odors aren't faster but simply more forceful. They may possess an ability to overpower a stench and find their way to a nasal target. Consideration of the fact that pleasant odors are more welcome than many stenches should be included in the model of the study.

The procedure, the standard operating procedure for those unfamiliar with scientific endeavor, needed to be carefully crafted to encourage participation of as many subjects as possible in the experiment. The direct phrase, "Here, smell this," was probably lacking in tact and detail the participant would insist upon before agreeing to the procedure.

Not long ago Calvin found himself in the city at a regional shopping mall. I will ignore the circumstances brining him to the city because it is not my custom to labor the reader with unnecessary detail. He was walking through one of those large department stores because the best parking is just outside their doors. If you want to enter the mall by any way other than these anchors it requires parking in so remote a location you may need a map to find your way back and a book of common translations to communicate with the locals in their native language.

As Calvin passed the perfume counter he noticed how bright and pleasant the display area was kept. He admired the uniquely shaped bottles, colorful labels, clever names for scents, and the convenience of the stools used to waylay pedestrians as they were lured into purchasing yet another unneeded product.

Just ahead as he was walking through, Calvin saw a young lady spray a mist into the air to sample the scent. Unthinkingly, he strolled through the cloud of vapor and could not help experiencing the sensory event. The acrid stink that enveloped him was nauseating. He redirected his steps to evade further exposure, but he had already done the damage.

"What possible motive could drive a young lady to douse herself with this reeking mixture?" Calvin wondered. The desire to attract a young gentleman is strong, he recognized, but what lady would want a man enticed by this stuff? Women employ a variety of tactics in the battle between the sexes.

Some notably brilliant women appear dumb when trying to attract men, thinking ignorance is attractive to them. Other talented women appear to be without artistic inclination to lure the attention of some schlub, believing culture and manners are a turn off to men. Still other athletic women demonstrate a lack of coordination, missing lay-ups and double dribbling, supposing that letting a man defeat her will endear her to him. These strategies are frequently effective or they would not have endured as long as they have. The gambit using stinky perfume, though, seems to represent flawed logic and is far beyond the scope of the more familiar deceptions.

Calvin exited the department store into the mall promenade trying to escape the expanding cloud. His choice of lunch hour to visit the mall meant his pace was slowed to a staccato shuffle. Having put a good distance between himself and the department store, he was surprised he could still smell that rancid scent. The stark reality of his situation began to sink in. The spray was on his clothes and he was now the source of the stench!

He could see people fifty feet away looking around, convinced something smelling that bad would be easy to identify. Shoppers next to him solved the mystery quickly. As Calvin passed strangers, they would glare at him as soon as they recognized him as the source. Old ladies stopped, intending to give him a piece of their mind, woven with tips on personal hygiene, only to shrink away unable to survive the rigors of close contact. Toddlers would wrench free from their parents' hands and flee in hysteria. Infants cried in their mothers' arms.

Breaking clear of the food court crowd he made better time. Regretting the esthetic carnage he was wreaking in that public place, Calvin searched for the nearest exit. He returned to his car, walking around the outside of the building where the absence of walls would allow the stench to dissipate.

He was trying to recall the safety procedure appropriate for the situation and was having no success. 'Stop, drop, and roll," didn't seem to apply. It would only delay his exit. He thought a bath in tomato juice might be just the ticket but he couldn't arrange it in the mall; he would have to get out of the building and go home.

Calvin continued to walk faster, sensing increased urgency, even if it wasn't there. As his stride and pace increased, his wits began to return to him. Taking note of his increased velocity, he believed he observed the smell to diminish in intensity.

He began to experiment. By varying his pace, he noted the intensity of the odor increased when he slowed and decreased as he moved faster. He could no longer detect the odor when he was walking the fastest, just before he broke into a trot. "At last," Calvin believed, "An experiment that can be duplicated!" With his mind occupied with the minute matters of research, the odor didn't bother him during the car ride back to the Institute for Idle Science.

Trying to keep subsequent experiments as close to the original experience as possible; Calvin tried to purchase the same perfume that had polluted him before. He shopped around Blandtrap but the drug store carried a limited selection of scents, most of which smelled like cherry cough syrup or eucalyptus. He failed to get the name of the product the saleslady was spraying which made finding it again a most ponderous task. He had to return and ask department store staff.

The same saleslady was not working when Calvin returned. The staff working said they would need the name of the perfume because they didn't believe they sold anything smelling like Calvin's description. He noted the clever product names on the perfume bottles on display and decided he would try guessing the name. "Pure Putrification?" was his first guess. He took a stab at "Dead Nine Days," and gave up after the snickers that "Satan's Underpants" elicited. As he was being lectured on the subjective nature of scents by the supervisor of the perfume counter, a customer sprayed a nearby sample into the air. It was not the original scent but it was reprehensible enough to do the job.

Calvin recruited me to help him with the experiment. I accompanied him bringing with me a stopwatch and a measuring tape, tools of the procedure. Reticent as I was to visit the mall any time other than the mandatory Christmas shopping trip, the promise of science and the welfare of mankind outweighed my apprehension. We began the experiment.

Calvin walked through a cloud of the stuff and began walking. We had already chalked distances on the floor of the promenade and I was ready with the stop watch. I would record distance and time when Calvin told me the odor was gone. I had refused, as a matter of principle, to allow the perfume to be sprayed on me. We collected more distances and times on subsequent laps.

It was Calvin's intent to duplicate the experiment several times to increase the reliability of our data. Mall security, responding to complaints of odd behavior and unusual smells, invited us to leave the premises and escorted us, guaranteeing compliance with their request. Calvin said they have a short memory and he has plans to return at a later date to refine his calculations. Preliminary data suggests the precise speed of smell to be 5.3 miles per hour.

So, not only is scientific research important in Blandtrap, it is ongoing in groundbreaking areas of science. We are delving into new and exciting topics where more conventional scientists fear to tread. It is a dedication to science unfamiliar to you folks in the city.

Respectfully Submitted,

Harry Ellis

Harry Ellis

238 Persimmon Street

Blandtrap

To the Editor of the Tiskilwa Bureau Valley Chief

RE: European Vacation

Dear Sir:

You must survive this week without my usual report from Blandtrap. Edith and I have taken a holiday. I will enjoy the splendor that is Europe. Without my wise advice I am sure you will flounder, but if you stir those settlings you use for brains, certainly you will survive until I return.

We rode by plane to Germany. There are other ways to get there; we chose to fly. Time was the reason for our choice, not because it is so rare these days but because the supply seems to be dwindling.

Society, on a plane, has rigid structure and is designed to curry envy among passengers. The airlines promote it hoping you will covet better accommodations to a point where you will be willing to pay for the privilege. You sit facing forward with all of the passengers who could afford better accommodations ahead of you. They may be nice folks in regular conversation. You cannot talk with them. You can only sit and watch as they are pampered and coddled.

A full view of the elite is not to be had. No, that would be unseemly. Flimsy attempts are made to obstruct full perception. Perhaps this is done to deter mutiny on the part of lesser passengers.

Things viewed through a filmy veil always seem more interesting than the bare, unvarnished truth. Fashion designers employed this tactic with aplomb for centuries before the current trend of exhibitionism grew to popularity.

Now, those who can wear popular fashion without a pronounced bulge or sag are fewer than those who do. Congress investigates matters well beyond its authority every day without measurable purpose. They should direct their attention to those who sell revealing clothes to unfit, overweight, and otherwise unattractive saps. One can barely divert one's glance in time to avoid the pain and self-conscious embarrassment a bare flabby midriff or exposed underwear cause the casual observer. "Beauty is in the eye of the beholder," it is said, and it is true. Ugly is there too. Offense and degradation fill the racks in clothing stores at the mall.

Envy is the seed and service the water that makes it thrive. While resting somewhat uncomfortably in your narrow seat with a piece of protruding metal designed to separate you from the passenger next to you, while it inflicts discomfort falling short of severe pain or leaving a permanent scar, you can see flight attendants hovering about the better class passengers. You see but a glimpse of that life. You imagine you hear "Another muffin, Masseur?" or, "A warm towel, mien Herr?"

Conjecture runs wild through your brain as you sit with neither muffin nor towel while joined in your seat to an unwelcome neighbor with an annoying habit like humming or moving his lips while he reads. You try to be tolerant. Letting bygones be bygones you sue for peace but are denied when he refuses to allow you to read his magazine as he turns the pages.

Priority is the sunshine that grows our little garden of discontent. You can guess what service you might get because it previews with those ahead of you: Beverage? Dinner? Common courtesy? Acknowledgement of any kind? What will be my next surprise? Harsh reality is likely what you will find your class of ticket has purchased.

Just when you think you can tolerate their treatment no more, your shoulder begins to itch. An itch is an irritation easily quelled by the scratch of a finger. Like those imprisoned in stocks or restrained with shackles, you discover relief from the itch is not found without contortions. What would have been an affliction unworthy of mention, when left alone to grow in intensity, becomes a mind-controlling obsession. The urge to scratch has grown to a life goal and surpassed welfare of family and concern for friends in importance.

As you writhe in your seat in feeble effort to reach the source of your pain, a vision of the passengers behind you lights your eye. There they are. At last, exactly what you have been looking for, sad creatures in such poor accommodations; they look up to you. Knowing they are seeing you in the same way you are viewing the pompous slugs ahead of you warms your heart in a wonderful way. You relax and enjoy the flight. A smile paints your face as you drift off to slumber-land in contorted comfort. Indeed, it must appear a smug smile to those aft of your section.

It was a large plane with two exits. To disembark was a simple and orderly event. Envy stops at the threshold. Sure, first class is allowed to leave through their private door before the rest of us, but the second door makes it seem as if all have equal status. Customer service, after all is considered, is just that; making the customer feel satisfied whether or not they have received anything of value.

The inexperienced international traveler, a club in which I am at least an officer, if not president, believes that the journey is over once the doors are open and the plane is empty. It has merely begun at that point. People move like ants. Maintaining a line, single file, we march to the customs desk where government agents ask travelers a few questions and observe their behavior as they respond. They have an instant to discover whether a traveler might be part of a plan of destruction. Only a few seconds are allotted to uncover a plot that may have had years of preparation. Their job is nearly impossible.

Although questions are never repeated verbatim they are, in the end, only two: "Are you a bad chap?" and "Do you mean us harm?" It is unlikely that anyone who was a bad chap or who meant harm would answer in the affirmative. Customs folks are aware of this so they have added another test.

In my youth it used to be called the 'hairy eyeball.' A customs agent may raise one eyebrow and peer mightily through that orb to examine the mental process in situ. It is much like holding a magnifying glass over an ant to learn its behavior. If you hold the glass over the ant long enough, you can see what he is made of and can examine him more closely than with the naked eye; but, if you hold the lens too long, you fry the ant and the knowledge you seek is lost.

I could almost hear the wheels spinning in the agent's head as he checked me out. He might be saying, "I like the cut of his jib," or, "Let's examine the camera bag more carefully." It is more likely, though, that he was thinking "Why would anyone wear plaid shorts and a 'She's with Stupid' sweatshirt?" Edith said I should pay closer attention to how I dress. I am eventually discharged to the next ordeal without ceremony. Edith avoided the more sever scrutiny I attracted.

The next stop was to reclaim luggage in the baggage claim area. It is always downward to baggage claim. The work of engineers, I assume, because gravity is doing most of the work of moving bags. Engineers are lazy folks and will steal free energy from gravity rather than employ an engine that will earn the energy consumed. Planes arrive at ground level and every time bags are handled they lose altitude until the bags are sorted and delivered to the desired carousel located in the deepest dungeon of the airport.

Baggage claim is really the greatest equalizer of a travel experience, bringing men of all stations of life and throwing them into identical situations. First Class, Business class, coach class, economy class, each have their own rights and privileges until you arrive at Baggage Claim. Prince or pauper, all their checked bags are summarily dumped onto the revolving carousel from a conveyor belt.

Every piece of baggage will arrive there scuffed, torn, and occasionally stained with mysterious substances. There is no order to the sequence of the suitcases. First Class passengers, with their 'Me First' expectations are left standing, sometimes long after lesser passengers have left. Economy class passengers often win this lottery and their grips slide down the shoot first. There is something Biblical in this lesson. "The first shall be last" is what I mean.

One of my bags failed to arrive. No doubt it took the opportunity provided by foreign soil to make a run for it. It is no small surprise bags might feel this way. The reputation of baggage handlers, a notoriously gruesome group of workmen, is appropriate. They are famous for ruining materials advertised as indestructible.

We waited until all the bags from our flight had been removed and those of the next two arriving flights. I was out of luck and patience. I informed Edith I would put in a claim for a lost bag and we could get on our way. New clothing wouldn't damage our budget too badly. After getting directions to the lost luggage claim office three times, the last in a language I understood, we dragged ourselves and the skin of several cattle in that direction.

Passing a carrousel three down from ours, something caught my eye. It was a stroke of luck. Peeking out from behind a thirty-two inch wheeled bag I could see a corner of my bag. I could tell the bag was discouraged, thinking it had won the game of hide and seek.

After collecting our belongings, we had to lug our bags, scaling stairs and clinging to escalators like so many Sherpa forced to scale a Nepalese crest until we found enlightenment at street level. Disappointed a guru did not await us, we had to rely on the wisdom of traffic attendants for the answer to life's immediate questions.

Sadly, there is no flag to set on the peak and no fame to be had by reaching the zenith. What is the reward for this extraordinary effort? Privilege. One who achieves the near impossible by balancing baggage and self on a slow-moving stairway while clutching wallet, passport, tickets and itinerary in what is never a free hand is rewarded with the honor of standing in line for taxi or rental car.

The bags we found were piled outside the tiny office so I could give full attention to the counter representative, or sales agent, or rental associate. Each country has its own titles for the person renting you an auto and titles are very important to these people. Should you use the wrong nomenclature, you will be immediately and firmly corrected. The offended will hold a grudge throughout the transaction, if not for life. This was enough to make me uneasy and wonder if the associate might create some mischief among the rental documents to get even with me. I would always fear but never know if the threat was there.

I tried to avoid trouble by granting them the respect they think they have earned by referring to them as "Your Highness" and other terms of honor and recognition. This language was not met with general approval. They began peppering me with questions unrelated to our travel.

Custodian, car washer, and clerk were all perturbed with me. Rental people, as far as I could tell, expected me to inquire as to their position and assign them the honor and deference their status commanded. Being unfamiliar with foreign pecking orders left me ignorant of their customs and prone to unintended social insults at every turn. What I believed to be a menial position was, apparently, a big deal by their standards.

Having completed the paperwork, I inquired as to the location of the vehicle. "It's down the hall and through the gauntlet," they said…well, that's not what they said, but I discovered that was what was meant.

Wheeling a precariously loaded cart of zippered leather, nylon, and mesh compartments down a hall filled with swinging elbows, protruding chair arms, children running without looking, and automatic doors three quarters of an inch too small for the cart proved to be a task for which I was inadequate. I un-shuffled and re-stacked the luggage no less than three times before reaching the car.

Up to that point I had been in full charge of the cart and its contents, including; all piling and dragging necessary to arrive at the auto, but once there I was quickly demoted. In an instant I can be reduced to a lackey and was at that moment. Edith's scrutiny was necessary for me to complete the job with any degree of satisfaction.

"Move that bag to the side," she said. "No, the other side; it will get crushed by the other bags if it is not moved."

My response was simple. "Any delicacy this bag once contained was certainly lost under the crushing weight of baggage handlers or as it cascaded down the escalator, or when it was slammed by the automatic doors. Even if it should have survived those insults, those two children chasing each other and using the bag as if it were second base, certainly finished the job."

Vehicle inspection is the last hurdle to leap before we were freed from airport confines. We walked around the car with the rental representative, scrutinizing the auto for dents and scratches, noting each on a small form.

Rank is not unimportant in America, yet it has boundaries. The smallest unintentional slight, such as calling a customer service representative counter staff rather than agent, is met with ridicule and disdain. We tried to be careful to avoid any address suggesting position in the company to circumvent the associated brusque correction and down-dressing. There is often some kind of negotiation when documenting observations and challenges to one's opinion.

"There's a mark here on the hood," I said pointing to the spot of concern.

The rental representative approached and examined the mark closely. He didn't use a microscope to examine the hood but I could tell he wanted one. "It looks like tree sap," was his conclusion.

Impulsively, I responded "Get a lot of tree sap in the covered parking deck, do you?" while looking around in futile and sarcastic search for indoor trees leaking sap.

"Noted," was the representative's response. He handed me a form and while he had me sidetracked, disappeared like a magician in a circus sideshow. After the business was over I had a hundred questions about what route to take and what to avoid in different countries. Once he could be helpful to me he vanished leaving us alone.

Behind the wheel at last, I was the master of my fate again. Checked and carry on cargo loaded, maps recently referenced, and navigator at hand, I wheeled the car out of the parking garage onto the freedom of the open road.

Driving is a simple pleasure. Leisurely cruising along a new road with unexpected and delightful sights is a joy equaled by few others. Edith and I enjoy a good drive and find it revitalizes us, recharging our batteries, so to speak. The Autobahn in Germany does not come to mind when I think of a relaxing drive.

On this notorious highway, at speeds approaching insanity, Germans take to the left lane with gusto. Speed limit signs are prominently posted yet they serve not as laws nor as guidelines, but as mere suggestions, somewhat like daily specials on a café menu. German drivers seem to be up to the task. In spite of questionable judgment, we saw no accidents on our journey and noticed very few dents in their autos.

In our country, dents are to the populace what medals are to the armed forces. Dents communicate to the observer the depth of commitment the driver is willing to demonstrate even under the most desperate circumstances. They say clearly "Stay out of my way. I'm willing to hit you if I have to." Dents show you how often a driver has been challenged and how he faired as he held his ground.

Not all dents are alike. The ones earned on the road are badges of honor, coming from battle with another driver trying to exercise his will over yours. Dents acquired in parking lots of retail stores show the cowardice of other shoppers. They make their mark, jump in their car, and flee the scene in fear of physical or insurance retaliation. There is no honor, no dignity in behavior of that sort.

Edith played the role of concerned passenger trying to live through a challenging experience rather than her more familiar role of wife of the village idiot. At one point or another during the drive she was heard to say:

"Don't tailgate him, he'll jamb on the brakes," or, "Watch out! He's turning left from the right lane!" or, "Slow down, he's running that stop sign!" or, "Speed up, he's going to ram you from behind!"

I learned they can attack at any time from any side. A man driving alone has little chance to avoid disaster, but if he can fill the car with watchful passengers not interested in comfort but committed to vigilance; and he can maintain the driving skills of a Grand Prix racer, it is possible to narrowly escape peril.

Like most things in life, you must adapt to change, allow for innovation, or ignore it and go on with life. Speed is a matter of opinion anyway. You find your niche and that is where you travel. I found my place at about 150 KPH. To those traveling slower I was a demon speedster careening down the highway at break-neck speeds. To those traveling faster I was a speed bump on a race track, an ox-cart among racehorses, molasses in a quicksilver world.

Jetlag, the time difference, and sleep deprivation from a long flight were ganging up on me so I had to pull over to rest three times on the trip from Frankfurt to Montreaux. The first glimpse of Lake Geneva, or Lac LeMan was breath taking. We had skirted the mountains while following the Rhine River south. Even from Geneva to Montreaux I had been tired and focused on the road rather than scenery. With a chance to slow down and pull over, the lake and the mountains take over your mind and imagination. It is a truly beautiful and romantic sight.

Finding the hotel proved more difficult than I anticipated. As you would guess, a road surrounds the lake sometimes right up to the shore and other times a few kilometers away from water. The hotel was somewhere on that road.

Our directions, which had served us well in the beginning, began to lose their luster. Montreaux is no metropolis; however, with the Jazz Festival in full swing hotels close to town were beyond our budget. "He's too cheap," would be Edith's comment on the matter. I would call it 'frugally conscientious.'

With less than an hour of daylight remaining I broke character, swallowed my pride, and asked for directions. Anywhere you seek driving directions is a crapshoot at best, and the reason why most men don't like to ask directions. Well, it's among the reasons.

Asking for directions and then following them assumes too much for most men, me in particular, to be comfortable with the situation. Why, you ask? Because it assumes the one giving the directions knows the difference between North and South, left and right, real and imaginary, present day and ten years ago. It also assumes they are familiar with the road. One can drive for weeks and never see a fork in the road, but get directions and forks appear like tulips in springtime. "Do I bend left or veer right?" I will ask, espying the imminent decision before me.

Edith will respond by burying her head in the map, trying to reason her way through the dilemma. She refuses to do anything productive like tossing a coin. In a situation with a fork dead ahead, I don't need the right answer as much as I need any answer if I am to avoid crashing into a guardrail.

My plan was to ask directions to our hotel. Certainly one hotel would know the location of its competitors and the grand brotherhood of benevolent innkeepers would assist each other's guests and direct them accurately. To my chagrin, innkeepers are as cutthroat and competitive as undertakers. Not one hotel had any idea where any other hotel was located, let alone the one we were looking for.

"I am sorry, Masseur, I do not know of that hotel. Besides, I heard there were no vacancies there. We have some very nice rooms here. Do you want to sign in?" they each would say pushing the registration book toward me and smiling the smarmy grin of a huckster.

Our first problem was that we were not staying in Montreaux proper. Neither were we staying on the outskirts of Montreaux. Cully was the nearest settlement to our hotel, but it was far enough away it took clear weather to see Cully from the establishment.

Our second problem was that country folk are the same wherever you go. There is an eerie commonality in the way they give directions. Locals don't give directions in the present, but in some recent or distant past. "Turn left where the old oak tree used to be," or "turn right where Earl Swenson's cow was hit by a tractor." Distances must be converted into useable units. "About a mile," means, "I have no idea how far it is." "A ways down the road," means you may not be able to drive it in one day.

Add to this difficulty the language barrier. A limited vocabulary is a horrible handicap. Not surprisingly, an impressive obstacle occurs when two words in the foreign language sound like words in your familiar language. Proper names excepted, relying on the similarity in sound to translate to similarity in meaning can be a disastrous assumption.

All reason exhausted, I resorted, at last, to dead reckoning. This proved no less fruitful than the other tactics I tried. One by one, eliminating roads that must be or had already earned that designation, I stumbled upon the correct path and we arrived at the hotel. Edith accused me of driving past it once. I admitted no error, claiming it was a victory lap. A late repast and we were off to bed for that sleep that is so sweet when physical and mental exhaustion meet at the same moment.

The next morning, late morning or early afternoon dawned with great promise. Lake Geneva offered spectacular views. Enchanting, I suppose, described the emotion a view from our window evoked. The mountains rising across the lake were far enough away that detail could not be discerned. Imagination filled in what the eye could not see. I felt as if I knew the folks in that misty village across the water. Providing, of course, it was a village and not a rocky crag.

Few events graced our itinerary. The goal was to relax. A tight schedule would have been counterproductive to the purpose of our trip. The jazz festival was one event on the short list. We arrived early the day we visited the festival, losing our way only twice. Booths were shut up and not many businesses were open yet. People were scurrying about and that was what I came to see. A parade of local citizenry proceeded by so Edith and I got a good look at what they had. Tall, short, thin and portly, albeit not as many portly people as I am used to seeing in America, we got the lay of the land well before groups would perform. They gave every appearance of being intelligent but it was hard to tell given our language deficiency.

Sitting in a sidewalk café with a cup of coffee, we saw the procession pass in a continuous line. From our vantage point Edith and I could witness transactions as the booths began to open. Capitalism is the same wherever you go. Product comes in the back door and is sold out the front door, or window, in the case of booths. Profit is the money you manage to hold on to in between. Some customs differed from country to country but the dance is the same.

The buyer is enticed by the merchandise and stops to take a closer look. The merchant approaches the buyer from his blind side if he can find one. The element of surprise can be as advantageous in merchandising as it is in warfare. The prospective buyer points out several deficiencies in the product. The seller knows it wasn't a defect that attracted the buyer, rather some allure of the product. So the seller continues to expound on virtues of the product and the buyer resists with protests, excuses, and unanswerable questions.

As in nature, where the antelope will either elude the attack of the lioness or will be devoured, the buyer will either escape negotiations or leave with some worthless trinket, and the seller will drag off the cash to feed his pride. You see it every day on nature shows.

The festival itself was delightful. Although we hung about for most of the day, entertainment didn't really get started until late afternoon. I have no idea how late the affair lasted. I am not accustomed to keeping such hours. I enjoy the product of musicians, artists, and performers but I could never work on the production line. The useful hours of my day end before theirs begin. They seem to prefer the dark of night to the light of day.

Performers we saw were delightful. One singer stood out from the rest. It was a young lady, Anna Grafton, from Columbus that sparkled like a star. Truly, it was a moving performance and a privilege to catch the act.

Edith reminded me she had met the girl. She was the niece of the silk ribbon lady who lectured on crafts and such. The Quilting Society had been trying to lure the lady to Blandtrap for years. Her fee was beyond the means of the Quilting Society budget even if they forsook benevolent projects for a year. Still, they pestered the lady.

I could see darkness coming on the horizon, so we headed east around the lake as we cruised back toward our hotel. Once in the neighborhood, we decided to enjoy our evening meal before unloading Edith's purchases from the car. I yo-yoed back and forth past Cully, where we had decided to explore culinary offerings. I felt like I won the lottery when I found the only road into the village.

Slaloming the car through gates formed by pedestrians and Vespas, we wove our way to the center of the village where we spied a restaurant. A place to park was at a premium. We found a couple of public parking lots, but they were already full. Parked up well beyond their designed capacity, a ticket, a tow, or both was certain if we risked leaving our car in either. I was looking for food, not adventure.

On a second pass through a narrow alley Edith saw a cab driver getting into his vehicle. I waved to him to get his attention. It had been my experience that gaining his attention would be easier than gaining his understanding. "Is there someplace we can park the car?" I begged, forgetting that fewer words were better than more. A confused look and a shake of his head led me to rephrase my request. "Park?" I simplified and mimed, changing gears on an imaginary steering column.

A smile came to his face and he nodded. His English was pretty good and we wrote down his directions. Thanking him profusely we headed off to park. Meticulous attention to the route he designated led us back to the same parking lot we had twice cruised and was as full as it had been earlier.

We drifted about the settlement for a few minutes. The village was very small and I could only get lost for a few blocks at a time before I came across a familiar street or landmark. Edith spotted the taxi driver ahead. He had seen us as well and motioned to us to follow him.

Down narrow lanes and up footpaths they were using as streets our mammoth auto traveled. When the road opened into a parking lot at the train station, we pulled in and walked. The cabbie had traveled at speeds that made me uncomfortable. I braved certain death to keep up with him. We couldn't afford to get lost again. I couldn't wait to lose my lap and get feet under me. We locked the vehicle and set off walking.

The parking lot at the train station was at the edge of town away from cafés we saw in the middle of the village so we were in for a hike. It was a beautiful evening so a hike was not a chore, however, a day of walking and gawking at the Jazz Festival had reduced my normal gait to a meander. Passing under a viaduct we passed a sign on a building. I wish I could remember the name of the place. It was named the Café Cully or the Cully Tavern or something of that ilk. The menu was displayed outside on a small poster-like marquis.

The menu was in French, of course, and this language thing does tend to rear its head from time to time when you are abroad. I had had my fill of pasta and cream sauce since we arrived and I was in the mood for steak. The menu had several choices, one of which appeared to be steak. It may not have been steak as I knew it but it was, at the very least, a dish that featured cow appendages among its primary ingredients. Convincing Edith, we went inside.

The establishment featured six tables and a small bar. We took a table near the kitchen. A couple with a young child was sitting at the table next to ours and the gentleman spoke English fairly well. We communicated; he in English, and I in what I had come to call French, although most of those who spoke French fluently seemed baffled by my idioms. I attributed their confusion to the depth of my thoughts rather than anything lacking in my French. The Swiss tended to gesture more after I spoke than before. When locals become agitated, foreign gestures bear a striking resemblance to those I have experienced in America.

Edith wanted pasta with a tomato sauce, tiring of cream sauces as I had so the order seemed simple. My request for steak and fries went without hassle. I couldn't be sure until the meal arrived but there was rarely a question after I pointed to the desired item on the menu. Once I established the steak should not be in an omelet it was smooth sailing.

We quickly nailed down the pasta part of Edith's order, but when we requested tomato sauce we got a raised eyebrow in response. We repeated, "Pasta with tomato sauce," trying ever so hard not to speak in disrespectful tones.

"Pasta and tomato sauce?" she repeated inquiringly.

We nodded.

"No. I won't do it," was her tart response.

After some pleading she disappeared into the kitchen and returned brandishing a bottle of Heinz Ketchup saying, "Pasta and tomato sauce? No!"

The gentleman at the next table who obviously spoke some English intervened on our behalf. The waitress laughed at the confusion and held up the ketchup bottle pronouncing, "For fries!" She left the bottle for me and disappeared into the kitchen to prepare our meals.

Her departure gave us an opportunity to chat with the couple at the next table and thank the man for helping out with our order. Like most of the Swiss we met, he and his wife said they spoke only a little English yet they were seldom stumped by the meaning of our conversation even when our choice of words was questionable.

The only other patrons in the establishment were two old men both with huge noses as if they were competing for the largest facial obstruction in the country. One had tiny knobs on his proboscis. They weren't warts; his nose was just knobby. The other's olfactory organ glowed ruddily. The two were playing cards with great zeal. Each hand seemed to have greater significance than the previous even though play never ended. Each nursed a carafe of red wine at his elbow and referred to it from time to time for guidance in the game. Whether enjoying a grand lead or digging out from outrageous circumstance, they consulted their friend often.

They had made their own table cover for the game. It seemed to be green felt but it was difficult to be sure looking through the decades of wear. When one would perceive he had an advantage over the other he would pound the cards on the table with great gusto and mutter what I only could assume to be insults in the face of the other. The loser would scowl and mumble back what I am sure must have been threats or insults of a more personal nature.

I leaned over to the couple seated at the adjacent table and inquired of them what game it was the old men played. "I do not know," answered the man, explaining that, as far as he knew, it was only played in Cully and a few of the surrounding villages. The game has a name, I suppose, but he either didn't know it or lacked confidence in my ability to play it intelligently.

"What is the prize they are playing for?" I asked.

"I am sure I do not know," was the man's response. "Maybe they just get to play another game and drink more wine."

I think the stakes are bigger than that. The future fortunes of Cully are fastened to the struggle between these two men, in their minds at least. The outcome of the battle is not what is important. These men contend with each other because their armies, the men and women of Cully, have mutinied and now pursue whatever each thinks best. They no longer listen to the experience of those who have already defeated the enemies they face: trouble in marriage, rearing difficult children, holding down a successful career, a relationship with God, and peace of mind amid the strife of life.

They anger at villagers' needless suffering; they spar with each other out of frustration. Sitting at their table playing a simple game and drinking the wine of their labors while they overhear the fear and agony suffered by the young is what they must endure each day. Youth seeks no counsel; no one explores their experience. When they offer unsolicited advice they are repaid with polite smiles to their faces and rolling eyes or snickers to their backs. The village believes they are blind and deaf. I'll bet they don't even bother with the town anymore. They will play their game, sip their wine, and die with untold secrets of life because none would take the time to listen. They have been molded into wretched men.

It was hard to say good night as we left the small tavern. It had begun to feel like home. People cared about us, or at least our culinary choices. We had made new friends. Old friends are best but new friends are exciting for a while. I regretted we lacked the time to become old friends.

Edith said the bed in the hotel was just beginning to feel good when it was time to check out. The festival had closed and we had a few days left to meander around Europe. Holding differing opinions on where we should go, we flipped a coin to choose our route and went the way Edith wanted to go.

We traveled up the French side of the Rhine River. The region is called Alsace in the version of English I speak. The people were interesting and engaging, the food was marvelous, and attractions were plentiful. Our days dragged on much too late into the night for my taste.

We rolled into a small village after nine thirty in the evening. Pushing up the road to make good time like manly Americans do, I had neglected to allow time to acquire lodgings for the night. We were hungry and tired. Edith and I had been together night and day for what seemed to be forever. Enough is enough. We needed space between us, even if it was from across a hotel room.

Two inns graced the main street we took into town. We chose the first we saw because patrons were still dining on the sidewalk in front of the inn. The other inn had customers inside but the street was dark.

We parked and went inside to see what accommodations remained in their hotel. The inn had no vacancies, in fact, they no longer let rooms. Our good fortune continued when the wait staff informed me the chef had rooms to let in an apartment building two blocks away. She gave us a price, we were interested, and before I knew what was happening, we were in a foot race with the waitress to view the room before we rented it.

"Hurry! The kitchen is only open for another fifteen minutes." She shouted as she ran in front of us. Scampering up stairs, she showed us a room with a shower and sink and where the toilet was down the hall. It looked like heaven to us, as a bed of nails would have at that point in the evening.

Thinking we could relax, the waitress cracked her whip, telling us we had less than ten minutes to submit our order to the kitchen. Edith went with a seafood selection while I chose the familiar beef entrée. We were in France now and nonsense over omelets was over. I come from the best beef country in the world.

No one raises better cattle than in surrounding counties. The beef served to me was without a doubt the worst piece of beef I have ever encountered in my life. However, it was also the most flavorful steak I ever sunk my teeth into. They may not know good beef over there but they know what to do with what they've got.

Perhaps the chef was emptying the pantry. My steak came in a Pinot Noir sauce and no less than six tiny side items. I enjoyed every morsel on my plate. In the States, they would have tossed us from the joint a full hour before we left the inn. I enjoyed a second glass of red wine. Not sure of the vintage, it tasted of asparagus and mushrooms. It was the perfect compliment to the meat and sides. I suspected genius.

I have fond memories of the village and hope to return one day. Our last night was a scramble to the vicinity of the airport in Frankfort, Germany. Hospitality was not among the concerns of local restaurants. Although bars were open late, their kitchens closed early and were unwilling to provide sustenance for us. Residents didn't have our problem getting served.

The airport in Frankfort was the way we left it, sterile and efficient. An unfortunate error in packing caused two bottles of white wine to break in our luggage. The scent was unmistakable. Europeans are snobs when it comes to wine. They couldn't leave it at white wine; they would guess "Chardonnay?" or "Leifenbraumlich?" They would turn and stomp away in disgust when I confessed I had no idea what kind of wine it was.

I slept most of the flight back to the States. Fatigue is a friend when long spans of time must be endured. Sleep becomes a blessing. Edith busied herself with puzzles and magazines while I snored.

Deplaning is not easy after having slept in an airplane seat. At my age the body doesn't respond the way I expect. Sitting in a contorted position for an extended period of time leaves me deformed. I could have starred in a bad horror movie as I hunkered down the terminal walkway on my way to retrieve luggage.

We waited the mandatory two hours before one of our bags could be officially listed as lost. During the eternity we were required to linger, I scoured every carousel in the airport hoping to find the elusive bag so I could drag my aching bones home. My search yielded no bounty.

Anger begins as a tiny seed, little more than an irritation or annoyance. Time is the soil in which rage grows; inconvenience the water that sustains fury's life; and boredom the fertilizer that nourishes wrath until it flourishes. This is the garden that is my ire.

When the baggage agent finally accepted my claim, he became fearful. It was clear to him he was in danger. He knew with the wrong question or impertinent remark I could snap, and so may several of his fingers.

Recognizing his perilous position, the attitude of the baggage agent instantly changed from "You will comply with all lit signs and all requests of the flight staff under penalty of federal law including fine and imprisonment," to "Hey, nobody's perfect."

"Can you describe the bag?" He asked.

"Faithful and loyal, it has never failed me before. Even now I suspect it is not the bag's fault. It only associates with the finest luggage and never ventures alone into unsavory parts of the airport. In the end, I am confident you will discover the bag had nothing at all to do with its own disappearance and perhaps is even being held against its will." Let me testify that you should trim sarcasm from your lips before airline personnel call for security. Detention can be endless and there is no where they are unwilling to look for things whether they expect to find them or not. You will regret inspiring them to want to search. Everyone is so sensitive these days.

"What does it look like?" He quickly clarified. "Does it look like one of these?" He then thrust a paper with diagrams and pictures of various and sundry luggage each of which looked a little bit like my bag except for several distinct differences.

"It looks like A7, but with handles like E2 and wheels like C9," I offered, pointing to pictures all over the form. Finally I ended the identification process probably because the agent tired of the game rather than satisfied he had a useful description of my luggage. The attendant commenced writing on a small form. It was impressive how many words and how much time he consumed scribbling on this small scrap. I, with nothing to do but audience the scribe, began to dig for information. "When do you expect the bag?" I asked hopefully.

"Can't really say; don't know where it is," as he continued to write.

"Where do you think it will be coming from?" I pressed on.

"I said I don't know where it is." The attendant was louder now and signs of irritation were displaying themselves: reddened face and bulging veins are usually the first clues.

He, however, was undaunted in his documentation. Novels have demanded less effort than this author put forth.

Cleverly, I tried another tack. "Do you think Eskimos will be returning the bag?"

"Sir! If you fill out the form, as soon as I know anything regarding your bag, I will call you and inform you of it. Until then, sir, I bid you good day!" and he disappeared through a door much to the chagrin of the line that had formed behind me. As I left, a man tried to trip me, and there arose a grumbling from others that didn't fully muffle their insults.

Next week you will find a more characteristic representative of my missives. I will update you with what has been happening in my absence. Until then, you must use the divining rod you used before my informative efforts began to grace your desk.

Respectfully Submitted,

Harry Ellis

Harry Ellis

238 Persimmon Street

Blandtrap

To the Editor of the Tiskilwa Bureau Valley Chief

RE: Painting the House

Dear Sir:

I have finished yet another of your articles about the deeds of charitable organizations in your city. The populace is, no doubt, better for their service. In Blandtrap, charity is performed more by individuals than groups, carried out by people rather than formal agencies of mercy or organizations of philanthropy.

Our churches have Ladies Aid Societies and are proud and eager to meet specific needs but most charity here is quietly done by the person who sees the need, without dragging others into the matter. We do it because it needs to be done. No consideration is given to what recognition is to be had or whether photographers are nearby as is your custom.

Time is a precious commodity and I hate to waste it. They say "time marches on." In the war that is my life, I find time more of a tank than an infantryman. Rain falls against my house. Wild wind and scorching sun barrage the thin coating that is the paint on my home. It wears away much faster than a river cuts a canyon, so it seems. I find myself, once again, at the point in time when the house is in need of a paint job. It's beginning to look tacky, a condition Edith will not endure.

Michelangelo labored for years on the ceiling of the Sistine chapel. Raphael was wrought with angst over his compositions. Van Gogh was mutilated at his own hands before his art matured to the point where he released it. I have much lower standards than these, my predecessors. All I want is a coat of paint on the sucker and be done with it.

A man of my vintage is always concerned with cost. I am not a cheap man. I want this clearly understood; I am frugal. Edith may say I'm frugal to a fault, but the value of a dollar was taught me at a young age and I am painfully reminded of what I had to do to earn every dime I spend. It's more mindful than miserly, more economics than eccentricity.

As time continues its march, it takes a toll on men and houses alike. Men like to be known for the number and value of their possessions if they are wealthy; and for the condition of their possessions, if they are not. I fall into the latter category. Not that we live in a state of need or that desperate circumstances have befallen us; we are comfortable by the standards of this country which means we are wealthy beyond the wildest dreams of most people in the world. Comparison is a tricky science. Envy complicates the process of reasonable comparison rendering what you have to seem less than what some others have. 'The grass is always greener' the adage goes.

Accidents while doing household chores have become all too familiar a topic of conversation lately. Edith keeps a watchful eye on whatever tasks I dare to tackle. Tripping and falling seem to be my most frequent offenses and she has become wise to the trend. She realizes nothing can be done about my clumsiness, a malady escorting me all my life. It is a remnant of an uncoordinated youth that in adulthood blossomed into a garden of ineptitude.

Falling is what Edith fears most. Her opinion that advancing age and a lack of dexterity spells certain doom has been shared with me on numerous occasions. I believe her findings have reached a fallacious conclusion. I fear my ladder privileges will soon be permanently revoked so I restrict use of the device to emergencies and times when Edith is away from the house. I am comforted that my independence is preserved and only slightly concerned that a minor accident may result in the demise of my freedom. Men must be men or they cease to be. I suppose its one of those lose – lose situations.

A job like painting the house was bound to trip Edith's radar. She would certainly see potential damage to my person if I tried to do the work alone. It would have been in my best interests to call professionals before the last shred of credibility suffered irreparable damage. Thought of the expense of professional craftsmen curled the hair on the back of my neck, especially after Stu explained the way they charge for their work. They were frightening details to learn. He told of an hourly charge, a charge for special techniques, some colors required multiple coats of paint, and the best painters in Blandtrap required a security deposit against weather to preserve your place in the schedule. He had me as scared as a miser at a charity auction.

I would have to navigate some pretty choppy waters if I was to avoid paying retail for a job I had always done myself. Retail pricing is a specter that has haunted me during every large purchase. Edith tends to tip for odd jobs done by strangers or passers by. It's a trait that endeared her to me when we were dating, but after our monies were merged in marriage, has irritated me ever since. I don't get tipped if I do an exceptional job sweeping the garage or cleaning the gutters. Why should strangers benefit from average workmanship when I am unrewarded for stellar performance?

Our home has been white since we bought the place. Meager efforts at residential archeology led me to believe it has always been white. I assumed we would paint the house white again, but experience has taught me that would be a rash and potentially dangerous assumption. Color is a controversial topic between men and women, particularly between husband and wife. Whenever shade or pigment is discussed, the entire spectrum of the rainbow is thrust to the forefront of discussion with each nuance of hue a real possibility.

If a man were to paint a picture of the American flag, the colors red, white, and blue would immediately spring to mind. He would be right only in the most general sense. A cautious man would not proceed without a fashion consultant. 'Which shade of red?' 'What tint of white?' 'Exactly how blue?' become pertinent questions. It is no wonder Betsy Ross sewed the first flag alone. Had she asked for input, her progeny would be stitching to this day, still bickering over coloration.

Men and women disagree over matters of color more than any topic other than finances, entertainment, child rearing, vehicular transportation, religion, logic, art, cinematography, social justice, politics, and arithmetic. Their differences in each of these areas are deep and fundamental.

Men believe that color is a palate and there exist an infinite number of colors creating one of the greatest wonders the world holds. If imagination were applied, any color could work in any given situation.

Women, on the contrary, believe there is one perfect color for the front of the house and it hides among paint swatches at the hardware store. It can be uncovered through a process of excruciating elimination by comparison. "Do you prefer this shade or that one?" It often deteriorates into a double elimination tournament of taste; the winner of which gets applied to the exterior of our residence. My observation reveals there is no quick or rational resolution to this conflict.

Men have only a few names to describe colors. Common among them are red, green, yellow, and orange. Although we recognize tint and hue among colors, we consider colors similar in appearance are interchangeable in application. We don't use names for colors that include geological phenomena, meteorological events, or geographical locations. Colors should have one name unless a suitable modifier is necessary to distinguish similar shades; terms like dark blue or light yellow are acceptable.

Women prefer colors with names like 'Dusty Mesa,' Misty Lake,' or 'Bermuda Beach.' These names express feelings from fond memories or anticipation of future adventure. While such descriptive labeling are favorites of women, these names elicit an entirely different response from a man. If a man's opinion is sought regarding what he thinks of 'Bermuda Beach,' he is likely to ask "Is than down I-74?" instead of pointing to a swatch.

Unequipped to provide intelligent input into the process, I surrender color to Edith's clutches and start preparatory work required by a large undertaking like painting the house. The garage, or at least a portion of it, would have to be cleared to form a base of operations where I can open paint cans or store tarps and the like. Sacrificing the space already filled with our useless possessions would mean compromise or combat with Edith. In matters of clutter they are the same.

I could give up my anvil collection. I heard somewhere anvils have limited appeal. It makes them all the easier to collect. Once I locate one, I can pretty much name my price. Once, unknown to me at the time of negotiation, it included a hernia. Edith thinks they are a waste of time and money and just suck up valuable garage space.

I admit that I have never used an anvil for anything resembling its intended purpose and have no immediate plans to do so. Even though I do not own a horse or know anyone who would lend me one, I derive great comfort from the knowledge that if I built a forge, bought some appropriate hammers and some iron stock, I could shoe my own horse…if I had one, that is. Edith keeps dragging me back to that point. Sometimes she is such a wet blanket.

My vote, as it has been on many previous occasions, was to throw out some of Edith's ceramics. The completed projects don't bother me as much as the green ware, particularly the ones large enough to be considered statuary. Possessing fragility until these works-in-progress were fired in the kiln, safe storage was murder on a guy like me. Accidents happen all the time. I knew she hadn't worked on any of them for years. If she had, she would have discovered several pieces contained more contact cement than ceramic material.

Edith laughs at my dirty, rusty anvils and asks how I can compare them to the artistic grace of her pre-formed masterpieces. I have to be careful in these waters or I will run my ship aground. With many words and as much compassion as I can fake, I explain the eternal nature of an anvil, its very mass and solidity command respect while the delicate features of ceramics, which can be blown over by a stiff breeze and can shatter from incidental contact, are just whole for fleeting moments in time. People can be like that too. Often they are more fragile than the most delicate object.

The better course of action was to first tackle boxes on the shelves lining the back of the garage. Filled with invaluable heirlooms and objects eliciting emotion-filled memories, they had been stored so long writing on the boxes had faded away and they had to be opened to reveal contents. Rummaging through a few boxes I recognized as mine, I was able to discard two large trash bags of memorabilia that had lost its luster or its grip on my memory.

Edith's boxes were more clearly identifiable than mine so I pulled many of hers down making her task easier. I left the results of my work in plain sight to inspire Edith to at least sacrifice to the same degree as had I. It's a ploy that seldom works in situations like this. I'm a dreamer at heart which explains why I continue to ply the scheme.

Not wanting to irritate her during the day when we were to select the final color that night, wisdom told me to avoid the contentious subject that ended in argument more often than resolution. I put a few of her boxes back on the shelves. By agreement we recognized the impasse and did not discuss the topic except at a formal meeting. It was taboo to discuss the topic at any other moment.

Sunset could bring an arrangement of inexplicable brilliance. We would stand next to each other or arm in arm admiring the spectacle. Appreciation for God's own work of art painted on the canvas of the sky could well up in us until it overflowed into words. We would turn to one another, gaze into the other's eyes and say "isn't it pretty." That's all the farther we dared go until the matter was over.

We called said meeting. Armed with reason, practicality, and knowledge of how the job needed to be done, I came to the table and sat across from Edith who had proved herself a worthy adversary in struggles past. She had prepared for battle using esthetic competence, good taste, and a sense of fashion. I admit she had me on my heels for a while but I dug in my heels and held fast to the end. Our agreement was to paint the house white again, clearly a victory for me. With strict limitations of paint manufacturer, brand, and hue of white, she also considered it a win.

The idea that there could be shades of white exceeded my threshold of giggle. I managed to avoid insulting her by covering my mouth and snickering into my hand. Had I laughed out loud or my amusement been detected in any way, we would have scrapped our progress and started negotiations anew.

In my youth I would have approached a job like this with gusto and had done so for decades. Prudence and Edith suggested another plan was necessary. It was the ladder issue again. I had grown weary of the argument over the last decade. Edith was sure to bring it up during color selection negotiations. Any time she felt she was losing a point she would introduce ladder travesties. Gravity had become her best friend and constant debate partner. I would have to enlist the help of men whose wives still allowed them to climb if I were to return to my home in peace.

The available labor force was temporarily thin in Blandtrap. I could call my best friend Stu and know he would come to my rescue; but with the restrictions Edith holds over me and constraints placed on Stu by his wife, we would need a third person to perform dangerous tasks like opening paint cans and cleaning brushes. Throwing our lots in together would propel us backward, not forward.

Having the brainwork covered, what we needed was a strong back. The power to reason was nonessential to our purposes. Heavy lifting like moving ladders and relocating decorative planters would have to fall to Clovis. No one tackles a job requiring brute force with the same gusto as Clovis. As with any task around the house, there is some component needing to be done delicately. A weighty and awkward ladder must be placed gently against clapboards if marks on the wall are to be minimized and pictures hung on inside walls are to remain off the floor. Not every laborer equipped with great strength also possesses the agility to avoid breaking windows. Clovis did not fall into this category. He was immensely strong, while being curiously clumsy. Although it would cost me nothing, Clovis was an asset, but one to be used sparingly and only in appropriate situations.

Tommy Hunter was my first choice for hired help. An amazing boy, he was not just fit, willing, and able; Tommy could project himself into the place of another. It is rare for anyone, let alone a young lad, to understand this talent, extraordinary for an adolescent to possess it. I've seen him do it over and over while he worked for Hugginbough. A customer would ask for a broom, for instance, and if it was a male customer Tommy would assume it was to sweep the garage or basement and give him a corn broom. If it was a female customer making the request, he would assume it was for use inside the house and give them a broom with synthetic bristles cut at an angle and suggest a dust pan to go with it since she would be removing her sweepings rather than pushing them into a corner like a man is apt to do. In either case, as he was getting the appropriate broom he would ask them what they were using the broom to sweep, just in case his assumption would in some way offend the customer. When Tommy was done waiting on you, you were a satisfied customer.

Valiant and noble qualities made Tommy a hard commodity to acquire. Of course, he made top dollar without demanding it and was clearly worth every penny he was paid. The line that formed to bid for his services was formidable. Only after family obligations, school demands, and sports requirements did Tommy look for work. Hugginbough Hardware and Lumber was at the front of that line. Offering the same top wage and providing more regular hours than any one else could afford, they came first. The village was grateful he had shown little interest in girls or there would have been no time remaining of Tommy to sell to the citizenry. Blandtrap would certainly fall to pieces once a girl finally caught his eye.

My fall-back plan was an adaptation of the Tom Sawyer gambit. You know, make the work seem like fun so everyone would want to do it for you. Tom Sawyer had charisma that drew people to listen to his syrupy language until they were won over. Lacking a way with words, I was counting on icy cold beverages and fried chicken to do the job of the silver tongue I lacked. Having seen it work for others, I thought I'd give it a shot myself.

Before pitching an idea to Edith I had to dress it up some so the foolishness would not jump out and poke her in the eye before she heard me out. Bolstering my courage, I approached her one night. It is fundamental to get the support of those close to you before you undertake an important project, particularly if you are relying on them to perform necessary tasks such as frying chicken and running interference for hair-brained decisions.

It has been a cornerstone of our relationship that I seek out Edith's views on a matter and listen to her concerns and worries before I go ahead with my original plans. In the past when I have shirked this courtesy, events have not gone as I imagined they would.

To my surprise she had few real concerns regarding my painting plans. There were typical apprehensions: extra cooking, dirty dishes, excess garbage, and the accumulation of the usual unsavory characters showing up as spectators whereever hard work is being done. Not only do they fail to contribute in any meaningful way, they have a knack for causing work for others and ticking off hard workers to the point they leave before the work is done. Vowing to surmount these obstacles and leap additional unexpected hurdles we were bound to encounter, agreement on the plan was reached without harm to either.

The attraction to Edith was the finality a painting party brought to her situation. In our home, a job of this scope, inside or outside the house has been known to last longer than the most liberal estimates for completion. It happened the last time I painted the house alone. It had never taken me more than two weeks from first scrape to last brush cleaning, although I should admit it seldom took less time either.

About five years ago I scraped and primed most of the house the first weekend. On Monday morning, Mrs. Pomerene called with a cat emergency, rerouting my energy to Paw Paw Lane on a mission of feline mercy. Edith came with me to translate because I don't speak fluent widow and hope to die in that condition. When two speak different languages, misunderstandings lead to arguments, more work, and wasted afternoons. I just wanted to get back to painting.

Thinking it rude to pass the homes of Mrs. Wing and Maybelle Oufsbacher without stopping in to say hello, I was able to yank Edith free of the widows' conversational pull to get us home at sunset. Tuesday was consumed with driving Edith all over the county doing favors the widows had made her swear she would do for them. There were buttons to be purchased in Butte Crossing and a leg of lamb to be gotten in your city with five or six stops between. I felt like a tourist on vacation, determined not to miss a local attraction no matter how small and unimpressive.

Wednesday brought rain: a slow, soaking, all-day rain. I spent the day on a folding chair in the garage regretting I had wasted the previous two days of sunshine playing errand boy for the widows. Vowing not to waste another day being distracted from the job, I sat Edith down at the kitchen table and explained in clear, direct terms how important it was to finish a job in a timely manner. It was necessary for me to keep a sound mind and a good reputation among men in the village.

While putting finishing touches on my brilliant closing argument, the telephone rang. Edith was quick to grab the receiver as she tends to be while I am talking perfect sense. She learned of serious medical problems her aunt in Georgia was enduring. Dire was her condition and alone she was, so Edith and I packed that night for an early morning departure.

The mountains were beautiful in the bright sunlight. I don't wear sunglasses on a regular basis but found them requisite to drive the five days we were gone. Sunshine is like fruit. If not plucked from the tree when it is ripe, it will rot and fall to the ground unusable. Edith asked me if I thought I was a movie star. I told her no, I still had a rational mind and a shred of moral responsibility so I couldn't possibly act in movies.

The health of the ailing aunt improved until the hospital released her. A few days of Edith's care got her back on her wobbly feet again. Having covered all the bases common decency demanded, we were free leave. As hours in the car passed, skies began to darken. Winds picked up and rain fell. The storm grew in intensity as we continued on our way.

A monsoon struck Blandtrap as we pulled into the village. The rainy season lasted three days causing me to lose my will to paint. Wandering from diner to bank to hardware store and back home, I felt like I was on the track team running laps. Exerting lots of hard effort, I was ending up right where I started. The circuit took a few hours depending on whom I ran into along the way. On a good day I could do four of five laps. Unable to tend to personal matters and keep to myself as is my custom; I began to volunteer to help others with tasks weather couldn't curtail.

By the time skies cleared, my dance card was pretty full. Stu needed a hand cleaning his basement. It's hard to refuse a favor for a good friend, especially after you have benefited from his generosity as often as I have. Calvin Farnsworth needed help with some research at the Institute for Idle Science and I signed up to work with him for two days. Seth Hugginbough was reworking the nail display at the hardware store and Tommy was unable to work due to family obligations. We would work on it Saturday night and Sunday after church.

It was nearly three months before my schedule eased and I could return to the painting chore. Edith had long since contracted with professionals to do the work. Their task was larger than mine. Months of bare wood exposed to the elements created new repairs I had not faced. I learned much by observing their techniques. I glean pleasure from supervising the work of those who know what they are doing.

Edith presented me with the bill upon their completion. Needless to say, I was shocked at the amount. I had to consult my records to see if I was paying more to paint the house than I had originally paid to own the house. Mortgage interest tipped the scale in favor of purchase. I vowed never to fall prey to scandalous professional painters again! It was fear of that kind of exposure that drove me to my present idea.

Deciding on a date for the painting party was a bigger mountain to climb than I figured it would be. It was a surprise to me that Edith's schedule was more important than mine. Most hostesses, even in Blandtrap, would drive into the city, pick up a few buckets of chicken at Lance Corporal Sander's Chicken, a shameless rip off of the more familiar national chain, and present it to uncaring hungry workers as their own creation. Not so with Edith.

Aware that ladies from the church and others would undoubtedly drop by to rate her food and presentation, she was more concerned with meeting her own high standards than feeding the starving. Imagine a cross between Mother Theresa and Betty Crocker and you'll get a picture of what I was dealing with. If Edith was satisfied with her effort, there was nothing to worry about from the critical, gossiping eye of another.

The mechanics of the stove and oven would be planned to more detail than brush strokes on trim boards. What was a means to an end for me was seen by her as an opportunity to shine in Blandtrap society. Hospitality was important to Edith, far more important than how the house was to be painted.

For two evenings we sat at the kitchen table in silence, each of us planning our own phase of the painting party. Edith had her planning pad open on the table. She asked me questions periodically to help her grasp the scope of the event. She wanted to know how many would be invited, would they bring spouses or children, and how long would it last.

I hadn't worked out all the glitches yet and the agenda was still a bit fuzzy in my mind. To get a good day's work done you need to get an early start. If you try to start too early, though, men will cancel rather than be late due to some small but essential household chore. If you start too late, they'll get in the middle a project before they leave home and stand you up to finish their task. Timing had to be balanced. Asking around I discovered nine thirty is currently the acceptable time. Nine is too early and ten too late.

I thought Edith's inquiries were good questions and a credit to her insight and preparation. I had no idea how to answer her. Some questions I could guess at right then, while others would take some research before I could manufacture a reasonable response. Seeing she was stuck until these questions were answered, I gave her the ammunition she needed to start firing away in the kitchen. There was no sense in holding her back until I calculated a number that would amount to wild speculation anyway. We could always adjust the target should more accurate information present itself later.

Rooting around in the basement for old wash tubs I knew were lurking among the priceless, dusty debris, I produced two tables that would be perfect to support the tubs. It took the better part of an hour to unearth them. Basement storage is a system of compacting large and unwieldy items into a minimum space. It is necessary to entangle one heirloom with another in order to defy the law of physics that states two bodies cannot occupy the same space at the same time. The person who came up with this theory obviously never owned a basement.

Packing things away in a basement is a process similar to how diamonds are made. The raw material for the gem is neither rare nor precious. It is carbon. What transform charcoal residue into a DeBeers treasure is time and pressure.

Likewise, the material stored in a basement has little to no intrinsic value except in the mind of one of the occupants, an opinion rarely shared by another. Old furniture in need of expensive upholstery; end, coffee, and side tables with weak legs or marred finishes; and chests of drawers and bureaus are intermingled with lamps, knick knacks, and paintings of questionable quality and origin.

Pressure is applied from floors above. The compelling human desire to improve, or at least change our environment causes us to acquire newer, sometimes older, household items to replace what has worked for years and continues to do its job admirably. Our affection for the replaced item is not diminished; it is simply exceeded by our zeal for the new possession. We don't want to get rid of the old, we want to relegate its life to some form of furniture semi-retirement where it may be called into duty should the winds of fashion suddenly change direction. Still holding sentimental value, we force the item into a basement with no room to receive it.

The adventure begins with two burly chaps grabbing the ends of an object possessing an odd number of sides. Flesh is removed from knuckles as movers wrangle varnished wood through doorways. Rare is the house that lacks a turn at the top, bottom, or middle of the basement staircase. Massive objects must be twisted, turned on their side, or stood on end to continue descent past one of these obstacles. At the foot of the stairs, reality will slap them in the face as they see no space exists to receive the new artifact.

They will manage to jamb it in among or around what's already there. Looking around, they will promise to get rid of much of the junk lying around, a sentiment lost during the walk upstairs. A tall glass of iced tea will dispossess the part of their mind once owned by the tidiness urge.

The element of time passes without help from us. Attention to family consumes our lives leaving us only occasional glimpses at the clock to measure passage of our brief span on earth. Good intentions ripen and rot on the vine for lack of time to complete them. We go to bed young and rise as old folks. Such is the curse of time.

When pressure from greed and sentimentality are applied over the period of time that escapes our grasp, diamonds are formed in our basements; gems created in the cellar. We forget the beauty of a diamond lies not in the rock removed from the mine, but in careful cutting and polishing after it is removed from the earth. They should be dug up and given to those with the need for them and the skill to make them gems in their own homes.

From the diamond mine in my basement I unearthed two buried wash tubs and the two tables to support them. Another table, perfect for hot beverages, was also found protruding from the dust. Cleanup was simple. I decided to cover them with a cloth.

The painting party idea was a timesaving invention for me. I hoped to accomplish in one day what would take two weeks to complete alone. Most time saving inventions are machines created to do the work people had to do regularly. The washing machine was such an invention. In the time it used to take people to walk down to the rock in the stream to pound their clothes, they are washed and dried in their personal laundries. Other devices have had similar timesaving benefits: the automobile, the vacuum, and the gas stove.

Working independently, but just as hard are the clever folks who invent time- wasting devices. Movies, television, radio, and role-playing games are designed to occupy our minds, distract our focus from more urgent and important matters. As I grow older, I find I have more free time than in younger years. The temptation of time-wasting devices is a siren call that would destroy the last days of my life should I yield to its beckoning. I confess I am not always diligent and stray from my vows against the frivolous use of my time.

The night before the painting party, Edith shifted into high gear. All four burners on the stove were in full production. Behind my back she added coleslaw and potato salad to the menu. She was being considerate to workers by providing a more complete and balanced meal. I would have preferred to see what kind of job they did before upping their salary. Her upscale plans interfered with my scheme to watch a ballgame and turn in early. Peeling potatoes doomed the ballgame idea and when Edith kept me at the kitchen table chopping celery, onions, and eggs, I feared my sleep pattern would be permanently disturbed.

I could have retired an hour earlier but I stayed up to help Edith with the dishes. Sleep, when it finally came was sweet, but merely resting with my wife is one of the great pleasures of life. Going to bed without her would seem like abandonment. Sleeping alone just isn't the same. I helped out until she was comfortable leaving the rest until morning and would join me in rest.

We rolled out of bed early the next morning. The daunting task of the day was upon us. Edith headed for the kitchen and I for the yard. We would be working together for the same end but our tasks were independent of each other.

A plan for arranging food and beverage tables had been rattling around my empty skull for several days. When I asked Edith's opinion on the issue, she made it clear she had all the responsibility she was willing to accept. Remaining minor details would need to be handled by someone else. I believed she meant me but I didn't think it would be prudent to further clarify her statement. I was confident she would correct me if I made a glaring error.

Food would be presented on a three by six foot folding table I recovered during a recent archeological dig in the garage. It was my intention to shanghai the first responsible looking boy to guard the food against neighborhood dogs, cats, and freeloaders. I don't want to be sexist about the job. A young girl could do the job as well as any young boy, but the boy would approach the job of chasing dogs and cats with rocks and sticks with more zeal than a girl. Also, young girls tend to attract young boys who will eat the food and do stupid things to impress the girls. I haven't the wisdom to convert boys' endless energy into useful work under these conditions.

The trickier part of food and beverage arrangement would be keeping the teetotalers separated from the elbow benders. The two groups don't mix well at any time, but particularly at an event like this. Due to disparate definitions of appropriate icy cold beverages, conflict soon arises. Both sides hold fast to their convictions and express them freely and loudly. There is something about seeing someone drink an alcoholic beverage that makes a teetotaler's blood boil. On the other hand, two drinkers can't abide a man who declines a more interesting concoction for a soft drink. Each is compelled to proselytize the other. Debate escalates into heckling, resulting in conflict that may include fisticuffs. If the situation deteriorates to physical violence, meaningful work ceases.

It took thought and experimentation to design a workable layout for beverages. The table containing coffee, iced tea, water and soft drinks were separated form the table with stouter liquids by a corner of the house and an unwieldy hedge I had overlooked when trimming the others. Temperance could not view Indulgence unless they were looking for a fight. I labeled one table 'iced tea and refreshments' and the other table 'the other brewed beverage.'

Once workers gathered and savored their first cup of coffee, I was relieved of all authority regarding the work at hand. A new chain of command quickly established itself and it excluded me. Those who know how were in charge, organizing the efforts of those who could do, assisted by those who wanted to learn to do. I would not need to inject my thoughts or opinions into the process. If I did, it would slow the work or lead to egregious error.

My remaining duties were few: to keep washtubs full of beverages and ice, and to chase away loiterers, back seat foremen, and those whose goal was intoxication rather than paint application. Anticipating I would feel funny asking people to leave my home, it was a relief to find it pleasurable. We have been nothing but hospitable our entire married life, tolerating unearned insult and social slight in the name of etiquette. Edith prides herself on being a gracious hostess - it is her trademark.

Urgency of the day changed my otherwise pleasant nature and she joined me in my ardor to retain control of workers and eschew idle and curious pedestrians. I would scour the crowd distinguishing real workers from the merely thirsty. Putting an arm on their shoulder in apparent friendship, I would look back to Edith who sat on the porch chair in her moments of rest. She would nod 'yes' or 'no' to signal her judgment that would seal the fate of the accused much like Caesar on his throne. The welcome guest I walked to the garage to prepare for work while the condemned man got the bum's rush and was pushed on down the street.

Community came together that day. Two coats of latex were applied in a few short hours, a task only possible with ample staff on a warm, dry day. I suppose you can cite examples of charity or community spirit in your town.

If it happened in your city, it would earn full mention in your newspaper. Notoriety would follow, being talked about for months around water coolers. In Blandtrap, however, it is a way of life, a daily happening. It is who we are rather than some rare, shocking event; normal rather than odd behavior. From my newly painted, shiny, white house I wish you well and hope some day you enjoy an experience similar to mine.

Respectfully Submitted,

Harry Ellis

To the reader:

We'll pick it up from here next time.

Harry E. Grafton